National Trust Guide

Santa Fe

National Trust Guide
Santa Fe

America's Guide for Architecture and History Travelers

RICHARD HARRIS

PRESERVATION
PRESS

John Wiley & Sons, Inc

New York • Chichester • Weinheim • Brisbane • Singapore • Toronto

A cooperative publication with the National Trust for Historic Preservation,
Washington, D.C., chartered by Congress in 1949 to encourage the preservation of sites,
buildings, and communities significant in American history and culture.

This text is printed on acid-free paper.

This publication is designed to provide accurate and
authoritative information in regard to the subject
matter covered. It is sold with the understanding that
the publisher is not engaged in rendering legal, accounting,
or other professional services. If legal advice or other
expert assistance is required, the services of a competent
professional person should be sought.

Library of Congress Cataloging in Publication Data:
Harris, Richard, 1947–
        The National Trust guide to Santa Fe / Richard Harris.
           p.   cm.
        Includes index.
        ISBN 0-471-17443-2 (Wiley : alk. paper)
           1. Historic buildings—New Mexico—Santa Fe—Guidebooks.
        2. Architecture—New Mexico—Santa Fe—Guidebooks.   3. Santa Fe (N.M.)—Buildings,
        structures, etc.—Guidebooks.   4. Santa Fe (N.M.)—Guidebooks.   I. National Trust for
        Historic Preservation in the United States.   II. Title.
        F804.S23H37 1997
        917,89'56—DC21   97–2042

Printed in the United States of America
10 9 8 7 6 5 4 3 2 1

Contents

Preface

The day I started writing this book, I went to the New Mexico Historic Preservation Department offices in the big, bleak old building that used to be Santa Fe's hospital and told Mary Ann Anders what I was planning. She burst out laughing. "Do you have any idea how many historically significant buildings there are in Santa Fe?" she asked.

"Well, not exactly," I admitted.

"About ten thousand," she said. "Give or take a few."

Flipping through some of the file cabinet drawers where applications for listing on the State Register of Cultural Properties and National Register of Historic Places are kept, I soon arrived at the conclusion that a lot of buildings, though historic, are not particularly interesting.

A case in point: Recently, a private foundation unveiled plans to build the Georgia O'Keeffe Museum, presenting the works and life of northern New Mexico's most celebrated painter. The museum, to be located on Johnson Street behind the Eldorado Hotel, would be housed in two historic homes and a former art gallery. The plan called for demolition of a fourth structure, a boxlike building that had been a small abstract company office.

The museum foundation presented the plan to the Santa Fe Historic Design Review Board and were stunned when the "H-Board" denied permission to demolish the fourth building. As a spokesperson for a local historic preservation group observed, the building was historically significant as "an example of the small, quiet buildings that used to be much more prevalent in Santa Fe." In a city where extraordinary architecture is the norm, being plain and ordinary can make a building special!

Some visitors come to Santa Fe for the shopping and restaurants and can do no more than feign mild interest in old buildings. Ambience, after all, requires no explanation. But for anyone who wants to understand "The City Different," architecture holds the key. In this book, I give historic buildings a chance to tell their stories, adding up to the story of Santa Fe itself. It is written with travelers and newcomers in mind, and this orientation has guided me in deciding which buildings to include.

While considering the scope of this book, I thought back on when I moved to Santa Fe and remembered how disorienting "Santa Fe style" buildings were to me then. I had trouble telling commercial establishments from people's homes. I found it almost impossible to judge a building's interior size from the sidewalk in front of it. The visual cues I was accustomed to were missing: no glaring electric signs, few large display windows, just low buildings of unpredictable shape made from sun-baked clay—or at least stuccoed and painted to look as if they were. In winter they blended into the dry clay hillsides; in summer they almost disappeared into the foliage of fruit trees planted more than a century ago when the city was already very old. Little by little my eye grew accustomed to this radically different architecture. As my understanding of Santa Fe Style buildings deepened, the culture shock newcomers experience when they find themselves no longer tourists but not yet locals melted away, and my love for the city grew. It's this kind of understanding that I want to share with you in this book.

Thinking back, I remembered the shock of discovering how many of the Spanish colonial style adobe-look buildings in old Santa Fe are actually of twentieth-century origin and built of materials other than adobe. I felt somehow deceived by this "adobe Disneyland," this artificial historic zone that seemed to have been fluted up for the tourists. Only later did I realize that nothing could be further from the truth. "Fake adobe" was in fact nothing less than the culmination of a thousand-year heritage.

By preserving the appearance of adobe long after it had been made economically impractical by the introduction of cheaper, more durable alternatives, Santa Feans honor the Spanish settlers who brought the art of adobe brickmaking to the southwest. We honor the Pueblo and Anasazi Indians who developed the fundamental elements of what is now known as Spanish Pueblo Revival architecture in ancient cities like the one at Chaco Canyon. And we honor the artists of 1920s Santa Fe who, in building their own adobe houses, brought to the traditional architecture a spirit of creative innovation that is still very much alive in contemporary Santa Fe–style building design. The blending of these varied influences makes Santa Fe architecture a symbol of the city's multicultural unity.

Adobe does not last like stone does. Fail one year to plaster over the cracks left by winter's freezes and thaws, and the entire structure turns to mud in summer thunderstorms. That was the original idea. Homes were built from the very earth on which they stood and would return to the earth in time. Permanence was not part of the bargain. The legacy of our ancestors was less the buildings themselves than the concept, the shape, and the spirit of them.

In selecting the buildings to include in this book, I started with the city's major landmarks, those of recent vintage as well as those of historical significance. I then added less-known structures that help us visualize what Santa

Fe must have looked like in each era of its development. My selection criteria included whether a noted artist, writer, politician, or other public figure ever lived there, whether it incorporates unique design features, or whether the place comes with a good story.

Although some private residences are included, when possible I have preferred to choose buildings that are open to the public instead. This is partly because the book is designed to serve as a tour guide and is most useful when it leads you to places you can enter and explore. It is also out of deference to the right to privacy. A few years ago I lived in an old place east of downtown when a book of local ghost tales came out, listing my home as a haunted house. I had never encountered a ghost there myself—or even heard about one until I read the book—but soon curious faces started peeking over the top of the coyote fence that surrounded my yard several times a day. When a local guide started including my house as part of her ghost tours, I knew it was time to leave. (The house I moved into apparently was haunted. I was careful not to tell anybody.) Please, don't let this book guide you through people's front yards.

While I wrote this book with visitors and newcomers in mind, I hope that it holds something of interest for longtime Santa Fe residents as well. I know I learned a lot while researching it that I hadn't known after living in Santa Fe for two decades. For instance, I found out why all four corners of the big block where the post office and federal courthouse stand are rounded—because it used to be the city's horse racetrack. Now I sometimes drive around the loop five or six times just for fun. It adds a whole new dimension to looking for a parking space.

I hope that reading this book brings you as much pleasure as writing it has brought me. Special thanks to my research assistant, Devin Kleiner, and mapmaker Deborah Reade for helping make it possible.

Richard Harris
Santa Fe, August 1997

National Trust Guide
Santa Fe

1

The Evolution of Santa Fe Style

Zozobra stands 40 feet tall. He looms over the crowd, his wrathfully twisted visage horrible to behold, roaring out maledictions that carry all the way to the far side of the city. The Fire Dancer approaches the hem of Zozobra's long, white robe in a graceful dance, holding him at bay by means of threatening gestures with a torch. The giant snarls in anger and grows agitated, waving his arms wildly. The crowd begins chanting, "Burn him! Burn him!" and the Fire Dancer obliges by setting Zozobra's garment aflame. He groans and screams hideously during the fire that engulfs him, which eventually reaches his head, setting off the fireworks inside. As sparks fly everywhere, shouts of "¡Viva la fiesta!" rise into the sky with them.

The burning of the huge puppet Zozobra at the beginning of Santa Fe's annual fiesta has been described by travel journalists as the most dramatic pagan ritual still practiced in the United States. Cultural anthropologists have studied the event as an example of community catharsis, with roots reaching back to the mass sacrifices of the Aztecs and the traditional effigy burnings known as *huelgas de Dolores* in Central America. In Spanish, *zozobra* translates literally as "sinking" or "capsizing" and has come to mean "worry" or "anxiety." In Santa Fe, the effigy Zozobra is also known in Spanish as El Rey de los Diablos and in English as Old Man Gloom. The ritual marks the end of summer and disperses the cultural tensions that tend to build up during tourist season.

Opposite: Zozobra burning, Santa Fe Fiesta, 1942. *Photograph courtesy Museum of New Mexico, neg. 47327.*

Many visitors who come to Santa Fe to see the burning of Zozobra do not realize that the tradition is of recent origin. The event was created by local artists Will Shuster and Gustave Baumann in 1926. It was calculated to set a new, livelier tone for Santa Fe's fiesta, which had become religiously somber, self-consciously historical—and closed to outsiders. The free, flashy new version of fiesta was designed in equal parts to kindle civic spirit and to attract tourists.

Like Zozobra, virtually every other aspect of the the Santa Fe experience today is a twentieth-century invention, an unabashedly romantic and selective revival of exotic elements drawn from various periods of the city's cultural growth. Blue corn tortillas, green chile stew, piñon nuts, fiesta dresses, bright-colored cowboy boots, turquoise-and-silver jewelry for every occasion, Navajo rugs, Georgia O'Keeffe greeting cards, painted wooden coyotes, art shows, Indian vendors, *ristras, vigas, farolitos,* flamenco, and elegant tailgate parties at the opera are all part of what is commonly known as *Santa Fe style.*

Santa Fe style properly refers to the city's architecture, which reflects a character unlike that of any other city in the world. One hundred years ago, Santa Fe looked a lot like every other small western city and was growing more "modern" every day. Then, in the early years of the twentieth century, a small group of archaeologists, architects, and artists decided to divert Santa Fe culture onto a radically different course. They were aided and abetted by a range of people, from railroad tour organizers seeking to promote tourism to residents whose families had lived here for centuries and who dreaded the loss of old traditions. The transformation took less than 20 years and reshaped Santa Fe for generations to come.

Q: How many Santa Feans does it take to change a light bulb?

A: Five. One to climb the ladder and screw it in, and four to stand around saying they liked it better the way it was.

Every Santa Fean knows the truth revealed by this old joke: Paradoxically, while almost all residents place a high value on preserving time-honored traditions, the city's history has often been characterized by sweeping transformations. In the last century, New Mexico changed hands so often that its people lived under four flags in less than 50 years, some of them more than once, and the language used in public changed from Spanish to English. Santa Fe's appearance changed apace, and by the time New Mexico became a U.S. state in 1912, the city's architectural looked nothing like it does today. Then, driven in equal measures by tourism, preservationism, and artistic inspiration, the Santa Fe style architectural revival took shape with astonishing speed.

What seems almost to have started as a fad was codified into law 45 years later in the Santa Fe historic zoning ordinance, the most comprehensive and detailed architectural style ordinance that had ever been devised in the United States. The law was unusual in that it did little to mandate the preservation of historic buildings themselves. Instead, it required conformity to one of two spe-

Detail of vigas, 1860's, note drilled holes, left, for dragging viga. *Bouquet Historic District, Pojoaque. National Register of Historic Places.*

cific architectural styles: Spanish Pueblo Revival style and Territorial Revival style, collectively called Santa Fe style. The requirement applied only within the city's historic district, which included downtown and Canyon Road. More historic districts have been added, but it was not until the 1990s that the ordinance was amended to require the preservation of historic buildings.

Today, even outside the districts where the Santa Fe historic zoning ordinance applies, almost all residential buildings (although not all commercial and government buildings) conform to Santa Fe style as set forth in the ordinance. The reason is simple: Adobe-look houses sell for much higher prices than do more conventional houses. Past homeowners have stuccoed over practically every masonry and wood-frame house in town and painted it earthtone. Homebuilders today would never consider turning away from Santa Fe style, and architects find it flexible enough to allow plenty of room for innovation.

This book is designed to reveal Santa Fe's unique spirit, history, and culture through its architecture. Beginning with the city's historic districts and progressing outward to Indian pueblos and ghost towns in the far corners of the county, in each chapter an overview of the area covered, past and present, is presented, along with a suggested walking or driving tour of the area and site-by-site descriptions of the historically significant structures along the route. Toward the latter part of each chapter a historical context is offered. Chapter 2 features historical background on the entire three centuries of Spanish colonial, Mexican, and territorial history. Various aspects of twentieth-century development, such as the rise of tourism, the artists' and writers' colonies, and political insights, are described in succeeding chapters. The final chapters, which deal with rural Santa Fe County, include an examination of the area's American Indian heritage, which is inextricably entangled with all that came afterward.

Around 1916, a railroad publicist coined the slogan "The City Different" for Santa Fe, and it fit so perfectly that it continues in wide use today. Looking (and being) different draws both visitors and artists in exceptional numbers. Yet to view Santa Fe style as a device for promoting tourism and boosting real estate prices is to miss the essence that has made it uniquely successful. Recent Santa Fe style is the direct descendent of building traditions that span three continents and reach far back into antiquity. The spirit within the architecture is one of harmony with the surrounding mountains, piñon-forested hills, and high desert studded with chamisa and sage. Buildings crouch low in natural vegetation. Sensuously curved walls mirror rolling ridgelines. Hard-edged brick copings recall canyon walls. They sing of ancient times.

SANTA FE'S ADOBE ROOTS

The oldest capital city in the United States, Santa Fe was founded by Spanish colonists from Mexico City in 1610. It is 110 years older than San Antonio, Texas, and 171 years older than Los Angeles, California. Its unique architecture echoes the colonial cities of old Mexico and the great pueblos of the pre-Columbian Anasazi culture.

Spanish Colonial Santa Fe was built of adobe—large bricks of native clay bound together with straw, laid to form masonry walls and coated with smooth protective layers of clay—with flat roofs supported by ponderosa pine beams called vigas. The use of adobe bricks originated in the deserts of the Middle East and spread to Spain during the Moorish occupation (A.D. 719–1248). Spanish colonists brought the Moorish building methods to the New World.

With the exception of mission churches, early adobe buildings did not incorporate the more sophisticated elements of Middle Eastern architectural traditions, such as true arches or domes. As far as history records, none of the early settlers of Spanish New Mexico possessed any formal training in architecture, and their structures were utilitarian and plain. Adobe bricks were simply the most available building material. Adobe also proved to be uniquely suited to the high desert climate. It held the warmth of the day through chilly nights and provided shady coolness through the midday heat.

The do-it-yourself adobe construction of New Mexico's colonial period owed as much to Pueblo Indian influence as to Spanish–Moorish technology. Separated from the major cities of New Spain—as Mexico was then known—by the vast, hostile Chihuahuan Desert, New Mexican settlers adapted to the arid landscape by emulating the indigenous people, who had been building large multistory structures throughout the region for more than 500

Adobe ruin under reconstruction. *Photograph by Richard Harris.*

years. The Indians built their walls of either bricklike slabs of flat rock or "puddled" adobe—successive layers of wet clay poured along the tops of walls and allowed to dry. The Spanish showed the Indians how to make adobe bricks, and the Indians showed the Spanish how to make flat viga-and-latilla roofs and low energy-efficient doorways with rough-hewn pine lintels.

Among the distinctive elements of early New Mexican architecture that have been carried forward into modern times is the portal, a simple type of portico placed over sidewalks to protect pedestrians from intense sun, rain, snow, and ice. In the colonial (1610–1821) and Mexican (1822–1848) periods, portals were often laid across extensions of viga roof beams and were supported by round posts made from the trunks of ponderosa pines and topped with decoratively carved corbels to spread the weight-bearing area of each post.

Since colonial times, it has been customary throughout northern New Mexico to paint residential window and door frames blue. Exactly where the practice originated is unclear. The color blue is sacred to both the Pueblo Indians, whose traditions hold that turquoise stone possesses magical properties and that blue corn is holy, and to Mexican Catholics, who associate blue with the spirit of the Virgin Mary. Window and door frames are now painted blue in both Indian pueblos and Spanish villages throughout northern New Mexico. Many New Mexicans believe that blue doors and windows prevent evil spirits from entering the house.

The floors in seventeenth-century Spanish colonial buildings were of dirt, which the occupants would cover with rugs. Following the Pueblo Revolt of 1680, when the Spanish were driven out of New Mexico, Indians

Puye pueblo ruins. *Photograph by Richard Harris.*

converted the Palace of the Governors in Santa Fe to a pueblo-style residential building. They paved the floors with puddled adobe for a smoother, harder surface, an idea that caught on among the Spanish after they returned to Santa Fe 12 years later. Through the eighteenth and nineteenth centuries, it was common practice to cure the adobe floors with ox blood, which made for a harder, shinier floor surface.

In contrast to the simplicity of houses, stores, and government buildings in colonial times, the mission churches built by Franciscan brothers at Spanish settlements and Indian pueblos in northern and central New Mexico strived to express the grandeur of the church in adobe. The nave was lighted by rectangular windows placed high in the walls, often on only one side. The walls of the sanctuary were usually carried higher than those of the nave, permitting a one-story opening above and in front of the altar that illuminated it from an invisible light source to create a supernatural effect. The interior walls were plastered with adobe and whitened with gypsum, then muraled in traditional Indian patterns. The vigas and corbels were often carved with Spanish–Moorish designs.

One relatively modest mission church, San Miguel Mission, can be visited in downtown Santa Fe; others are still in use at the Spanish mountain villages of Las Trampas and Chimayo and several Indian pueblos, notably Acoma and Isleta. The ruins of some of the largest seventeenth-century missions can be seen at Pecos National Monument, Salinas Missions National Monument, and Jemez State Monument. With their lofty ceilings, thick adobe walls, and massive buttresses, the mission churches were designed to double as fortresses against raids by nomadic Indians from the outlands. When twentieth-century architects were developing the Spanish Pueblo Revival style, they viewed the old adobe mission churches as the only true examples of large public buildings in colonial New Mexico.

Aside from the churches, only a few adobe structures from colonial times still exist in Santa Fe in anything like their original form. The adobe architecture of the territorial era (1848–1911), which began when New Mexico was ceded to the United States at the end of the Mexican War, incorporated elements that were in vogue for brick buildings in the eastern United States during the years leading up to the civil war. Foremost among these elements were Greek Revival door and window frames, which can be recognized by the triangular pediments on the tops of the frames. Milled wood frames such as these were brought west in large quantities by wagon on the Santa Fe Trail. They represented a transition style designed to modernize and "Americanize" adobe architecture long before other kinds of building materials from the east became available in Santa Fe.

Territorial architecture retained the traditional portal but used square posts, sometimes slightly tapered and sometimes beveled at the corners.

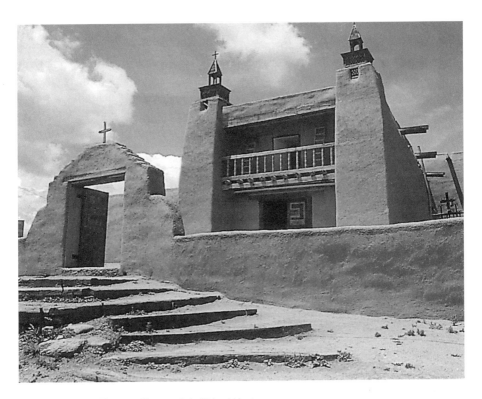

Mission Church, Las Trampas. *Photograph by Richard Harris.*

The Inn of the Anasazi, showing the main features of Spanish Pueblo Revival style: protruding *vigas*, battered walls, buttresses, and hand-hewn corbels and lintels. *Photograph by Richard Harris.*

Portal posts in this style, as well as window and door frames, were typically painted white. (White window and door frames and portal posts are identifying features of Territorial Revival style today. It is customary to paint the round portal posts of Pueblo Mission Revival style dark brown.) In the Territorial era, it was also common to place a low white balustrade along the edge of the portal. Sometimes these portals were reinforced to serve as balconies; other times the ballustrades were for purely ornamental effect.

Most buildings newly constructed in Santa Fe during the territorial period had pitched roofs, another symbol of Americanization. Although more difficult to built, the sloping roofs were less susceptible to damage from winter's daily freezing and thawing and are still widely used in northern New Mexico mountain villages. In the twentieth century, pitched roofs were rejected for aesthetic reasons by both the creators of Territorial Revival style and the drafters of the city's historic styles ordinance. Today, whether a Territorial-style building has a sloped or flat roof often reveals its true age. The distinctive red brick coping along the roofline of Territorial Revival–style buildings derives from territorial-era renovations of older adobe structures such as the Sena House on Palace Avenue. The oven-baked bricks, unknown in New Mexico before the opening of the Santa Fe Trail, were more weatherproof than adobe, so using them to cap exterior walls extended a building's life. Red bricks were too heavy to transport by wagon in large quantities, so there were never enough to build an entire house; the few bricks used for

Territorial-style copings were expensive and gave buildings an elegant, even ostentatious appearance.

The arrival of the railroad in 1880 increased the availability of building materials. Not only could more tools and materials be imported from the east, but the large-scale mining of coal to power locomotives also provided fuel for kilns, making red brick available in sufficient quantities to build entire houses for the first time. From approximately 1880 to 1910, Santa Fe saw sweeping urban renewal efforts aimed at eliminating old-fashioned adobe buildings, which many newcomers saw as an embarrassment, and replacing them with more conventional Victorian styles of the era. Victoriana represented a collection of revival styles based on the architecture of various European countries in the nineteenth and early twentieth centuries. In Santa Fe, where coal for brick ovens was readily available for the mines of Madrid, Italianate styles (including the Railroad Commercial style used for new office and retail construction around the Plaza) were more popular than the wood-frame Queen Anne Revival style that is meant by "Victorian" in most other parts of the Rocky Mountain west.

Within a generation, however, Victoriana was swept away by a new, uniquely Santa Fean architectural revival movement. Like Victorian styles, Santa Fe style came about through the resurrection of elements from earlier periods, applying them in innovative ways with the use of modern materials and techniques. Like Victoriana, Santa Fe style was actually a collection of distinct styles—Spanish Pueblo Revival (sometimes called Spanish Pueblo Mission Revival) and Territorial Revival.

An unlikely mix of archaeologists, architects, artists, and old-timers played key roles in the invention of Santa Fe style, which took about 20 years to fully develop. It was another 30 years before the rules governing "recent Santa Fe style" became law within the city's historic districts. Today, more than 95 percent of all buildings in Santa Fe—not only in the historic districts—are in Spanish Pueblo Revival or Territorial Revival style, and surprisingly few contain elements of both.

THE ARCHAEOLOGISTS

Although the usual subject matter of southwestern archaeology is pre-Columbian Indian ruins, one of the most ambitious archaeological projects ever undertaken in New Mexico was the restoration of the Old Palace (now known as the Palace of the Governors) in 1909. The controversial project marked the beginning of Santa Fe's stylistic transformation, which would continue through the 1920s.

The Palace had served as the seat of government and the living quarters of New Mexico's Spanish, Mexican, and U.S. territorial governors for nearly 300 years. Due to a shortage of funds for maintenance, however, it deteriorat-

The Hotel Plaza Real, showing the main features of Territorial Revival style: decorative brick coping, Greek Revival–style pedimented windows, a balustrade, and square portal posts. *Photograph by Richard Harris.*

ed badly during the late nineteenth century. Governor Lew Wallace, who occupied the Palace from 1877 to 1881, offered this description of the governor's quarters, where he finished his classic novel, *Ben-Hur: A Tale of the Christ:* "The walls were grimy, the undressed boards of the floor rested flat upon the ground," Wallace recalled in his 1906 autobiography. "The cedar rafters, rain-stained as those in the dining-hall of Cedric the Saxon, and overweighted by tons and tons of mud composing the roof, had the threatening downward curvature of a shipmate's cutlass. ... [T]he ghosts, if they were ever about, did not disturb me; yet in the hush of that gloomy harborage I beheld the Crucifixion, and strove to write what I beheld."

Wallace requested a $30,000 federal appropriation to renovate the Palace, but the U.S. Congress turned him down. Instead, they decided to erect a new territorial capitol building in Santa Fe. It was completed in 1889, and a portion of the Old Palace became a post office. Other parts served as law offices and a fire station.

When the new capitol burned down in 1892, territorial government offices were moved back into the Old Palace, but the exorbitant cost ($2000) of repairs to the crumbling adobe walls was more than the U.S. Congress wanted to spend on a decrepit 300-year-old building in a remote part of the southwestern territories. Construction of another territorial capitol building, designed by Colorado architect Isaac Hamilton Rapp, began in 1898 and was completed in 1900. Extensively renovated, the structure still stands within the state capital complex and is now known as the Bataan Building. As for Isaac H. Rapp, the territorial capitol commission elevated him to the status of leading architect in the region. Sixteen years later, he would create the first Santa Fe style building.

A series of political maneuvers followed in which various government entities tried to rid themselves of responsibility for maintaining the Old Palace. As soon as construction of the newest capitol building began, the federal government transferred ownership of the Old Palace to the Territory of New Mexico. The governor, Miguel Otero, responded by trying to persuade the Smithsonian Institution to make the Palace a western branch of the National Museum. After nearly two years of debate, the Smithsonian dismissed the proposal as a "scheme for making a local museum at the expense of the National Government." Another proposal, to declare the abandoned edifice a national monument, also met with failure.

By 1908, the Old Palace had fallen into such a state of ruin that local businesspeople were receiving serious consideration of a proposal to demolish it and sell the prime downtown real estate to developers for construction of modern commercial buildings. But although nobody wanted financial responsibility for this "white elephant" of a building, it was the nation's oldest public building. At the last minute, several groups, including the New Mexico Historical Society, the local chapter of the Daughters of the American Revolution, and the Santa Fe Archaeological Society, came up with a new plan to avert its destruction.

Under the plan, the Washington-based Archaeological Institute of America would take over ownership of the Old Palace as the permanent location for its new School of American Archaeology. Part of the Palace would become the rent-free headquarters of the New Mexico Historical Society. Another part would be operated by the Archaeological Institute as a museum, which would be known as the Museum of New Mexico, in exchange for initial restoration funds and an annual appropriation from the territorial legislature. As elaborate as the plan was, it suited perfectly the needs of all parties involved. Within four months after it was first proposed, the arrangement was signed into law.

The school and museum were staffed by one of the most eminent teams of archaeologists ever assembled. The director, Edgar L. Hewitt, was the leading southwestern archaeologist of his day and the driving force behind enactment of the Antiquities Act of 1906, which protected ancient Indian ruins in the United States. His associate, self-taught American Indian scholar and archaeologist Adolf Bandelier, had spent the past 34 years excavating postclassic Pueblo ruins on the Pajarito Plateau west of Santa Fe, where a large national monument would later be named after him.

The job of supervising repairs to the Old Palace went to a junior staff member, Jesse L. Nusbaum, whose official job title was archaeological photographer; he was the only archaeologist there with practical experience in the construction trades. Nusbaum recruited the help of an old college chum, Sylvanus Morley, who left his assistant teaching job to join the School of American Archaeology as a specialist in Central American studies. Nusbaum and Morley brought such fervor and youthful vision to the task of fixing up the old building that the project was transformed into a chance to prove their progressive ideas, which would soon revolutionize the field of archaeology.

Until then, the concept of archaeological restoration was virtually unknown. Archaeology, particularly in the remote ancient sites of the Americas, had previously been a matter of systematic, academically sanctioned looting of artifacts for museums. Ruins were rarely excavated; instead, they were mapped by digging trenches that were later filled in. Adolf Bandelier, who had begun his studies without formal training, had shocked the academic establishment by excavating Pueblo ruins, stabilizing them, and leaving them exposed to public view, but even he had not presumed to rebuild walls that had collapsed.

Nusbaum and Morley became the leading proponents of a truly radical idea: that restoring ruins to the point where untrained visitors could visualize the way they had been when people lived there would capture the public imagination, elevate the status of archaeology, and result in much higher levels of funding. In later years, the pair would preside over the restorations of the two biggest archaeological tourist attractions in the western hemisphere today. Morley would spend more than 20 years overseeing the reconstruction of the Maya ruin of Chichén Itzá in Yucatán, Mexico, while Nusbaum would

Palace of the Governors, 1868. *Photograph by Nicholas Brown, courtesy Museum of New Mexico, neg. 45819.*

become the superintendent of Mesa Verde National Park in southwestern Colorado.

In 1909, the mere suggestion of opening ancient archaeological sites to tourists would have gotten Nusbaum and Morley fired and banished from their profession. Their commission to fix up the Old Palace offered a way to put their radical philosophy into practice in a way that would pass unnoticed until it was too late.

When Nusbaum began the project, he surveyed the palace and described it in his journal in these words: "The walls were falling in many places, and everywhere inappropriate restorations were in evidence, a hodge-podge of ill-conceived additions conforming to no particular style of architecture. The plaza space behind the building had been filled up with trash and manure from the stabling of livestock in there, to such a level that it was well above the sills of the rear windows. ...I arranged for native workmen with teams for the immediate removal of this and it took 2100 small wagon loads for the removal of 1000 cubic yards of this material."

The restoration took four years, with occasional intermissions as funds ran low and Nusbaum undertook other missions, stabilizing the Cliff House at Mesa Verde and exploring the Yucatán with Morley. When completed, the interior of the Palace of the Governors was a idealized replica of what it had been when the first Anglos had arrived in the 1820s. Nusbaum's re-creation was not literal; he knocked out walls and built others, rearranging the floor plan to accommodate museum exhibits, a library, and offices. The style of the building, however, was purely Spanish-colonial New Mexican, stripped of all territorial-era adornments.

Near the end of the project, a controversy erupted. The Palace had a Victorian "gingerbread" piazza portico that blended in with the rest of the architecture around the plaza. Nusbaum wanted to replace it with a traditional eighteenth-century Spanish colonial portal. The museum board flatly refused to provide funds for the new portal. But a group of citizens voiced their concern about the ongoing loss of Santa Fe's traditional Spanish colonial atmosphere pressed for the change, and money was reluctantly made available to give the Palace a new front.

Nusbaum envisioned a restoration of all the buildings surrounding the Plaza. Even though he was never able to obtain the kind of funding such a project would require, the Palace of the Governors' new look inspired a revival style that would harmonize with it and provided preservation advocates with an inspiring example.

THE ARCHITECTS

In the climate of renewed appreciation for colonial architecture that followed the restoration of the Palace of the Governors, Isaac Hamilton Rapp is credited with "inventing" the Spanish Pueblo Revival style.

Palace of the Governors, 1880. *Photograph by Ben Wittick, courtesy Museum of New Mexico, neg. 15376.*

There was no formally trained architect firm in turn-of-the-century New Mexico. As a territory and not yet a state, New Mexico had no professional licensing boards, so credentialed architects avoided New Mexico in favor of the neighboring states of Texas and Colorado. When Isaac and William Rapp opened their practice in Trinidad, Colorado, just 13 miles from the New Mexico boundary, they became the closest licensed architects to Santa Fe. When he took on the challenge of creating the new style, Isaac H. Rapp had been designing Queen Anne–style houses, neo-Gothic churches, and castle-like schools and banks around Colorado and New Mexico for 25 years. In Santa Fe he was best known as the architect of the 1900 New Mexico Territorial Capitol.

Rapp was the natural choice to create the New Mexico Building for the Louisiana Purchase Centennial Exposition in St. Louis in 1904. This early attempt at creating a distinctively New Mexican look resulted in a California Mission Revival–style building that bore little resemblance to any in New Mexico (although it looked like the trademark train stations that the Atchison, Topeka & Santa Fe Railroad would soon be building across the territory). He kept experimenting with various types of traditional Spanish architecture. In 1909, at the same time that Jesse Nusbaum was beginning restoration of the Old Palace, Rapp's Scottish Rite Temple, modeled after a portion of the Alhambra in Spain, was being built a few blocks away. Today, the temple stands as one of the Santa Fe historic district's most eccentric structures.

Rapp's first true Santa Fe style building, constructed in 1909, was built not in Santa Fe. It was a Colorado Supply Company warehouse in Morley,

Palace restoration, 1913. *Photograph by Jesse L. Nusbaum, courtesy Museum of New Mexico, neg. 13037.*

Colorado, just north of the Colorado–New Mexico boundary at Raton Pass. The company's owner wanted the warehouse, which would be in plain sight of rail passengers, to be a true landmark: a replica of the old Spanish mission church at Acoma Pueblo, a mesa-top pueblo in western New Mexico inhabited by descendents of the ancient Mesa Verde people. The original church was in ruins and would not be restored for another 15 years, so elements of creativity and archaeological guesswork came into play. The old warehouse no longer stands, but Rapp built another, the Gross–Kelly warehouse in the Santa Fe Railroad yards, from the same plans in 1914.

Rapp and his brother were then hired by the state to go to San Diego, California and design the New Mexico Building for the Panama–California Exposition in 1915. New Mexico had recently become a state, and there was a good deal of curiosity about this exotic, distant land. The railroad was promoting Santa Fe tourism in an unprecedented national publicity campaign. Again, Rapp took his inspiration from the eighteenth-century Spanish mission church at Acoma. The "Cathedral of the Desert" captured the public imagination, and unlike other buildings in the exhibit, it was never torn down. Extensively remodeled, it still stands today in San Diego's Balboa Park.

Edgar Hewitt, who had grown beyond archaeology in his role as director of the Museum of New Mexico, wanted to build a separate art museum in the next block west the Palace of the Governors. After watching the creation of the New Mexico Building in San Diego, he commissioned Rapp to create the new museum based on a more refined version of the same design. Completed in 1917, the New Mexico Museum of Fine Arts has defined Spanish Pueblo Revival style ever since. Rapp's other Spanish Pueblo Revival

Scottish Rite Temple. *Photograph by Richard Harris.*

buildings in Santa Fe during that period included the Santa Fe School for the Deaf (1916) and Sunmount Sanitarium (1914 and 1920, now the Immaculate Heart of Mary Seminary).

In 1920, Rapp accepted the job of designing the La Fonda hotel for the Harvey Company. Located at the site of an old one-story inn that had stood since early Santa Fe Trail days, the hotel was to be diagonally across the Plaza from the Museum of Fine Arts. The design of La Fonda, the largest building in downtown Santa Fe at the time of its completion, was Rapp's last large project. It was a departure from Rapp's series of mission church replicas, which had culminated in the Museum of Fine Arts. The jagged rooflines of the hotel's staggered facades suggest the skyline of a ruin; the inspiration might have been an ancient Indian pueblo, although a bell tower included in the original plan resembles that of a crumbled old adobe mission church.

Surplus World War I army tanks were used to demolish the old adobe inn, and construction began on the new three-story hotel. Before it was finished, Rapp's brother and partner, William, died of pneumonia upon returning home from a visit to Santa Fe. The next year, the Rapp firm's 47-year-old junior partner, Arthur Henderson, died of a heart attack after accompanying Rapp to inspect a mining claim. Leaving the bell tower of the new hotel unbuilt, Rapp returned home to retirement in Trinidad at the age of 68. He lived for 14 more years but accepted no new projects. Upon his death in 1933, his wife, Jean Morrisson Rapp, returned to Santa Fe, where she built an adobe house based on one of her late husband's designs and spent the remainder of her life as a watercolorist and active member of Santa Fe's artist colony.

John Gaw Meem, the architect most closely associated with Santa Fe style, took over where I. H. Rapp left off and put his creative stamp on more of the city's classic buildings than any other architect before or since. Meem practiced in Santa Fe from 1927 to 1957, the year his concept of Santa Fe style was enacted into law.

As a junior executive of a New York bank, Meem had been sent to Brazil, where he had contracted a tropical virus that was mistakenly diagnosed as tuberculosis. In 1920, he came to Santa Fe for treatment at Sunmount Sanitarium, one of the country's top three tuberculosis centers, where he spent the next two-and-a-half years. During his stay, total immersion in I. H. Rapp's novel southwest-style architecture caused Meem to discover a new vocational interest.

Upon his release from the sanatorium, he spent 18 months as an apprentice in a Denver architects' firm but suffered a relapse of his illness and returned to Santa Fe in 1924. Soon after, he renovated his first house (the Galt house at 805 El Caminito) and tried his hand on several other home renovations and additions in the Canyon Road–Acequia Madre neighborhood over the next three years. He went into private practice in 1927 and over the next few years, designed a number of modest adobe residences inspired by I. H. Rapp's Spanish Pueblo Revival style.

As his reputation grew, Meem acquired wealthier clients with more formal tastes. To satisfy them, he developed a new approach that would evolve into the Territorial Revival style, patterned loosely after such residences as El Zaguán and the Borrego house, both on Canyon Road. An early example, built in 1929, was the Robert Tilney house at 1014 Old Santa Fe Trail.

Museum of Fine Arts construction, 1917. *Photograph courtesy Museum of New Mexico, neg. 13009.*

Although the house seems classically New Mexican from a present-day perspective, its details—such as large, louvered shutters and elaborate arched transom windows—owe more to the late Georgian style common on the east coast than to any structure previously built in Santa Fe.

National design competitions were often used to attract the talents of major architectural firms to the challenge of defining Santa Fe style. While entrants came from as far away as San Diego and Boston, the winners always turned out to be Santa Fe residents, and among them John Gaw Meem was the acknowledged champion. One notable instance was the design for the Laboratory of Anthropology, sponsored by John D. Rockefeller, Jr. Among the five finalists, who received cash awards of $1000 each, was the Denver firm of Fisher & Fisher, where Meem had begun his apprenticeship just a few years earlier. But it was Meem, not Fisher & Fisher, who won the commission.

In the 1920s, Meem designed a new facade for the First National Bank (1926) and an expansion of La Fonda (1927–1928). His great opportunity came when Cyrus McCormick, Jr., a Chicago businessman who owned a summer home in Santa Fe, sponsored a prize competition in 1930 for the best exterior redesign to bring the other building facades around the Plaza into harmony with the Palace of the Governors, the Museum of Fine Arts, and La Fonda. McCormick almost seems to have rigged the contest with Meem in

Territorial Revival. Alfred M. Bergere house, 135 Grant Avenue, built 1870 in adobe with flat roof. *National Register of Historic Places.*

mind, for the rules barred elements of nonlocal Spanish-inspired styles, such as Moorish ornamentation, Mediterranean tile roofs, and California Mission curvilinear facades. Shunning the obvious, Meem won the contest and its $400 cash award not with a Spanish Pueblo Revival look but with something new — Territorial Revival style.

With its straight, clean lines, the adaptation of the Greek Revival adobe synthesis style of the mid-nineteenth century was more suited for adapting the existing brick buildings, which Meem saw as too precisely rectangular to transform easily to the curves and nonparallel walls of Spanish Pueblo style. Although his design was not used, and the renovation of the Plaza was put aside for future consideration, it brought recognition to Meem and his Territorial Revival style. The new, more formal look would be used in renovations of virtually all city and state government buildings.

Meem's other major commissions around the city included the Santa Fe Indian School (1931), the Santa Fe County Courthouse (1938), the First Presbyterian Church (1939, remodeled 1947), Cristo Rey Church (1939), a new facade for the F.W. Woolworth Building (1939), the stabilization of St. Francis Cathedral (1940), the downtown Sears & Roebuck Building (1948), the Museum of International Folk Art (1950), a second facelift for the First National Bank (1954), the Santa Fe Jewish Center (1952, now Temple Beth Shalom), and the First Baptist Church (1959). Between 1939 and 1954, he remodeled eight of the buildings facing the Plaza — none of them in the Territorial Revival style he had originally proposed. Throughout his career, Meem displayed equal fluency in both Spanish Pueblo Revival and Territorial Revival architecture — yet never combined elements of the two styles.

Meem chaired the Santa Fe City Planning Commission from 1944 to 1951. He served on Plaza improvement committees in 1950 and 1955; the resulting plans, like Meem's 1930 plan, were never implemented. Perhaps his most lasting achievement was the historic zoning ordinance of 1957, drafted by a blue-ribbon committee that Meem headed. He retired two years later, at the age of 65. His final accomplishment, however, came in 1966, when he emerged from retirement to design the present portales around the Plaza. The architect, who had come to Santa Fe for treatment of a chronic, life-threatening illness more than six decades before, died in Santa Fe in 1983 at the age of 89.

THE ARTISTS

The construction and renovation of large public buildings after the Palace of the Governors was, for the most part, the special province of professional architects. Santa Fe style residences were another matter. People had been building their own adobe homes for centuries without formal training in either architecture or the construction trades. One of the reasons that artists began to congregate in Santa Fe around the same time that the Santa Fe style renaissance was transforming the town was that they could build their own homes very inexpensively from adobe bricks made, in accordance with long-standing Spanish tradition, of earth dug from the land where the house would stand. Adobe homebuilding came to be viewed as a visual art, similar to sculpture. Many innovative concepts in Santa Fe style came out of this artistic experimentation.

The first artist to move to Santa Fe permanently was Carlos Vierra, a Californian of Portuguese descent. Vierra had studied art and photography in New York and become a well-known cartoonist there, but respiratory disease forced him to return to the west and check into a small Santa Fe tuberculosis sanatorium. As his health improved, Vierra opened a photography studio on the Plaza, and when the School of American Archaeology came to Santa Fe soon afterward, director Edgar Hewett hired him as the official photographer for the school and the Museum of New Mexico. One of Vierra's first official assignments was to travel around New Mexico photographing old mission churches, haciendas, and other structures as guidelines for the restoration of the Palace of the Governors and, later, the design of the Museum of Fine Arts. Vierra also traveled to the Yucatán and Guatemala with expeditions from the school, photographing the ruins of ancient Maya cities and drawing his conceptions of what the ancient cities had looked like in their heyday; his murals showing the work of Franciscan missionaries among the Maya grace the walls of St. Francis Auditorium in the Museum of Fine Arts.

In 1919, Senator Frank Springer, a member of the museum's board of regents, gave Vierra a life estate in a piece of land on the south edge of town, and Vierra spent the next three years building his own adobe home there. The house, located at Old Pecos Trail and Cordova Road, was a definitive example of early Santa Fe style residential design. Like many artists' houses of the era, it combined visual beauty with engineering naiveté. Its curvilinear gateway, apparently the original prototype for the type of archlike gate that is common in Santa Fe walls today, echoed the mountain skyline in the distance as viewed from the portaled patio; but the large north-facing windows made the house almost impossible to heat.

William Penhallow Henderson, a well-known painter, came from Chicago to Santa Fe in 1916 with his wife, poet Alice Corbin, a tuberculosis patient at Sunmount Sanitarium. Henderson built an adobe house for himself and his family along the country road that led to the sanatorium. In doing so, he cultivated such enthusiasm about Santa Fe style homebuilding that he not only helped other artists build their own houses nearby but also started a building supply company where they could buy such necessities as vigas, roof tar, and window glass. Although he had no formal training or pro-

Will Shuster house. *Photograph by Richard Harris.*

fessional license, Henderson achieved prominence in Santa Fe by winning several competitions and went on to restore Sena Plaza and design and build the Wheelwright Museum of the American Indian.

Henderson's enthusiasm was shared by his neighbors and fellow artists, Frank Applegate and B. B. Dunne, who also built their own homes and went on to show more recent newcomers how to do the same. Henderson's leading protégés were Will Shuster, Fremont Ellis, Willard Nash, Walter Mruk, and Josef Bakos, known in Santa Fe lore as Los Cinco Pintores. The five young painters had come from various parts of the world to study with Henderson and other painters then living in Santa Fe. Faced with the practical difficulties of making a living on the frontier, they pooled their savings to buy land adjacent to Henderson's and Applegate's, then worked communally to build houses there.

A classic Cinco Pintores ("five painters") story recounts how, on their first attempt, Will Shuster dashed over to warn Fremont Ellis that his wall was leaning precariously and looked back just in time to see his own wall topple. Nobody had told them that adobe brick walls were supposed to interlock at the corners. Nevertheless, under the tutelage of Henderson and Applegate, the five built their houses, which are still in use more than 70 years later. They lived in the first houses while building second houses, then sold or rented the first houses for income to sustain them in their not-always-lucrative painting careers. It became common practice in Santa Fe's art colony to build a guesthouse first and live in it while finishing the main

23

house, then rent it out as an income supplement. Many rental units on Santa Fe's east side today are such guest houses, known locally as casitas suegras ("mother-in-law houses").

SANTA FE STYLE LAWS

In the 1950s, a group that included architects John Gaw Meem and Irene von Horvath, along with author–historian–archaeologist Oliver La Farge, advocated legal measures to preserve the unique appearance of downtown Santa Fe. After five years of months of study and nearly a year of heated public debate, the city council adopted the Santa Fe *historic zoning ordinance,* later renamed the *historical district ordinance* but locally known as the *historic styles act.* The ordinance established the Santa Fe historic district, the first of several contiguous historic districts that exist today, encompassing the downtown and Canyon Road areas. As originally enacted, the ordinance did not mandate the preservation of existing buildings within the district. Instead, it required that all new construction conform to either old Santa Fe style or recent Santa Fe style, defined each in painstaking detail, and created a historic design review board to judge whether architectural plans conformed to the styles. The 1957 ordinance was one of the first of its type in the United States, and its design requirements remain in effect today (Santa Fe City Code, Sec. 14-70, as amended).

Old Santa Fe style includes the substyles commonly called Territorial style and Pueblo Spanish style. (The latter, also known as Spanish–Indian style or Spanish Pueblo Mission Revival style, is the design developed by Nusbaum, Rapp, Meem, and others in the early years of the twentieth century, incorporating traditional Spanish colonial and Pueblo Indian elements.) Old Santa Fe style is described in the ordinance as follows:

- With rare exception, buildings are of one story, few have three stories, and the characteristic effect is that the buildings are long and low. Two-story construction is more common in the Territorial substyle and is preferably accompanied by a balcony at the level of the floor of the second story.
- Roofs are flat with a slight slope and surrounded on at least three sides by a firewall of the same color and material as the walls or of brick. Roofs are never carried out beyond the line of the walls except to cover an enclosed portal or porch formed by setting back a portion of the wall or to form an exterior portal, the outer edge of the roof being supported by wooden columns. (Skylights and chimneys are permitted.)
- Facades are flat, varied by inset portales, exterior portales, projecting vigas or roof beams, canales or water-spouts, flanking buttresses and wooden lintels, architraves and cornices, which, as well as doors, are frequently carved and the carving may be picked out with bright colors.
- Arches are almost never used except for nonfunctional arches, often slightly ogive, over gateways in freestanding walls.

- All exterior walls of a building are painted alike. The colors range from a light earth color to a dark earth color. The exception to this rule is the protected space under portales, or in church-derived designs, inset panels in a wall under the roof, in which case the roof overhangs the panel. These spaces may be painted white or a contrasting color, or have mural decorations.
- Solid wall space is always greater in any facade than window and door space combined. Single panes of glass larger than 30 inches in any dimension are not permissible.
- True Old Santa Fe style buildings are made of adobe with mud plaster finish. Construction with masonry blocks, bricks, or other materials with which the adobe effect can be simulated is permissible, provided that the exterior walls are not less than 8 inches thick and that geometrically straight facade lines are avoided. Mud plaster or hard plaster simulating adobe, laid on smoothly, is required.
- It is characteristic of Old Santa Fe style commercial buildings to place a portal so that it covers the entire sidewalk, the columns being set at the curb line.

Recent Santa Fe style is a series of design standards intended to achieve harmony with historic buildings by using similar materials, color, proportion, and general detail. The requirements of the ordinance include:

- No building may be over two stories in height in any facade unless the facade includes projecting or recessed portales, setbacks, or other design elements.
- The combined door and window area in any publicly visible facade may not exceed 40 percent of the total area of the facade except for doors or windows located under a portal. No door or window in a publicly visible facade may be located nearer than 3 feet from the corner of the facade.
- No cantilevers are permitted except over projecting vigas, beams, or wood corbels, or as part of the roof treatment described below.
- No less than 80 percent of the surface area of any publicly visible facade must be adobe finish, or stucco simulating adobe finish. The balance of the publicly visible facade may be of natural stone, wood, brick, tile, terracotta, or other material subject to approval by the design review board.
- The publicly visible facade of any building and any adjoining walls must be of one color, simulating a light earth or dark earth color, matte or dull finish, and of relatively smooth texture. Facade surfaces under portales may be of contrasting or complementary colors. Windows, doors, and portales on publicly visible portions must be of one of the Old Santa Fe styles, except that buildings with portales may have larger plate glass areas for windows under portales only. Deep window recesses are characteristic.
- Flat roofs may not have more than 30 inches of overhang.

The same ordinance also contains restrictions on signs within the historic district. Only signs advertising a bona fide business on the premises are allowed. No sign may be placed so as to disfigure or conceal any architectural feature or painted on a wall. Spotlights, floodlights, visible bulbs, neon tubing, and signs that flash, blink, revolve, or move are prohibited. In addition, the ordinance restricts dimensions of a sign, with different rules depending on location and whether it is a hanging, projecting, or flat sign.

In 1983, the historical district ordinance was amended to subdivide the original Santa Fe historic district into a core historic district, a historic review district, and a historic transition district, with different procedures for design approval. The city also created two new districts—the Don Gaspar area historic district in 1977 and the Westside–Guadalupe historic district in 1983—along the edges of the original historic district.

Under the original ordinance, property owners were required to seek review board approval before demolishing existing buildings in the historic district, but nothing prevented them from letting a historic building deteriorate to the point of condemnation, then tearing it down and replacing it with a recent Santa Fe style structure. In 1981, the city passed a new ordinance, similar to those now in force in many historic districts around the United States, imposing minimum maintenance requirements on all buildings within the districts. The ordinance contains specific provisions governing repairs and prescribing, for example, under what circumstances a replacement window must contain the same number of panes as the old one and what materials must be used for repaving adjacent streets and sidewalks.

Outside Plaza, an unusual example of recent Santa Fe style, blends elements of both Spanish Pueblo Revival and Territorial Revival architecture. *Photograph by Richard Harris.*

2

The Plaza

n most regions of the United States, a typical town started with a Main Street that served as a retail zone and informal social center. As the town's population grew, Main Street grew longer and side streets branched from it. With increasing numbers of cars, retailers migrated away from the congestion and parking problems of Main Street into suburban shopping malls. In less fortunate towns, the old Main Street business districts have been abandoned to decay and high vacancy rates; in more fortunate towns, tourism or a prosperous local economy has enabled the redevelopment of Main Street with cafés, boutiques, galleries, and other specialty shops.

Instead of a Main Street, a typical Spanish colonial town had a plaza (called a *zócalo* or *parque central* in many Latin American towns). The broad town square was flanked by the cathedral on one side, the government *palacio* on another, with a bank, an inn, and retail stores along the other two sides.

The plaza was the central feature of the Reales Ordenanzas, the most detailed city planning regulations devised by any nation during the colonial era. The Ordenanzas, declared by King Phillip II of Spain in 1573, applied to every city and town built in the Spanish colonies—more than 11,000 in all. The comprehensive uniform town plan was designed so that communities would grow symmetrically from the central plaza. The plaza was originally a broad, barren parade ground reserved for religious fiestas and military displays. Only gradually over the centuries of Spanish rule did it become a center of community life where residents came to socialize.

Santa Fe's plaza was laid out according to Ordenanza specifications requiring that it be at least one and a half times as long as it was wide, with

Opposite: Museum of Fine Arts. *Photograph by Richard Harris.*

Plaza today. *Photograph by Richard Harris.*

recommended dimensions of 600 feet by 400 feet, and that eight streets run from it—two at each corner and one from the center of each long side. The original town square, twice as large as the present-day Plaza, included what is now the Catron Block on the east side between the plaza and St. Francis Cathedral. As originally planned, the town center extended two blocks in each direction from the plaza, with farmlands beyond.

Historians do not know for sure whether the original plaza actually conformed to the town plan laid out by Governor Pedro de Peralta, the first governor of Spanish colonial New Mexico to make Santa Fe his capital. All government records from the era were destroyed during the Pueblo Revolt of 1680, leaving no historical documents except the scant descriptions of Santa Fe contained in reports by missionaries to their superiors in Europe. No map survives to show the layout of seventeenth-century Santa Fe.

Today, the Plaza has become less a traditional Main Street, as almost all retail stores geared to the practical needs of residents, with the sole exception of Woolworth's, have closed or relocated to Villa Linda Mall, Santa Fe's largest mall, on the southwest side of the city. Just as in earlier times, however, the Plaza is used for special events. They range from tourist-oriented extravaganzas, of which the largest is Indian Market, to events of mainly local importance, such as Community Day (nicknamed "Take Back the Plaza Day"), not to mention the formal religious processions, parades, and street dancing associated with the Santa Fe fiesta. The city sponsors free, live music on the Plaza several times a week during the summer months, and tourists and locals of all walks of life find its shaded benches and cool lawns a pleasant place to while away sunny afternoons.

In 1990, archaeologists excavated portions of the Plaza in a city-sponsored project intended to clarify what early Santa Fe actually looked like. Their less-than-startling conclusion was that the Plaza had in fact been the plaza since 1610. Artifacts, such as nails, chunks of coal, and a single piece of seventeenth-century *majolica* ceramicware from the Mexican city of Puebla, were discovered beneath the Plaza lawn to a depth of 5 feet. Since the original adobe floor of the Palace of the Governors confirms that ground level in the seventeenth century was only about 18 inches lower than it is today, the likely explanation for artifacts being buried so deep is that soil was eroded away by rainwater and replaced during windstorms by fresh deposits of dirt at the rate of a small fraction of an inch per year.

EXPLORING THE PLAZA

The Plaza is the natural place for visitors to begin seeing Santa Fe. Each period in the city's four-century history is reflected in the Plaza and the structures that surround it.

The first challenge when arriving in downtown Santa Fe is to find a place to park. Spaces are limited along the narrow old streets. There are a two-level enclosed municipal parking lot three blocks west of the Plaza and a municipal outdoor lot off Water Street at Don Gaspar Avenue south of the Plaza, as well as another municipal lot north of the Plaza at Sweeney Convention Center on Marcy Street. All the city lots charge parking fees. To park free means looking a few blocks farther from the center of town. Parking can usually be found in the Don Gaspar neighborhood across Paseo de Peralta from the state capitol; it's a five- or six-block walk among the buildings of the state government complex to the Plaza. Another option is Alameda Street, where parking can usually be found along the Santa Fe River; depending on how far up the river you park, you'll be seven to 10 blocks to the Plaza, most of it a pleasant walk on a paved path along the river park. The third possibility is to park along Prince Street, the road that separates Fort Marcy Condominiums from Mesa Park; follow Washington Street north past Paseo de Peralta, turn right on Artist Road (follow the Hyde Park/Ski Basin signs) and right again onto Prince Street. From the Cross of the Martyrs at the western tip of the mesa overlooking the city, a winding brick walkway descends into downtown Santa Fe. The only drawback is that it can be a long, hot climb back up to your car.

Once you reach the **Plaza,** find a shady bench and take a moment to appreciate the setting. Part open-air museum and part eccentric urban renewal project, Santa Fe's Plaza marks the spot where English- and Spanish-speaking American civilizations met for the first time in the American west.

To the eyes of many newcomers, the architecture surrounding the Plaza seems so unfamiliar that its subtleties go unnoticed. At least five separate architectural styles — Spanish Pueblo, Territorial, Railroad Commercial (Italianate), Spanish Pueblo Mission Revival, and Territorial Revival — are plainly visible in the buildings flanking the four sides of the Plaza. The buildings are unified by continuous portals, a typical colonial New Mexican feature that was restored around the Plaza in 1966. The differences between the various architectural styles are more visible to those who raise their eyes to the second-story facades and rooflines. Building silhouettes further unify the overall effect across the northwest and southeast corners of the plaza, where the First National Bank Building echoes the skyline of the larger Museum of Fine Arts and that of Packard's Indian Trading Company mirrors La Fonda.

Two commemorative monuments stand on the Plaza. The obelisk in the center was erected in 1868 by the territorial legislature to honor federal soldiers who had fallen defending New Mexico. A smaller black granite marker near the southeast corner of the Plaza, erected in 1910 by the Daughters of the American Republic, marks the end of the Santa Fe Trail. Although it does not say so, the spot was also the end of the earlier Camino Real, the King's Highway linking colonial Santa Fe with Mexico City, which entered the Plaza area by the route that is now San Francisco Street.

Running the full length of the Plaza's north side is the Palace of the Governors, which houses the New Mexico Museum of History. The commercial buildings that line the other three sides of the Plaza are of much more recent vintage, most dating back no further than the late nineteenth century. Across the street from the southeast corner of the Plaza is La Fonda, the city's most famous historic hotel. It stands as a living link to the early twentieth century and the arrival of tourism in Santa Fe. Diagonally across the Plaza, at the northwest corner, the New Mexico Museum of Fine Arts recalls the emergence of the city's artist community during the same era. Both buildings were defining examples of Spanish Pueblo Revival architecture.

Pueblo Indians display their jewelry and pottery for sale under the Palace portal, in the same spots where their ancestors traded for centuries. In the late 1970s, a law school graduate who was working as a jeweler while waiting for admission to the New Mexico bar filed a lawsuit charging racial discrimination when he was not allowed to sell his jewelry alongside the Indians. To preclude more such disputes, the Indians were officially declared an exhibit of the museum, which sets rules for them, including the requirement that all items must be made by the vendor or family members. Pottery and jewelry here are of the finest quality, and prices are negotiable. The city of Santa Fe licenses the non-Indian vendors who sell jewelry and other craft items from stands or pushcarts along the Plaza sidewalk across the street from the Palace. Until recently, peddlers' licenses on the Plaza were limited to a handful of vendors whose families had been selling there for generations, but within the past few years more licenses have been granted. The vendors are a subject of continuing controversy between those who would have the city ban commercial activities on the Plaza altogether and those (especially would-be vendors) who wish the city would issue more licenses. There are elderly Indians who have been wandering the Plaza and hotel lobbies with their jewelry for so long that no one cares to stop them.

The must-see tourist highlights around the Plaza are the **New Mexico Museum of History,** housed within the Palace of the Governors, and the New Mexico Museum of Fine Arts, one block west. The history museum contains permanent exhibits of maps, documents, old photographs, and such artifacts as spurs, firearms, pottery, antique clothing, and ceremonial death carts, tracing the history of New Mexico from the earliest Spanish explorations to statehood. Other rooms in the Palace include a restoration of the office of Governor L. Bradford Prince, the last territorial governor of New Mexico to occupy the Old Palace, as it was then known, and a magnificent replica of the interior of a Spanish colonial mission church. Oil murals around the walls of one room, where Indian artifacts are displayed, depict views of the Pajarito Plateau with Indians and ancient cliff dwellings painted in 1913 by early Santa Fe artist Carl Lotave. The museum shop contains one

Palace of the Governors today. *Photograph by Richard Harris.*

of the most complete selections of books on southwestern history and Indian subjects to be found anywhere.

The **New Mexico Museum of Fine Arts** is one of the largest art museums in the southwest. The galleries on the main floor contain changing exhibits from the museum's huge collection of paintings by twentieth-century New Mexico artists. Most of the thousands of paintings owned by the museum are stored in two climate-controlled subterranean levels, and only a few dozen are exposed to public view at any one time. Toward the rear of the original museum building, a wide hallway leads past an outdoor sculpture garden to the New Wing, the largest gallery in the museum, used primarily for traveling exhibits. Upstairs are several smaller rooms where works by early twentieth-century New Mexico painters are displayed. Georgia O'Keeffe, New Mexico's most famous artist, who would not allow the museum to show her work during her lifetime because of a long-standing dispute, now has the entire room at the top of the stairs devoted to her work. Other rooms contain works by Ernest Blumenschein, Andrew Dasburg, John Sloan, Nikolai Fechin, Los Cinco Pintores, and other members of the Santa Fe and Taos artists' colonies. **St. Francis Auditorium,** which occupies the west wing of the museum building, is decorated with large murals that were designed and begun by School of American Archaeology artist Donald Beauregard and completed after his death by Carlos Vierra and Kenneth Chapman. The murals recount the coming of Franciscan missionaries to the New World, beginning with Christopher Columbus's stay at a Franciscan monastery in Portugal and continuing through the conversion of the Maya in Mexico's Yucatán to the arrival of the friars in New Mexico and the construction of a mission church.

Before venturing off into the shops and side streets of downtown Santa Fe, take time to stroll through **La Fonda,** the third major public building at the town center, diagonally across the Plaza from the Museum of Fine Arts. The big, dim, tile-floored lobby, decorated in Spanish and New Mexican motifs, is an atmospheric masterpiece. Paintings by early Santa Fe artist Gerald Cassidy grace the lobby, along with folk-art murals by Ernest Martínez, the hotel's in-house artist since the 1950s. In the summer, a rooftop bar affords fine views of the Plaza, San Francisco Street, and St. Francis Cathedral.

The **Plaza** has been transformed many times during the four centuries that it has marked the center of Santa Fe. It has been a dusty parade ground, an Indian dance plaza, and a shady Eastern-style town square complete with a gazebo bandstand. At one time it was used as a community cornfield. A white picket fence surrounded the Plaza in the late nineteenth century, and the only entrances were through turnstiles designed to keep wandering horses out. The

Plaza has been the scene of thousands of community fiestas and celebrations, artisans markets, concerts, political speeches, religious processions, and street dances.

The inscription on the east face of the obelisk at the center of the Plaza reads: "Erected by the people of New Mexico through their legislatures of 1866–7–8 / May the Union be perpetual." The north and west faces pay tribute "To the heroes of the Federal Army who fell at the battle of Valverde fought with the rebels February 21, 1862" and "To the heroes of the Federal Army who fell at the battles of Canon del Apache and Pigeon's Rancho (La Glorieta) fought with the rebels March 28, 1862, and to those who fell at the battle fought with the rebels at Peralta April 15, 1862. The south face reads "To the heroes who have fallen in the various battles with the [...] Indians in the Territory of New Mexico." In the 1970s, an unidentified Anglo man wearing a hardhat used a hammer and chisel to neatly remove the word "savage" in broad daylight.

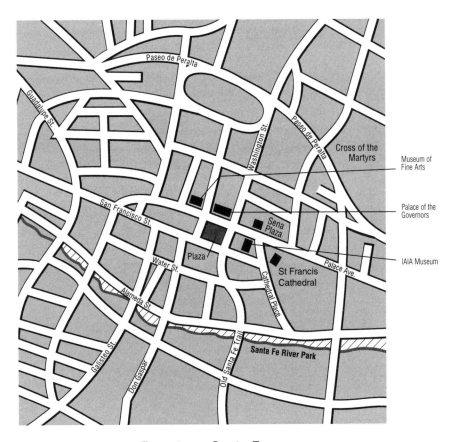

Downtown Santa Fe

PALACE AVENUE

The **Palace of the Governors,** which runs along the entire north side of the Plaza and has no street address, was built by Santa Fe's founder, Spanish conquistador Pedro de Peralta, in 1610, fourteen years before Manhattan Island (New York) was purchased from the Indians. Originally called the *casas reales* (royal houses) and later the Old Palace, it served as the seat of government in New Mexico for three centuries. Following the Pueblo Revolt of 1680, it was occupied by Tewa Indians for 12 years and converted into pueblo-style dwellings. Thereafter, it served as the official "mansion" and offices of Spanish viceroys and both Mexican and U.S. territorial governors. Although it was renovated several times in the eighteenth and nineteenth centuries, virtually all changes that were made in those times have been removed. The government abandoned the building in 1900, upon completion of a new territorial capital, and parts of it were used for everything from banking and grain storage to art shows. Beginning in 1909, the School of American Archaeology took over the decrepit Old Palace and, under the supervision of archaeologist Jesse Nusbaum, restored it to a semblance of its original seventeenth-century appearance. Portions of the present wall surface have been removed to reveal the adobe construction underneath, and holes in the wood plank flooring expose excavations that show the levels of adobe flooring in earlier centuries and the remains of walls left over from the Palace's years as an Indian pueblo. The Palace of Governors is open to the public. Admission is charged.

■ 107 West Palace Avenue

The **New Mexico Museum of Fine Arts** was designed by Colorado architect Isaac H. Rapp and completed in 1917 on a site previously occupied by administrative buildings of Fort Marcy, the U.S. Army command post established during the occupation of New Mexico after the Mexican War. One of the first buildings to be built in the Spanish Pueblo Revival style, the Palace Avenue facade of the museum is loosely patterned after a seventeenth-century Franciscan mission church at Acoma Pueblo in western New Mexico, while the Lincoln Avenue face was inspired by another old mission church at Laguna Pueblo. The museum is a refinement of three seminal Spanish Pueblo buildings that Rapp had designed in the previous few years: the Colorado Supply Company warehouse near Raton Pass, the Gross–Kelly warehouse in the Santa Fe Railroad yards, and the New Mexico Building (now the Balboa Park Club) in San Diego's Balboa Park. For many years the museum served as a center for the city's developing artists' colony. Exhibition space was provided on an "open door" basis to all resident New Mexico artists. A framing shop in the basement was also available to local artists, and wealthy patrons sponsored monthly artists' banquets upstairs. The spacious new wing at the back of the museum, designed by Edward Larrabee Barnes and Antoine Predock, was opened in 1982. The town clock in the shape of a giant pocket watch on the corner in front of the art museum stood on the opposite side of the plaza, in front of what was then Spitz Jewelers, from 1916 to 1967. When the portal was built in front of the old jewelry store, the son of watchmaker Salamon Spitz donated the clock to the city, and it was moved to its present location.

LINCOLN AVENUE

The buildings that line the west side of the Plaza date back to the mid-nineteenth century, when wagonloads of trade goods arriving on the Santa Fe Trail were unloaded in the Plaza. Older buildings occupied at least a portion of

Spitz clock. *Photograph by Richard Harris.*

Lincoln Avenue on west side of Santa Fe Plaza, 1866. *U.S. Army Signal Corps Photograph, courtesy Museum of New Mexico, neg. 11177.*

Santa Fe Plaza, 1881. *Photograph by William H. Jackson & Co., courtesy Museum of New Mexico, neg. 15282*

this block in colonial times, and early descriptions suggest that an Indian pueblo stood here at the time of the reconquest in 1692.

The **First National Bank Building** at the corner of Lincoln and Palace was originally the Territorial-style Perea & Company Building, one of the first two-story buildings in town when it was built in the mid-nineteenth century. It later served as the Z. Staab & Company general store (1874), the Capital Hotel (1886), and the *New Mexican* newspaper offices (1900). In the 1920s it was renamed the Cassell Building and converted into Santa Fe's first motion picture theater. John Gaw Meem remodeled it in Spanish Pueblo Revival style in 1953–1954 for the First National Bank, which was moving from its former location on the opposite side of the

Plaza. The double corbels and twin portal posts are an unusual feature intended to convey the same kind of solidity as that conveyed by the massive stone columns with Ionic capitals on the previous bank building.

The **Batts Building,** which houses the Plaza Restaurant and several gift shops, also dates from the early territorial era. A refurbishment in the 1950s transformed the ground floor, with its red brick facing and picture windows under the Territorial Revival portico, into the storefronts out of step with the Plaza's overall Santa Fe style architecture.

The Territorial-style **Ore House** restaurant is in the old Elsberg & Amberg Building, originally a dry goods store built in the 1860s. Although its whitewashed Victorian portico and covered balcony clash with most other Plaza

El Oñate Theater (now First National Bank), 1921. *Photograph courtesy Museum of New Mexico, neg. 10661.*

Ore House today. *Photograph by Richard Harris.*

architecture, it is probably the most historically authentic of all the commercial buildings on the Plaza. Photographs from the nineteenth century show the building facade looking much as it does today. During the intervening time, however, it was transformed to become the Claire Hotel, the major hotel on the plaza until La Fonda was built, and later restored to its former appearance.

Claire Hotel, 1916. *Photograph courtesy Museum of New Mexico, neg. 10671.*

SAN FRANCISCO STREET

As the terminus of El Camino Real, the Spanish colonial highway to Santa Fe, San Francisco Street has been lined with buildings since early colonial times. With the arrival of the railroad, most older structures in this block were demolished and replaced by red brick Victorian commercial buildings, which were later stuccoed over and renovated in assorted versions of Santa Fe style. The portal, mirroring that of the Palace of Governors but adorned with *canales* instead of exposed *vigas*, was added in 1968.

The **F.W. Woolworth Building** at 58 West San Francisco is treasured by locals simply because it is the last store on the Plaza—or, indeed, in the downtown area—that still sells everyday necessities, other Main Street stores such as J.C. Penney's and Sears & Roebuck having long since relocated to the shopping malls for lower rents and more parking.

The **Plaza Galería** at 66 West San Francisco was the site of La Castrense (also called the Capilla de Nuestra Señora de la Luz, or Chapel of Our Lady of Light), a Mexican Baroque–style military church that fronted on the Plaza from 1760 to 1859. It fell into disrepair after Mexican independence, and when the U.S. Army occupied Santa Fe after the Mexican War, it was used first as an armory and later as a U.S. District Courthouse. When citizens objected to using a church for these purposes, Bishop Lamy evaluated the possibilities for restoring the church but decided against it. He demolished the church, using its roof beams to restore the Santuario de Guadalupe. The ornate stone *reredos* or alterpiece in the church was stored in the St. Francis Cathedral for many years before being

Shopping on San Francisco Street, 1918. *Photograph by Wesley Bradfield, courtesy Museum of New Mexico, neg. 14142.*

installed in the Cristo Rey Church in the 1940s. After demolition of La Castrense, the Delgado Building was built on the site in 1859 to house a trading company. It later became J.C. Penney's and then Dunlap's Department Store. When Dunlap's closed in 1989, the building was gutted and converted into the Plaza Galería, an indoor mall containing 26 small galleries and gift shops.

The two-story buildings east of the Plaza Galería, which contain art galleries and fashion boutiques, are officially known as **Spiegelberg No. 2** and **Spiegelberg No. 1.** The first of them was built as a retail store in 1881 by merchant Jacob Solomon Spiegelberg, a German immigrant who had come to Santa Fe with Kearny's troops 35 years earlier and brought his four brothers west to join him. The second store was built the following year. Both buildings were of red brick adorned with the most elaborate Victorian ornamentation

on the Plaza, which was removed in the course of a Santa Fe–style renovation in the 1950s.

The single-story retail store on the corner across from La Fonda was originally the **Seligman and Cleaver Store.** Established in 1855, it is one of the oldest storefronts still standing in Santa Fe.

■ 100 East San Francisco Street

La Fonda (the name is Spanish for "the inn") was the largest building in Santa Fe when it was built in 1920. The hotel was originally conceived by a group of local investors, who sold it to the Fred Harvey Company prior to completion. The last major project designed by Isaac Hamilton Rapp, it underwent a facelift and expansion just eight years later at the hands of John Gaw Meem. The site where La Fonda stands, at the exact point where El Camino Real and the Old Santa Fe Trail met, was previous-

San Francisco Street looking east, 1897. *Photograph by John B. Reall, courtesy Museum of New Mexico, neg. 124334.*

Old Santa Fe Trail marker.
Photograph by Richard Harris.

ly the location of the single-story adobe Exchange Hotel, which was established sometime before 1855 and was the only hotel in town during the early territorial years. An older *fonda*, about which little is known, already stood on the site when Anglo traders began arriving in Santa Fe in the 1820s.

WASHINGTON AVENUE

The east side of the Plaza was vacant during colonial times. The Plaza extended all the way to the older church that stood on the site of St. Francis Cathedral. The entire block was developed in territorial times by James Johnson, a merchant and financier who

Meat market in former Exchange Hotel building, 1900. *Photograph courtesy Museum of New Mexico, neg. 105576.*

Farolitos on La Fonda, 1930. *Photograph by T. Harmon Parkhurst, courtesy Museum of New Mexico, neg. 54312.*

Johnson Block (Santa Fe Finishing School and U.S. Post Office), 1880. *Photograph courtesy Museum of New Mexico, neg. 1381.*

moved to Santa Fe from Maryland in 1852. The two-story Johnson Block contained the U.S. Post Office, the First National Bank, the *New Mexican* newspaper and law offices, and a girls' finishing school where the daughters of merchants and army officers could learn eastern-style etiquette.

The south half of the **Johnson Block,** now occupied by Packard's Indian Trading Company (which has operated at this location for more than 50 years) and Eagle Dancer Indian shop, was renovated in 1888 and converted into the red brick First National Bank, with a massive neo-Grecian columned facade. It was renovated in Spanish Pueblo Revival style after the bank moved to the other side of the Plaza in the 1950s.

The north half of the Johnson Block was rebuilt in 1888 as the Catron Block, financed by lawyer, politician, and

financier Thomas B. Catron, a leader of the notorious Santa Fe Ring. The ornate Italianate facade of the building, designed by a little-known architect named Brigham and built by the prominent firm of Palladino and Berardinelli (Italian stonemasons who had come to Santa Fe to build St. Francis Cathedral), has been preserved, although the red brick has been painted to harmonize with the other Plaza architecture and a Territorial Revival portal has been added. Although the words "Catron Block" are inscribed in the facade, the building is often known as the Blatt Building, after the merchant who operated Santa Fe's first full-line department store, the White House, there in the early twentieth century. The second floor of the Catron Block is the only building on the Plaza that preserves hints of the Victorian appearance that characterized turn-of-the-century Santa Fe.

Catron Building today—detail. *Photograph by Richard Harris.*

SPANISH COLONIAL SANTA FE

THE SIXTEENTH CENTURY

Spanish exploration in the southwest began in 1536 with Alvar Núñez Cabeza de Vaca, the royal accountant assigned to an ill-fated expedition to Florida led by conquistador Pánfilo de Narváez, shipwrecked in a storm off the Florida coast near present-day Tampa. The survivors built rafts from fragments of the ship but succeeded only in drifting west across the gulf to find themselves marooned once more near the location of present-day Galveston, Texas, where most died at the hands of cannibalistic Karankawa Indians. Cabeza de Vaca and three other survivors trekked across Texas, New Mexico, Chihuahua, and Sonora before encountering a Spanish slave-hunting expedition. The route and details of Cabeza de Vaca's journey are largely unknown. After returning to civilization, Cabeza de Vaca retired to his family estate in Spain, but his offspring returned to America to join expeditions to settle New Mexico. Today, more than 200 Santa Fe households carry on Cabeza de Vaca's name (often shortened to C de Baca or simply Baca).

Legend has it that he became the apprentice of an Indian shaman and traveled in safety because the indigenous people believed he had magical powers, but that he concealed this from all but his family, fearing to be branded a heretic by the Spanish Inquisition. Perhaps as part of a cover story, Cabeza de Vaca claimed to have visited Quivira, a city of great wealth that church leaders already had decided must exist in northern Mexico. The city in question was probably the Indian pueblo of Zuni, though whether Cabeza de Vaca actually saw it or merely heard about it is questionable. A 1539 expedition led by Fray Marcos de Niza to confirm the rumors ended disastrously, but the survivors straggled back to Mexico City with even more extravagant accounts of not one but seven cities of gold.

Encouraged by the stories, in 1540 the viceroy of New Spain sent Francisco Vásquez de Coronado, the 30-year-old governor of the northern Mexico province of New Galicia (now Chihuahua), to locate the seven cities. In an epic two-year journey that took him and his recruits as far as the Grand Canyon and the Kansas prairies, Coronado found not only Hawikuh (Zuni) but a number of other long-established Indian towns, including Taos and two now-ruined pueblos in the Santa Fe area—Pecos and Kuaua. They found that the Indian pueblos were much poorer than the cities of central Mexico and that there was almost no gold. In fact, there was no evidence of any precious metals to be mined in the rugged New Mexico mountains. Throughout three centuries of Spanish and Mexican rule, no gold would be discovered in New Mexico or elsewhere in the north. Gold strikes were made in areas that are now California, Arizona, New Mexico, and Colorado just three years after the northern Mexico territories were ceded to the United States.

After Coronado's empty-handed return, no further Spanish expeditions into New Mexico took place for more than a generation. In 1581, Fray Agustín Rodríquez led a group of missionaries into New Mexico, but all were killed by indigenous people. In 1590, Gaspar Castaño (for whom Don Gaspar, a major Santa Fe street and historic district, is named) mounted an unauthorized expedition to establish a colony in New Mexico, but the Spanish army hunted him down and he was prosecuted and sentenced to slavery. In 1592, adventurers Leyva de Bonilla and Juan de Humaña made another illegal foray into New Mexico, where both were killed—Humaña in a skirmish with Indians and Bonilla in a mutiny by his own recruits.

THE SEVENTEENTH CENTURY

The Spanish colony called Nuevo Mexico, or New Mexico, officially got its start in 1600 under the leadership of Governor Juan de Oñate, who financed the expedition with his inheritance from a family fortune made in the silver

Portals, Gregorio Crespin House, 132 E. DeVargas Street, built c. 1740. *National Register of Historic Places.*

mines of Zacatecas, Mexico. Oñate established Nuevo Mexico's first capital, San Gabriel, at the confluence of the Río Grande and Río Chama, about 35 miles north of Santa Fe near the present-day town of Española.

Few traces remain of San Gabriel today. It seems that Oñate's priorities in financing the new colony were skewed. For instance, in hopes of discovering the mythical Straits of Anian—a passage from the Mississippi River to the Pacific Ocean—he brought a full complement of sailors and shipbuilding equipment to the New Mexico desert; yet he failed to provide adequate provisions for the colonist families in his expedition, who were forced to depend on local Indians for such necessities as food and blankets. After Oñate's followers complained to the Viceroy of New Spain in Mexico City, the governor was removed from his post.

The viceroy was on the verge of abandoning the whole idea of a northern colony on the Río Grande when a report arrived from the contingent of 10 Franciscan brothers in Nuevo Mexico showed hope for missionary efforts among the Indians. Deciding to give the fledgling colony one more chance, in 1609 the viceroy appointed Pedro de Peralta as the new governor of Nuevo Mexico and ordered him to relocate the capital farther south, where it would be more centrally located between the northern and central Río Grande Indian pueblos. Other factors that inspired the choice of the new capital site were its proximity to the Santa Fe River, its 7000-foot elevation, resulting in a mild climate year-round, and the abundance of timber nearby.

Peralta named the new capital La Villa Real de la Santa Fe de San Francisco de Asis (the Royal Town of the Holy Faith of Saint Francis of Assisi), reflecting the key role played by Franciscan missionaries in the new colony. Shortened to "Santa Fe" in common speech even in colonial times and officially renamed Santa Fe when New Mexico became a U.S. territory centuries later, Santa Fe still formally retains its lengthy colonial name on the municipal seal and in the city charter.

Santa Fe in the seventeenth century was first and foremost a military fort. The Palace of the Governors, then known as the *casas reales* ("royal houses," or government buildings), was the front portion of a military compound that included an arsenal, a jail, a chapel, the governor's residence, and offices for other government officials. It covered about one-fourth of the occupied land area of Santa Fe. Each of the first Spanish civilian residents of Santa Fe was assigned two contiguous lots in the blocks that surrounded the Plaza for a house and garden, as well as fields on the outskirts of town for vegetable farms, livestock pasturage, vineyards, and olive groves. Aztecs and other Nahuatl Indians brought from Mexico to do the manual labor of building the capitol lived south of the river in the Barrio de Analco (*analco* is Nahuatl for "on the other side"; *barrio* translates literally as "district" but may imply "slum" or "ghetto"; nonslave districts in Santa Fe were called *vecindades*, not *barrios*). They, along with the Franciscan missionaries responsible for their spiri-

Don Diego de Vargas Zapata y Lujan Ponce de León, painting c. 1704. *Photograph courtesy Museum of New Mexico, neg. 11409.*

tual supervision, grew corn communally in fields along the south edge of town.

The majority of Spanish settlers in Santa Fe's jurisdiction lived away from the capital in *haciendas,* country estates owned by individual families under land grants from the king of Spain, along the Río Grande and its tributaries. The landowners lived in large, fortified residences, while farmworkers— mostly Mexican Indians—lived and worked on other parts of the land grants under conditions similar to those of serfs in medieval Europe.

Like the villages and haciendas of the surrounding countryside, the capital itself lived in almost complete isolation from the mainstream of Spanish colonial civilization. Supply expeditions from Mexico arrived as infrequently as once in three years. Festering in the colonial civilization of seventeenth-century Nuevo Mexico was hidden animosity against the Spanish on the part of the Pueblo Indians, whose towns shared the river banks with Spanish haciendas. In a certain sense, the indigenous people were fortunate: They did not face mass relocation or genocide as did Indian people in the eastern United States, because Spain based its right to colonize the Americas on a papal declaration conditioned upon assisting missionaries to convert native people to Catholicism. The usual plan was to convert the local people and put them to work.

In Nuevo Mexico, however, the Indian people outnumbered the newcomers and resisted any sort of social contact other than formal negotiations. Missionaries had considerable success in gathering communities of Christianized Indians and built impressive adobe churches at the majority of large Indian pueblos. Recent atrocities by Spanish soldiers against Indian tribes in western Mexico and South America had raised the church's concern for the welfare of American Indians, especially those who lived in established towns and thus were likely candidates for conversion. The Spanish brought their own Aztec slaves from Mexico but did not enslave the Pueblo Indians—well, not exactly. They required tribute from each pueblo in the form of firewood, salt, and other commodities that came from the wilderness. Then, too, the Indians were often caught up in the uneasy relationship between their protectors, the Franciscan missionaries, and the secular military government of Nuevo Mexico. As alliances between Spanish royalty and the Vatican waxed and waned, the Nuevo Mexicano government repeatedly changed the rules concerning dances and other non-Christian ceremonies.

Aside from jurisdictional disputes between tribal elders and the Spanish governor, the Pueblo people suffered in silence until the summer a terrible drought destroyed the crops of Indians and Spanish settlers alike. Spanish attempts to exact tribute in the form of corn from the starving Indians touched off the Pueblo Revolt of 1680.

De Vargas Pageant, 1912. *Photograph courtesy Museum of New Mexico, neg. 10793.*

The uprising, which was supported by all Río Grande pueblos as well as some groups of nomadic *indios barbaros* ("wild Indians," now known as Navajos and Apaches) from the western outlands, was fomented in secrecy by Popé, a San Juan Pueblo leader, who orchestrated simultaneous attacks on haciendas up and down the Río Grande in early August 1680, burning homes, scattering livestock into the hills for the nomads to capture, and killing 300 Spanish settlers. Upon receiving news of the uprising, Governor Otermín gathered all residents of Santa Fe inside the Palace of the Governors compound for self-defense. Over the next few days, survivors of the Río Grande massacres straggled into Santa Fe, swelling to more than 1000 the number of people huddled within the palace. The Indians took up positions along the south bank of the Santa Fe River, and the first seige of Santa Fe began.

The seige lasted five days. Then the Indians shut off the *acequia* that supplied water to the palace, forcing the Spanish to surrender or fight. Armored Spanish horsemen attacked and managed to set the Indians to flight, but there was no doubt that they would be back. Governor Otermín seized the period of respite to organize a retreat to the south, where he and his followers formed the settlement that would become El Paso, Texas. They lived there for 12 years before cavalry troops arrived from Mexico City to lead the Spanish reconquest of Santa Fe.

With the Spanish gone, Pueblo people took over Santa Fe. They burned the church, destroyed all documents they found, and subdivided the Palace of the Governors into dwelling units. According to one eyewitness to the Spanish reconquest, by 1692 at least 1500 Indians were living in the palace and in traditional pueblos from one to four stories high that they had built on the other three sides of the Plaza.

Local tradition clings to the myth that the Spanish reconquest of Santa Fe was a "bloodless victory." True, when conquistador and newly appointed governor Diego de Vargas and his army of 50 Spanish soldiers and 50 Mexican Indians reached Santa Fe in September 1692, he managed to establish diplomatic negotiations with the Puebloans and obtain their consent to the return of Spanish settlers. When de Vargas returned the following year with 70 families, however, the Indians would not let them into the Plaza. Facing a winter with inadequate shelter and too little food, de Vargas laid seige to the Palace of Governors for two months. The situation grew increasingly desperate with the onset of winter, as 22 Spanish settlers died of starvation and disease. Finally, de Vargas employed the same tactic that had been used against his predecessor: He dammed the *acequia* and cut off the Indians' water supply. Then he attacked the thirst-weakened Indians, killing 81 and scattering the rest.

It was at this point in history that Santa Fe's unique blend of Spanish and Indian architectural styles originated. As colonists returned from El Paso, many found themselves temporarily homeless pending determination of real estate claims, since almost all legal documents had been burned during the revolt. The pueblos that the Indians had built became temporary living quarters for the Spaniards and inspired them in rebuilding their own homes.

Hostilities and occasional violent skirmishes between the Indians and the Spanish continued through 1696. To protect themselves against punitive expeditions by the Spanish army, some Indians built defensive pueblos on mesa tops above the Río Grande, while others left their homes and fields to live among their Navajo allies in the desert wilderness to the west, where a new way of life was emerging built upon the domestication of sheep and horses captured from Spanish haciendas during the 1680 revolt.

In 1696, Governor de Vargas was arrested by his successor, Rodríguez Cubero, on charges that he had hoarded food during the shortages suffered in the first winter of the Spanish reconquest. De Vargas was taken in chains to Mexico City, where he proved his innocence after several years. He was reinstated as governor of Nuevo Mexico in 1703. His comeback may explain why two Santa Fe streets (Don Diego Avenue and De Vargas Street) were named after him, while Don Cubero and other colonial governors only merited one apiece.

THE EIGHTEENTH CENTURY

The eighteenth century was a time of growth and development for Nuevo Mexico. Traffic increased along El Camino Real, the wagon route that ran from Mexico City past the silver mines at Zacatecas to the desert towns of Chihuahua and El Paso before reaching its northern end at Santa Fe's Plaza. Although Apache Indians made the desert crossing a dangerous undertaking, trade with Mexico City gradually increased, and new settlers came to Santa Fe a few at a time. From 1700 to 1790, the population of Santa Fe more than doubled, to 2542 residents.

The biggest problem facing the Spanish colonists in the eighteenth century was Indian raids. Apaches and Utes posed the greatest initial threat, but as the settlement of Texas pushed indigenous people westward, the Comanches replaced the Apaches as the main enemies of Spanish settlers and Pueblo Indians alike. Isolated Franciscan missions such as the one at Pecos were abandoned because of Comanche raids. Pueblo people, settlers, and missionaries were forced to put aside past differences and unite against a common threat, giving rise to a live-and-let-live attitude that has characterized intercultural relations in northern New Mexico through most of its history.

In 1705, the governor ordered all Spanish settlers around Santa Fe to relocate their homes, gardens, and corrals as close to the central plaza as possible for security and defense from Indian raids. This approach, which coincidentally had been the concept for Indian pueblos over a span of 800 years, set a precedent for new villages in the mountains to the north of the capital, where many residents still live along narrow village streets and go to

Wagon train on the Plaza, 1861. *Photograph courtesy Museum of New Mexico, neg. 11254.*

work in the surrounding fields, meadows, and forests. In Santa Fe, however, it did not last long. As families grew, it was natural for succeeding generations to choose to build homes on their out-of-town acreages.

To increase security in Santa Fe and the Indian pueblos and Spanish villages along the Río Grande, the governor created villages of *genízaros*, Indians of uncertain origin who did not belong to a pueblo, along the outskirts of the region where Spanish settlers lived. The idea was that these villages would insulate the Spanish and Puebloans from attack by hostile Indians. A number of northern New Mexico towns, including Bernalillo (southwest of Santa Fe) and Abiquiu (northwest of Santa Fe), got their start as genízaro villages. At the same time, rural villages of Spanish sheepherders and woodcutters grew up in the pine-forested hills along the base of the Sangre de Cristo Mountains north of Santa Fe. Many of these villages, such as Chimayo, Truchas, Las Trampas, Cordova, Ojo Sarco, and Peñasco, have continued their tradition-bound community life ever since. Today, they offer rare glimpses into the lifeways of Spanish settlers in New Mexico.

Nuevo Mexico continued to be among the poorest Spanish colonies, hardly even measuring up to the modest economic resources of Yucatán or Guatemala. Its major exports were sheep and bison hides, which were traded southward to Chihuahua and Zacatecas. Colonial governors sent exploration parties to the wildest reaches of their domain but found almost no gold or silver. To make matters worse, Nuevo Mexico was the only Spanish colony in North America without access to a seaport, a severe limitation on economic development. Two centuries after its founding, Nuevo Mexico was still one of the most remote outposts of the Spanish Empire.

Late in the eighteenth century, around the time of the U.S. Revolutionary War, the Bourbon reforms restructured European colonialism. Where Mexico was concerned, the reforms amounted to budget cutbacks and belt tightening. As part of the reforms, King Carlos III of Spain reorganized Mexico's frontier colonies, consolidating them into *provincias internas*. The new northern border of the provinces, approximately the same as the U.S.–Mexican border today, stranded Nuevo Mexico outside the official jurisdiction of the viceroy in Mexico City and absolved Spain of any responsibility for subsidizing the colony. Supply trains ceased coming, and both the military and missionaries were abandoned without government support.

MEXICAN AND TERRITORIAL SANTA FE

THE NINETEENTH CENTURY

Soon after the turn of the century, the de facto governor of Nuevo Mexico sent a diplomatic mission to the Spanish government to plead for financial help and reinstatement as an official colony. The representatives returned to

Santa Fe emptyhanded. The Spanish Empire was shrinking worldwide, and the economic resources needed to sustain it were dwindling. Finally, in 1821, Spain abandoned almost all of its former colonies in the Americas, and Nuevo Mexico was declared to be a state in the newly formed nation of Mexico. (A few years later, for political reasons, it was demoted from a state to a territory.)

Mexican independence set the stage for one of the most portentious encounters in American history. Throughout the colonial era, trade with countries other than Spain was prohibited by law, and any hapless French or U.S. traveler caught in Nuevo Mexico territory was arrested as a spy and marched to Mexico City for interrogation. Mexico reversed the policy and threw its borders open to trade with the United States. Within a year, trapper William Bicknell started blazing a wagon route from Independence, Missouri, the U.S. gateway to the American frontier, to Santa Fe, the northernmost capital in Mexico. The distance between the two towns was 780 miles, a long journey but almost 300 miles shorter than the brutal desert road to Mexico City.

With the opening of the trail, Santa Fe residents prospered as never before. Trade caravans arrived frequently rather than once every few years. Anglo merchants brought factory-made goods that had been hard to get

Interior of St. Francis Cathedral. *Photograph Courtesy Museum of New Mexico, neg. 10020.*

under Spanish rule, such as cloth, jewelry, and firearms, and swapped them for commodities such as wool and furs, as well as mules, which had been almost unknown in Missouri—and the rest of the United States—until traders started importing them from Mexico. Santa Fe's Mexican governor, Manuel Armijo (commonly known among Anglos of the time as "His Obesity"), levied high tariffs on U.S. citizens importing goods to Nuevo Mexico. Soon half the traffic on the Santa Fe Trail was Mexican traders making the profitable journey to Missouri and back.

The people of Nuevo Mexico enjoyed about 25 years of unbridled prosperity before political earthquakes shook Santa Fe. The first rumbling came in 1837, when José Gonzales of Taos, who had been inspired by wars of independence in Texas and Yucatán, masterminded an ill-fated Indian and New Mexican revolt against the Mexican government. Four years later, the neighboring Republic of Texas sent troops to invade Santa Fe and secure the region as part of the independent republic. The little-known expedition, which numbered three times as many as the defenders of the Alamo, was arrested before reaching Santa Fe and taken to prison in Mexico by forced march.

Five years after that, in 1846, the United States went to war against Mexico. U.S. Brigadier General Stephen Kearny led a cavalry force to capture Santa Fe. For reasons unknown, Mexican Governor Armijo chose to flee to Mexico rather than fight in defense of Santa Fe. Kearny occupied Santa Fe, took over the Palace of the Governors, expanded the military compound behind it, and constructed a fort overlooking the city from a mesa half a mile east of the Plaza. Although the initial occupation of Santa Fe was bloodless, a resistance movement spread in secret. In 1847, a rebellion flared up in Taos, and Charles Bent, the first U.S. territorial governor of New Mexico, was assassinated. The following year, U.S. troops captured Mexico City, ending the Mexican War. In the Treaty of Guadalupe Hidalgo, Mexico signed over the territory of New Mexico (which included present-day Arizona and parts of Colorado and Utah) to the United States.

A debate raged in Washington for two years concerning New Mexico's status. Although New Mexico had enough population to qualify for statehood and, in fact, had more residents than any other territory in the Rocky Mountain west, many congress members believed that it should not be granted statehood because a large majority of New Mexicans spoke no English. It was formally declared a territory of the United States in 1850.

The most noticeable change that marked the beginning of the territorial period was the transformation of the Catholic church from the regional folk religion of missionary priests and *penitente* brothers to a more conventional, mainstream Catholicism. Lamy destroyed two adobe churches, built two European-style neo-Gothic ones, renovated another beyond recognition, and eliminated most Spanish-speaking priests. (See Chapter 4 for more about Archbishop Lamy and his churches.) Lamy's religious revival notwithstanding, gambling soon became the biggest industry in territorial Santa Fe. By the mid-1850s, casinos and brothels operated openly within two blocks of the Palace of the Governors.

Eleven years after New Mexico became a U.S. territory, the U.S. Civil War broke out. Texas, which had also become part of the United States not long before, seceded from the Union and joined the Confederate States of America. Texans had long believed that New Mexico was rightfully a part of Texas, and in 1862 they mounted a cavalry expedition to seize Santa Fe in the name of the Confederacy. The rebel troops were within 30 miles of Santa Fe when they and a hunting party of Union soldiers from Fort Marcy took each other by surprise. The ensuing Battle of Glorieta, which is faithfully reenacted by the local historical society every spring, involved a full day of shooting but minimal casualties. During the skirmish, a messenger from the Fort Marcy party managed to ride back to Santa Fe and notify General Kearny, who rallied his troops to repel the invasion. While Kearny was searching for the rebel invaders, they entered Santa Fe and claimed New Mexico Territory for the Confederacy. Five days later, after routing the rebels' supply wagons, Kearny and his men rode back to capture Santa Fe without serious incident. After the almost comic invasion was defeated, New Mexicans voted the territory anti-slavery, unequivocally separating themselves from Texas, and had no further involvement in the Civil War.

Perhaps the biggest problem facing New Mexicans in the mid-nineteenth century was quieting titles to land. Although the U.S. government had pledged by treaty to honor pre-existing Spanish and Mexican land grants, the reality was that land had been passed on for centuries by the old European custom of *livery of seizin* (physically giving the new owner a symbolic handful of dirt in front of witnesses) without written documentation. To make matters worse, in 1869, territorial governor William A. Pile sold the Spanish archives stored in the Palace of the Governors as waste paper, destroying most documents from the Spanish colonial and Mexican periods, including land records. Shrewd operators claimed title to huge tracts of land throughout the territory by fraud or forgery and held it with private armies of gunfighters, while on the local level real estate swindles clouded property titles all over Santa Fe. In 1891, Congress established a U.S. Court of Private Land Claims in Santa Fe—fortuitously, as it turned out, for the following year the territorial capitol burned down, destroying most legal documents, including land records. Arson was suspected but never proved. By 1904, the federal court had confirmed title to about 2 million acres of land around New Mexico, sometimes on the flimsiest preponderance of evidence. Land disputes dating back to territorial times are still common today in northern New Mexico.

The Atchinson, Topeka & Santa Fe Railroad reached New Mexico in 1880, but when unscrupulous land promoters tried to gouge the railroad with exorbitant prices for rights-of-way through the narrow pass between Pecos and Santa Fe, the company decided to divert its tracks to the formerly insignificant little town of Albuquerque instead. Although Archbishop Lamy later prevailed upon the railroad to run a spur line into the capital, Santa Fe would never regain its position as a commercial center.

New Mexico and Arizona remained territories for decades after neighboring Texas, Colorado, Utah, Nevada, and California had all achieved statehood. Repeated proposals to become a state failed because of reluctance on the part of some U.S. Congress members to recognize a state in which the majority of the people did not speak English. Attempting to sidestep this objection, in 1906 the territorial government submitted a proposal to Congress to admit the territories of New Mexico and Arizona as a single state. The bid failed again, this time because the people of Arizona Territory voted it down. Finally, in 1912, both territories were granted statehood. New Mexico became the forty-seventh state admitted to the Union, with Santa Fe as its capital. Arizona, which took longer to adopt a state constitution, became a state five weeks later.

Santuario de Guadalupe. *Copyright © 1996 by Jack Kotz.*

3

Downtown
Santa Fe

anta Fe shambled into the twentieth century like an old cowboy, its
glory days fading into wistful memory and its place in the modern
world uncertain. The Santa Fe Trail trade declined rapidly with the
arrival in New Mexico of the Atchison, Topeka & Santa Fe Railroad,
and when the main rail route bypassed Santa Fe in favor of Albuquerque, the
commerce that had sustained Santa Fe in the nineteenth century collapsed,
leaving the city as nothing more than a local shopping center for the small,
isolated villages of northern New Mexico.

Santa Fe did not then, and does not now, have any economically significant manufacturing industry. Agriculture existed, and still does, only on the
near subsistence scale of family cornfields, chile patches, and alfalfa meadows. Then, as now, the statewide economy was based on exploitation of natural resources through cattle grazing on the arid eastern plain known as *el
llano,* timber cutting on hard-to-reach mountain slopes, and mining for low-
grade gold ore. There was not yet a market for New Mexico's major natural
resource, oil, and gas. A portion of the revenue from natural resource
exploitation found its way to Santa Fe in the form of taxes, providing government jobs, but both the levels of taxation and the size of state government
agencies were minuscule by modern standards. The city's economic
prospects appeared so doubtful that the population, which had almost
tripled during the nineteenth century, declined by 22 percent between 1890

Opposite: Loretto Chapel. *Photograph by Richard Harris.*

61

Sunmount Sanitarium cottage interior, 1913. *Photograph by Jesse L. Nusbaum, courtesy Museum of New Mexico, neg. 61398.*

and 1910 to a low of 5072 residents. On the eve of statehood, Santa Feans desperately needed a new way of bringing money into the local economy from the outside world.

Tourism held the solution. Today, virtually all retail businesses in downtown Santa Fe are geared toward tourists, and a large percentage of non-government jobs are in the hospitality industry. At the beginning of the twentieth century, however, pleasure travel was a luxury reserved for a wealthy few, and large-scale tourism was unknown in the United States.

The seeds of Santa Fe's economic dependence on out-of-state visitors got its start with health care as physicians came to recognize that the high, dry, mild climate was ideal for alleviating the symptoms of lung diseases. First the church-owned St. Vincent's Sanatorium and later the world-renowned Sunmount Sanitarium filled to capacity with refugees from the coal-smoke pollution of eastern industrial cities, seeking a cure for tuberculosis and other chronic respiratory illnesses that were often misdiagnosed as TB. Many people who originally came to Santa Fe for long-term medical treatment not only survived but stayed and prospered as artists, architects, and financiers.

Although tuberculosis is no longer the major public health problem that it was a century ago, Santa Fe has continued to sustain a reputation as a healing mecca of sorts. A legal and cultural openness to holistic therapies, rooted in the traditional tolerance of village *curanderas* and Indian shamans, has made Santa Fe an international center for alternative healing. Schools such as the Southwest Acupuncture College, New Mexico Academy of Healing Arts, and International Institute of Chinese Medicine draw students and practitioners from around the world. No fewer than 144 licensed acupuncturists practice in Santa Fe, along with Reiki energy healers, Rolfers, Ericksonian hypnotists, Mayan abdominal massage therapists, iridologists, Reunion therapists, and psychic surgeons. The number of psychotherapists in private practice in Santa Fe is more than 10 times the per capita number nationwide.

The idea of tourism, in the southwest at least, seems to have originated with the railroads, which saw it as a way to boost passenger travel on its routes through this sparsely populated region. Santa Fe's main tourist attraction in those days was the American Indian population of the nearby pueblos. Having relocated or exterminated most Indians east of the Mississippi River long since, people in the more "civilized" parts of the United States were renewing their fascination with indigenous people largely because of the new medium of motion pictures—many of them, such as Thomas Edison's experimental 1898 film *Indian Day School,* the 1912 Biograph films *Pueblo Legend* and *The Tourists,* and a series of 1914–1915 silent westerns starring Tom Mix, filmed in New Mexico. Many people believed that Indians were a vanishing race, due to federal policies of the time, which were aimed at eradicating native customs, languages, and dress with the eventual goal of eliminating Indian reservations and assimilating indigenous people into mainstream American life. The railroads saw big profit potential in inviting travelers to meet the country's most traditional Indian group, the Puebloans.

In the same year that New Mexico became a state, the Atchison, Topeka & Santa Fe Railroad began a decade-long advertising and promotion campaign to lure pleasure travelers to the southwest. They offered painters and illustrators free passage to Santa Fe to bring back romanticized depictions of the Pueblo Indians, their villages, and the natural landscape in which they lived. They sponsored art exhibitions in Chicago and most eastern seaboard cities, and they promoted Wild West shows and World's Fair–style expos featuring New Mexico and its Indians. The AT&SF began building their train stations throughout the southwest in a trademark Spanish Mission style of architecture to enhance the exotic image of what was then the most remote region in the United States. The promotion of railroad tourism reached its peak in the mid-1920s, when hotel entrepreneur Fred Harvey added La Fonda in Santa Fe to his chain of atmospheric southwestern hostelries, which also included the original lodge at the Grand Canyon. Tourists could visit the Indian pueblos in comfort on "Harveymobile" tours, then return to La Fonda in time for high tea served by gentile, uniformed "Harvey Girls," who soon became the subject of a popular movie themselves. At the same time, several annual community events started which have grown bigger each year since, including the revived Fiesta de Santa Fe and the Santa Fe Indian Market, each of which now draws hundreds of thousands of out-of-towners.

Candelario's "Original Trading Post". *Photograph by Richard Harris.*

Tourism increased tenfold in the late 1920s as establishment of service stations along U.S. Route 66 and other major highway routes made it practical to see New Mexico by private passenger car. Regretably, the Indians derived little benefit from early-day tourism. Their pottery and textiles, avidly sought by collectors and museums alike as artifacts of a supposedly vanishing culture, were bought for pennies by non-Indian businesspeople, many of whose lucrative trading companies are still in operation today. In the early years of New Mexico's statehood, the public fascination with Indian pueblos helped fuel the Santa Fe style architectural revival, until the city's neoantiquity became a tourist draw in its own right.

Today, both Indian and Spanish heritage — as well as revival architecture — continue to play key roles in Santa Fe's one-of-a-kind tourist allure, along with the cultural attractions of the opera and the art scene. In recent years the range of galleries that fill the downtown and Canyon Road historic districts has broadened to include not only Indian and Spanish art and works by resident Santa Fe artists but also an array of collectible-quality folk art from all parts of the world. Although the number of out-of-state tourists that visit Santa Fe each year is only about one-tenth that of the largest U.S. vacation destinations, Walt Disney World and Las Vegas, visitors to Santa Fe are on the whole wealthier and more sophisticated than their counterparts in most other tourist areas. Although Santa Fe is as tourist dependent as any community in the United States, it has no commercial tourist attractions: no giant water slides, wax museums, or theme parks. Its sightseeing highlights are museums, galleries, and churches, and its City Different ambience.

As for the Indians, they have transcended the artistic and cultural exploitation that kept them poor for decades while Pueblo arts and crafts made their way into museums around the world. The presence of the Institute of American Indian Arts has made Santa Fe the unrivaled center for both traditional and contemporary indigenous art. There, Indians from tribes throughout the United States learn not only techniques but also marketing strategies that have helped establish many Institute of American Indian Arts (IAIA) graduates among the most successful artists in modern America.

Santa Feans, new and old, regularly write letters to the editors of local newspapers complaining that the city has become an "adobe Disneyland." This viewpoint gives voice to the preservationist attitude that permeates the city, and no one who has watched the transformation of downtown Santa Fe since the late 1960s would challenge the assertion that tourism *has* made the city more elitist, much more expensive, perhaps less "human." Yet it takes only a moment's reflection to realize that other western cities of comparable size — say, Cheyenne, Wyoming, Ogden, Utah, or Pocatello, Idaho — have nothing like the selection of museums, fine restaurants, gourmet grocers, authors' appearances, or live stage performances that enhance the quality of life in Santa Fe.

A stroll through downtown Santa Fe today conjures up questions about the relationship between tourism and preservation. Clearly, the city's visual charms would not exist at all if not for generations of intentional efforts to stimulate tourism. The city's artists and preservationists have found in the tourist trade a sugar daddy offering apparently unlimited wealth. The same elements that attract visitors have been embraced by locals with such enthusiasm that Santa Fe style in all its manifestations has gained a cultural depth far beyond the romanticized superficiality of many other tourist destinations. Yet Santa Fe's success has made downtown shop space some of the most expensive in the United States notwithstanding the brevity of the tourist season, pushing more retailing into the hands of absentee owners, chain boutiques, and designer factory outlets with little or no connection to local heritage or tradition. Even as Santa Fe has become the model for "theme towns" from Salem, Massachusetts to Ashland, Oregon, its own future course is by no means clear.

DOWNTOWN WALKING TOUR

Downtown Santa Fe covers an area of roughly eight blocks north-and-south and eight blocks east-and-west. Guadalupe Street bounds the downtown area on the west; Paseo de Peralta loops around the other three sides of downtown. The Santa Fe River bisects the downtown area. The historic city center, including the Plaza, museums, cathedral and most other places described in this chapter, occupies the area north of the river. Barrio de Analco and San Miguel Mission are on the south side of the river, along with the sprawling Capitol Complex, which is described in Chapter 5.

A walking tour of the downtown area tends to take the form of a cloverleaf of several short loops. From the Plaza, the best walking streets radiate like a tic-tac-toe grid; pedestrians who detour diagonally into the corners of downtown may find themselves in little zones of blank walls, chain-link fences, and nonexistent sidewalks that are more confusing than interesting.

From the Plaza, head for the main sightseeing highlights first. Walk one block east along the north side of Palace Avenue. The portal-covered sidewalk runs along the front of a series of Territorial buildings, now filled with restaurants and art galleries, with interior courtyards. Be sure to stop into **Sena Plaza,** the city's most beautiful and peaceful public courtyard.

From the entrance to Sena Plaza, cross Palace Avenue (pedestrians have the right-of-way) to Cathedral Place. On the west side of the street is the **Institute of American Indian Arts Museum,** where after a few minutes' meditation in a dim, kiva-shaped entry room called the Welcoming Circle, you can see changing exhibitions from the National Collection of Contemporary Indian Art as well as works by major contemporary Indian artists, photography displays, and a sculpture garden dedicated to the memory of internationally renowned Apache sculptor Allan Houser.

Across the street, **St. Francis Cathedral** dominates a large area of past and present Catholic church property that includes **Marian Hall, La Residencia,** the **Villa Rivera Building,** and shady **Cathedral Park,** the site of outdoor art shows on summer weekends. Enter the cathedral through the door on the south side, which takes you into the transept. Walk around the front of the altar to the other side of the transept to see the church's most interesting feature, the ornate little chapel of La Conquistadora, the small seventeenth-century statue that is New Mexico's most cherished religious artifact. For those who find local church history fascinating, the small, little-known Museum of the Archdiocese of Santa Fe is located in a church administration building south of the cathedral.

Leaving the church grounds, proceed west for a block on San Francisco Street and turn south (left) in front of La Fonda. Follow Old Santa Fe Trail to **Loretto Chapel** on the grounds of the **Inn at Loretto.** The chapel is worth the nominal admission charge if only to see the Miraculous Staircase. Many visitors consider this chapel the most beautiful of all Santa Fe churches.

Continue walking south on Old Santa Fe Trail for one block beyond the bridge that crosses the Santa Fe River to reach **San Miguel Mission.** After visiting the mission church, take a few minutes to wander up East De Vargas, the narrow street beside the church, and see the houses of **Barrio de Analco,** some of the oldest remaining structures in the city.

Retracing your route across the river, walk west through the **Santa Fe River Park**. This long, slender park follows the usually-dry river for about 3 miles, continuing in both directions from the downtown area, and makes a pleasant walking route by itself. Reaching Don Gaspar Avenue, turn north (right) and continue past the **St. Francis Hotel** and more small galleries and restaurants to return to San Francisco Street near the southwest corner of the Plaza.

Turn west (left) on San Francisco Street. Originally the Camino Real, the main highway of Spanish colonial New Mexico, it was the first street in town to be lined with commercial buildings (although not the ones that are there today). The portaled sidewalk of West San Francisco runs past two-story buildings that contain a hodgepodge of fine arts galleries, shops, movie theaters, and sporting goods stores. Some larger buildings along the south side of the street have been converted into indoor malls full of tiny shops, since rents for retail space are so expensive in downtown Santa Fe that a department store-size building can no longer be rented in its entirety. While few buildings along West San Francisco Street today have much historical significance, several are architecturally intriguing, notably the **Original Trading Post** and the **Lensic Theatre**. The retail shops end at the intersection with Sandoval Street, two corners of which are occupied by the **Hilton of Santa Fe** and the **El Dorado Hotel.**

Sena Plaza. *Photograph by Richard Harris.*

Turn north (right) on Sandoval Street and follow it as it curves eastward to become West Palace Avenue, taking you past the **Felipe B. Delgado house,** the **Palace Restaurant,** and the entrance to **Burro Alley.** Some of the best art galleries in the city are located in the block of West Palace just west of the Museum of Fine Arts, between Grant and Sheridan Avenues. If historic buildings are your passion, however, follow Grant Street past the Grant Corner Inn and the **Pickney–Tully house** to the **First Presbyterian Church** (along the way, you'll pass an abandoned supermarket that has been converted to house several excellent contemporary art galleries). Then take Marcy Street two blocks east, passing the **Sweeney Convention Center** and **Santa Fe City Hall,** and turn back toward the Plaza on Lincoln Street. You can't miss the big, blank **First Interstate Plaza** on the corner. The **Old Sears Building** fills the middle of the block.

This route brings you back to the Plaza at the northwest corner, next to the Museum of Fine Arts. If you wish to continue walking, follow the Palace of the Governors portal past the Indian vendors and turn north (left) on Washington Avenue, which takes you past the **Museum of New Mexico Historical Archives** and the **Public Library** and leads to the curved intersection of Federal Place, formerly the city's horse racing track, to see the abandoned Territorial Capitol, now known as the **Federal Courthouse.** Beyond the courthouse, on the other side of Paseo de Peralta, is the neo-Moorish **Scottish Rite Temple.**

Turn right and follow Paseo de Peralta around the curve for about a block and a half, where you'll find the brick-paved **Commemorative Walkway,** which leads by switchbacks up the slope of a mesa on the east edge of downtown to the **Cross of the Martyrs.** The cross was erected during the 1970s in memory of 20 Franciscan priests who died during the Pueblo Revolt of 1680. It replaced an older Cross of the Martyrs on another hill to the north that was put up in 1920. Beyond the Cross of the Martyrs is **Old Fort Marcy Park** (not to be confused with another Fort Marcy Park on Washington Street; the entire near northeast neighborhood is called the Fort Marcy district). Dirt mounds on the mesa top are all that remains of the original Fort Marcy, a star-shaped earthern fortification overlooking the city. It is the best spot in town from which to watch the sunset. [You can also reach Old Fort Marcy Park by car, turning uphill from Paseo de Peralta on Otero Street, which becomes Artist Road, then uphill (right) again on Kearny Street to the park.]

After walking back down from the Cross of the Martyrs, turn south (left) on Paseo de Peralta. At the corner of Marcy Street is a small, triangular area of lawn called **Thomas Macaione Park.** Macaione, an Italian immigrant barber-turned-artist, was a familiar figure in Santa Fe's artists' colony as early as the 1940s. He fell into obscurity and was all but forgotten in the mid-1980s when the trailer in which he was living burned down, putting him on the front page of the local papers and reintroducing him to a new generation of Santa Feans. Thereafter, the white-haired septigenarian became a familiar sight on Santa Fe streetcorners, where he worked on his paintings every day. Invigorated by his newfound fame, Macaione ran for public offices, from mayor of Santa Fe to president of the United States, at every opportunity. After his death in 1993, one mayoral candidate ran on the claim that she was channeling Macaione's spirit. The park was renamed in his honor in 1996, and a slightly smaller-than-life bronze sculpture was placed there depicting Macaione at work with his paintbrushes and easel—a lasting example of the honor Santa Fe often accords its most eccentric residents. From the park, a three-block walk down either Marcy Street or Palace Avenue will bring you back to the Plaza area.

PALACE AVENUE

■ 109 East Palace Avenue

Trujillo Plaza, which now houses galleries and shops, served as a private residence in the early nineteenth century. It achieved historical significance much later, in 1942, when it became the official mailing address and reception office for scientists reporting for duty on the Manhattan Project (the first atomic bomb) at Los Alamos Nuclear Laboratory, then a top secret location 40 miles away among the rugged canyons of the Pajarito Plateau.

■ 113½ East Palace Avenue

Prince Plaza was originally the western half of the same property as Sena Plaza. The hacienda surrounding the Plaza was bought in 1879 by attorney Bradford Prince, later territorial governor and then state Supreme Court justice, who lived there for 40 years. Today the building at the back of the small plaza houses The Shed, one of Santa Fe's most popular lunchtime restaurants.

■ 125 East Palace Avenue

Sena Plaza was built over a period of nearly a century. In 1831, Mexican army major Jose D. Sena inherited a small adobe house about which little is known. To provide living space for his family of 11

children along with servants and livestock, Sena gradually expanded the structure into a mansion of 33 rooms surrounding the city's most picturesque courtyard and fountain. The Territorial Revival–style second story was added in 1920. Today, the ground floor houses specialty shops and two restaurants, La Casa Sena and Cantina.

■ 141 East Palace Avenue

The **Coronado Building** stands on the site of the Santa Fe County Courthouse in territorial times. County commissioners in the 1880s wanted to build the stately German municipal–style courthouse in the center of the Plaza, but in response to public protest it was located several blocks away on a lot formerly used as a roller skating rink. The red brick building was completed in 1887, burned out in 1909, rebuilt in 1910, and demolished in 1940, when banker Henry Dendahl bought the property and built a new Territorial structure on the site. The white balustrade, square portico posts, and large windows with frames designed to recall Greek pediments are typical of the style used for government and commercial buildings in the 1940s. The building, distinguished by Mexican ceramic tilework flanking the front entrance, served as doctors' offices during the period when St.

Prince Plaza. *Photograph by Richard Harris.*

Vincent's Hospital was located across the street, and is still used as office space.

■ 228 East Palace Avenue/ 820 Paseo de Peralta

The **Villa Rivera Building,** which contains the state government offices of Cultural Affairs, Arts Division, and Historic Preservation, was formerly St. Vincent's Hospital. The original hospital building was constructed in 1853 as a single-story parsonage behind the old church on the site where St. Francis Cathedral now stands. In 1865, Archbishop Lamy gave the building to the Sisters of Charity, a nursing order, who used it as a convent while adding a second story, then opened its doors as Santa Fe's first nonmilitary hospital. The building was renamed the Villa Rivera Building in 1982 in memory of Father Reynaldo Rivera, a priest at St. Francis Cathedral whose murder shocked the city that year.

The adjoining **La Residencia Nursing Home** was built in 1886 as a hospital annex and later became New Mexico Territory's first home for the elderly. Parts of the growing Sisters of Charity complex also served as an orphanage before the hospital grew to fill the buildings and necessitate more and more expansion. The two buildings were connected during a renovation by John Gaw Meem in 1953–1954. The hospital operated here until 1977, when a new hospital was completed on the south side of town. It is also called St. Vincent's Hospital, although it is no longer controlled by the Sisters of Charity.

A third building, **Marian Hall,** was added to the west side of the Sisters of Charity complex next to Cathedral Park in 1911. Originally a tuberculosis sanatorium, the hall was converted to residential quarters in the hospital's 1954 renovation, with lay nurses' housing on the third floor and a convent for the sisters on the lower two floors. Now connected to the other buildings in the complex, Marion Hall houses the State Public Utilities Commission and shares the address of the Villa Rivera Building.

Old St. Vincent's Sanatorium, before 1896. *Photograph from Archives. Sisters of Charity, Mt. St. Joseph, Ohio, courtesy Museum of New Mexico, neg. 67743.*

Old St. Vincent's Hospital, 1890. *Photograph courtesy Museum of New Mexico, neg. 15221.*

330 East Palace Avenue

La Posada, a hotel and casita complex on six landscaped acres just east of downtown, centers around the building that was originally the mansion of Abraham Staab, one of the town's wealthiest retailers in the late nineteenth century, who became a director of the First National Bank and the first president of the Santa Fe Chamber of Commerce. Staab bought the land in 1876 from the Baca family, whose hacienda had occupied all the land east of Paseo de Peralta before Palace Avenue was extended beyond the paseo, bisecting the Baca estate. It was not until 1884 that Staab built the magnificent three-story brick house.

Staab was a leader of the city's Jewish community, whose most prominent members lived on this part of East Palace Avenue. Yet he and his associates became the primary financiers behind the construction of St. Francis Cathedral. When Archbishop Lamy admitted that the church was unable to repay the loan, Staab agreed to forgive the debt—on condition that the Hebrew letters "YHWH" (signifying Jehovah) be inscribed above the cathedral doors; the inscription remains today.

Staab's wife, Julie Schuster Staab, suffered from severe depression for years before she died in 1896, at the age of 52, in an upstairs bedroom. Although Santa Fe boasts far more than its share of haunted house tales, no other ghost has been seen as frequently as Mrs. Staab, whose eerie apparition on the stairway is a familiar sight to the hotel's employees.

106 Faithway Street

The **Preston house,** at the end of the block-long street across Palace Avenue, is the only known example of a Queen Anne Victorian residence in Santa Fe. This three-story brick-and-frame mansion was built in 1886 by George Cuyler Preston, an attorney associated with the Santa Fe Ring. The exterior of the house has been covered over with stucco, decorative metal siding, a red metal roof designed to look like Mediterranean tile, and touches of contemporary gingerbread that accentuate its fairytale look. Entering the residence's interior, its nine-

Preston house. *Photograph by Richard Harris.*

teenth-century woodwork aglow, is like stepping into an earlier era. The mansion is now operated as the Preston House Bed and Breakfast.

355 East Palace Avenue

The **Francisca Hinojos house** is something of an oddity among the Victorian and Territorial-style residences along Palace Avenue east of Paseo de Peralta. Although the walls are adobe, the house was built by masons who had come from Louisiana to work on St. Francis Cathedral. They incorporated features that were common in brick houses being built in Louisiana at the time but were unheard of in adobe houses, such as a prominent bay window and a steeply pitched tin roof. Stone from construction of the cathedral was used to build a retaining wall in front of the house. It now contains law offices and commercial art studios.

729 East Palace Avenue

Originally called **"The Willows,"** this residence was built around 1915 for Aloysius Renahan, a judge and member of the territorial political machine known as the Santa Fe Ring. The lawn was originally a paved terrace for entertaining. The facade of the house itself has also been greatly altered over the years. It continues to be a private residence. Before construction of the residence, a brewery, bar, and bowling alley stood on the site. The same owners operated Santa Fe's first ice plant across the street and stored up to 3 tons of ice at a time in a cave in the hillside behind the brewery.

CATHEDRAL PLACE

108 Cathedral Place

The building that now houses the **Institute of American Indian Arts Museum** was orginally built as a U.S. Post Office. Designed by Isaac Hamilton Rapp around the same time as La Fonda and the Museum of Fine Arts, its twin-towered main facade resembles the architecture of the old cathedral that stood across the street before St. Francis Cathedral was built (and more than 40 years before this structure was built). The building is symmetrical, unlike most Spanish Pueblo Revival buildings of the era. The round, rough-hewn portal posts are topped by zapata corbels. The corbels and roof beams are carved with brightly painted "bullet" motifs. Exposed *vigas* supporting the semi-enclosed portal echo Nusbaum's restoration of the Palace of the Governors portal. Before construction of this building, a row of plain adobe and red brick structures with a long portico housed a school and the residence of James Seligman, a member of one of Santa Fe's first Anglo merchant families.

213 Cathedral Place

The **Cathedral of St. Francis** was designed by Jean Baptiste Lamy, the first Archbishop of Santa Fe, and built between 1869 and 1886 on the site where the city's main Catholic church had stood since 1626. The original adobe church was destroyed in the Pueblo Revolt of 1680 and another, known as La Parroquia, was built in 1714–1717. Lamy built the present cathedral around La Parroquia, demolishing the smaller church upon completion and carrying it out the front doors of the present edifice. The cathedral is built of huge blocks of yellow limestone that were quarried by Italian stonecutters 20 miles south of Santa Fe at the site of the present-day village of Lamy. The French Romanesque architecture uses square columns with ionic capitals to support the twin truncated towers and smaller, freestanding round neo-Corinthian columns to support the doorway arch and the distinctive double arches that adorn the tower. The large stained-glass rosetta, typical of many major European cathedrals, was imported from Clermont-Ferrand, France, and installed in 1884 as the finishing touch on the exterior. Lamy's plan for the church envisioned 160-foot-tall steeples atop the towers, but they were

Santa Fe Post Office, 1963; flag at half-mast for the death of President Kennedy. *Photograph courtesy Museum of New Mexico, neg. 65143.*

never built. Inside, a portion of the old Parroquía is preserved in the small chapel set into the north wall containing the small willow-wood figure of La Conquistadora, the oldest Christian religious statue in the United States. The cathedral was the seat of the Santa Fe Archdiocese for 100 years until 1974, when Archbishop Roberto Sanchez moved his headquarters to Albuquerque. The cathedral is open to the public.

OLD SANTA FE TRAIL

■ 209 Old Santa Fe Trail

The **Chapel of Our Lady of Light,** commonly known as **Loretto Chapel,** was the first stone masonry building in Santa Fe and the only one that was completed before the railroad arrived. Under the supervision of Archbishop Lamy, construction was begun in 1873 and finished in 1878, although the 10-foot-tall iron statue

of Our Lady of Lourdes was not placed atop the chapel until 1888. The small, elegant neo-Gothic chapel was built as the house of worship for the nuns and students of Loretto Academy by a team of the same construction workers who were building St. Francis Cathedral. As remembered in one of Santa Fe's most famous legends, before the chapel was finished, the church architect assigned to the chapel was shot dead by the archbishop's nephew, John Lamy, whose wife he had allegedly seduced. When the chapel was completed, it was belatedly noticed that there was no way to reach the choir loft. A carpenter appeared and built the remarkable double-360-degree spiral staircase without the use of nails and without central or visible support, then disappeared without asking for payment. The faithful believe that the mysterious stranger was Saint Joseph, the patron saint of carpenters; skeptical historians theorize that he

St. Francis Cathedral. *Photograph by Richard Harris.*

was an Austrian builder visiting from Colorado. Wherever the truth may lie, the wonder of the Miraculous Staircase speaks for itself.

▇ 211 Old Santa Fe Trail

The **Inn at Loretto** stands on the former site of Loretto Academy, a girls' school operated by the Sisters of Loretto next door to the Christian Brothers' all-male St. Michael's College. Built in 1975, the inn is perhaps the most harmonious attempt in recent years to build a large building in Spanish Pueblo Revival style. Loosely patterned after Taos Pueblo, the five-story hotel's bulk is concealed through a creative arrangement of terraces and recesses.

▇ 401 Old Santa Fe Trail

San Miguel Mission was the first church in the United States. Construction began sometime between 1610 and 1612 and was completed by 1626. Only two

other mission churches from before the Pueblo Revolt of 1680 still stand in New Mexico — at Acoma (1629) and Isleta (1630). The original walls are intact but no longer visible. Much of the church was destroyed during the Indian revolt, and when it was rebuilt in 1710, the walls were thickened to 3 to 4 feet, windows were moved as high as possible, and battlements were added around the roof so that the church could double as a fortress in the event of future conflicts, which never occurred. The church was originally built to minister to the Mexican Indian slaves who lived in nearby Barrio de Analco. After its reconstruction in 1710, the year inscribed on the main beam in the choir loft, it became the church for enlisted men in the Spanish army. The *reredo* (altar screen) was added in 1798 to display the mission's statue of its patron, St. Michael, which Franciscan brothers had carried through

La Conquistadora Chapel interior. *Photograph by Robert Brewer, courtesy Museum of New Mexico, neg. 65143.*

San Miguel Mission in ruins, 1883. *Photograph by Dana B. Chase, courtesy Museum of New Mexico, neg. 13969.*

San Miguel Mission today. *Photograph by Richard Harris.*

the villages of northern New Mexico in 1709 to raise funds to rebuild the church after the revolt. Among the paintings that hang in the church are several done on deer and buffalo hide which were used by early missionaries as visual aids for teaching the Christian Bible to local Indians. An old bell, dating to 1856, used to hang in the square bell tower and is now exhibited in the adjoining gift shop operated by the Christian Brothers. An excavation in the floor of the church reveals the vestives of an Indian pueblo that stood on the site before the arrival of the first Spanish colonists. Sunday mass is still held at the church, which is open to the public daily.

EAST DE VARGAS

■ 129–135 East De Vargas

The **Roqui Tudesqui house** probably dates back to the mid-eighteenth century, when it was part of Barrio de Analco, the pueblo of the Nahuatl Indians who had been brought from Mexico as slaves during the early Spanish colonial era. The ear-liest documentation relating to the house is from 1839, when it was sold to Tudesqui, an Italian immigrant who made his fortune as a trader on the Santa Fe Trail. The rambling old house was purchased in 1987 by the Historic Santa Fe Foundation, which rents it out as a residence.

■ 132 East De Vargas

The **Gregorio Crespín house,** one of the oldest homesteads in Santa Fe, was built sometime between 1720 and 1747, when Crespín (about whom little is known) deeded the house to Bartolomé Márquez, creating one of the few Spanish colonial real estate documents that has survived from the early eighteenth century. The house was converted to Territorial style, with red brick coping and a new portal, around 1870. Only a glimpse of the secluded house, which is still a private residence, can be seen from the street.

■ 215 East De Vargas

The **"Oldest House in Santa Fe"** bases its claim on archaeologist Adolph Bandelier's opinion that its foundation was

Barrio de Analco. *Photograph by Richard Harris.*

originally part of an Indian pueblo that stood on the site as early as A.D. 1250. The thick walls of the western part of the house are made of puddled adobe, a method used by the Pueblo Indians long before the first Europeans arrived. Tree-ring dating of the *vigas*, however, shows that they were cut from 1740 to 1767. The house is shown on the oldest known map of the city, the Urrutia map of 1768. At the time, it was part of the Barrio de Analco, the living quarters of poor Indian workers who were descendants of the Nahuatl slaves brought from central Mexico by early Spanish conquistadors. The exterior of the Oldest House has been given a protective stucco coating, but the interior is the last remaining example of the conditions in which the barrio's inhabitants lived during Spanish colonial times, with its dirt floor, low *viga*-and-*latilla* ceiling, and corner fireplace. An authentic merging of Spanish and Indian architecture, it embodies the authentic origins of the Spanish Pueblo style. The house was operated for many years as a small private museum and curio shop, which went out of business in 1995. The Oldest House is now the rear dining area of Upper Crust Pizza. Two neighboring structures that also were originally part of Barrio de Analco are now art galleries.

◼ 327 East De Vargas

The **Arthur Boyle house** is another old adobe hacienda about which little is known. It appears on the earliest detailed map of Santa Fe, drawn in 1766, but no public records relate to it until 1837, when it passed by will to members of the prominent Ortiz family. Adobe walls 4 feet thick and an old-fashioned *raja* (split wood) ceiling attest to the house's antiquity. Nineteenth-century renovations added some Territorial features. It is still a private residence.

◼ 338 East De Vargas

The **José Alarid house** dates back to approximately 1835, when it was built by Alarid, a disabled Mexican army veteran. It was later owned by Archbishop Lamy, by official state interpreter Epifanio Vigil, and by Anita Chapman, who was Adolph Bandelier's secretary and later the New Mexico state librarian, a position she held until 1937. The house was remodeled sometime before 1910 to add a pitched roof and a Greek Revival–style shaded porch with slender, milled posts lacking the traditional corbels.

◼ 352 East De Vargas

The **Adolph Bandelier house,** a large Territorial home dating to the mid-nineteenth century, is one of several homes in Santa Fe that were occupied at one time or another by Bandelier, the Swiss archaeologist whose excavations of postclassic Indian pueblos on the Pajarito Plateau are preserved in Bandelier National Monument, the most popular national park unit in northern New Mexico. Bandelier rented this house from landlord John F. Schumann upon his arrival in Santa Fe in 1880. Alhough he did not live there long, the house was bought 40 years later, soon after his death, by his niece, Elise Bandelier, and her husband, grocer Henry Kaune.

DON GASPAR AVENUE

▦ 210 Don Gaspar Avenue

The **Hotel St. Francis,** built in 1924 on the site where an earlier hotel dating from the 1880s had burned down, was originally called the De Vargas Hotel. Its location, just across the river from the old state capitol (now the Bataan Building), made the De Vargas the hotel of choice for politicians when they came to town for annual legislative sessions. The hotel deteriorated badly in the 1970s and early 1980s. Around the corner from the bus depot that used to be located where the

two-story municipal parking lot on Water Street now stands, it became a low-rent haven for transients and starving artists. San Francisco–based entrepreneurs acquired the building in the mid-1980s and returned it to its former glory with a lavish Victorian-style restoration. High tea is served daily in the elegant lobby.

WEST SAN FRANCISCO STREET

▦ 201 West San Francisco Street

Built before 1883, the building that is now called the **Original Trading Post** was constructed in the Italianate or Railroad Commercial style. The present Old West wooden facade was added around the end of the nineteenth century and has weathered over the years to the point where it looks older than any other downtown building. Although the original trading post claim may not be quite accurate, the curio shop that occupies this building was one of the first specifically tourist-oriented retail stores in town.

▦ 211 West San Francisco Street

The **Lensic Theatre** was built in 1930 by entrepreneurs Nathan Salmon and John Greer on the site where Doña Tule, Santa Fe's notorious first lady of vice, had oper-

Hotel St. Francis. *Photograph by Richard Harris.*

Lensic Theatre. *Photograph by Richard Harris.*

ated a monte casino in the mid-nineteenth century. The theater's Mexican Baroque Revival facade, ornamented with fanciful miniature towers and sea monsters, is unique in Santa Fe. The interior decor, well cared for, though worn, recalls the opulence of old-time movie palaces. The Lensic still operates as a motion picture theater.

■ 309 West San Francisco Street

The **Eldorado Hotel,** the largest hotel in the city (216 rooms), became Santa Fe's most controversial construction project when it was built in 1986 on the site of a former hardware store and lumberyard. Many local residents objected that a masssive five-story building at this location would change the character of Palace Avenue and the entire downtown area by blocking the mountain view to the west, but city planners apparently found the potential tax revenues from the big, expensive hotel irresistible. When an old adobe house that occupied part of the hotel site became a *cause célèbre* of preservationists who hoped to block the construction, developers sidestepped the issue by leaving the walls of the house

standing as they built the hotel around it. Refurbished and reinforced until nothing of the original house is visible today, the preexisting structure became the Old House Restaurant just off the main lobby.

SANDOVAL STREET

■ 100 Sandoval Street

The Albuquerque-based international hotel chain founded by New Mexico native Conrad Hilton built the **Hilton of Santa Fe** in 1972 around the old Ortiz hacienda, ancestral home of one of Spanish colonial Santa Fe's oldest and most prominent families, which had stood on the site since early in the eighteenth century. It was sold in the 1860s and converted into a trading company and later a brothel, then restored to respectability as a retail store before Hilton purchased the property. No visible trace remains of the original hacienda.

WEST PALACE AVENUE

■ 142 West Palace Avenue

The **Palace Restaurant,** at the corner of Palace Avenue and Burro Alley, stands on

Palace Restaurant. *Photograph by Richard Harris.*

the site of a saloon, gambling hall, and brothel operated by Santa Fe's leading madame, Doña Tule Barcelo, from the early days of trade on the Santa Fe Trail until her death in 1853. It formed the entrance to Burro Alley, Santa Fe's rowdy red-light district. At various times she also operated casinos nearby on the sites now occupied by the Santa Fe County Administrative Offices (formerly the District Courthouse) and the Lensic Theatre. The Palace Restaurant building, constructed in 1959, was loosely modeled after the architecture of Sra. Barcelo's establishment. It still marks the entrance to Burro Alley, now a narrow, walled-in street whose few retail shops are quite respectable.

■ 124 West Palace Avenue

The **Felipe B. Delgado house,** a two-story home, was built in 1890 by Delgado, a native Santa Fean who operated one of the largest wagontrain shipping companies on both the Santa Fe Trail to Independence, Missouri, and El Camino Real to Chihuahua, Mexico. He bought this lot in 1877 to park wagons and tether horses for

both his own expeditions and those of other Santa Fe Trail traders. After the railroads replaced wagons for commercial shipping, Delgado used the lot as the site for his elegant home. The exterior, authentically Territorial in style, is essentially plain but decorated with a second-floor balustrade and portico. The overhanging roof eaves reveal the building as authentically Territorial in style, not a Territorial Revival renovation. The interior of the house is Victorian, with wainscoting and ornate hardwood trim. The house was a private residence until 1970; it is now used as bank offices.

GRANT AVENUE

■ 122 Grant Avenue

The **Grant Corner Inn,** an 11-room brick bed and breakfast inn, was built 1908 and 1913 as the in-town residence of a prominent New Mexico ranching family. It was renovated in Early American style in the 1980s by innkeepers Pat Walter and Louise Stewart, who added the large porch.

■ 135 Grant Avenue

The **A. M. Bergere house** is one of two Fort Marcy officers' residences remaining of the six that originally stood in the army presidio adjoining the Palace of the Governors. The other survivor is now attached to the Museum of Fine Arts on the Lincoln Street side. Those that were demolished were replaced by the Sears Building. Built in 1870, the house was occupied by General Ulysses S. Grant during his visit to Santa Fe in the summer of 1880. It was abandoned by the army in 1894 and used as rent-free housing for various government dignitaries, including Alfred M. Bergere, court clerk of the First Judicial District, who bought the property and added the second story. The house was remodeled in 1926, adding a conglomeration of Spanish Pueblo Revival and Territorial Revival elements. It is presently used as church offices.

■ 136 Grant Avenue

The **Pickney R. Tully house,** now retail space that has recently housed an herb shop and clothing boutique, presents a unique reversal of the Santa Fe Style stucco trend: Although built from adobe in 1851, it was stenciled in 1890 to look like red brick, a feature so unusual that it was restored when the house was taken over by the Historic Santa Fe Foundation in 1974. The 1890 makeover also concealed the house's Spanish Pueblo origins with the addition of a bay window. Tully, a partner in the Ochoa & Tully Company, which developed a trade route between Santa Fe and Tucson, Arizona, in the 1860s, lived in the house for only three years before deeding it to his son-in-law, Oliver P. Hovey, publisher of New Mexico's first English-language newspaper, the *Santa Fe Republican*. Other notables who lived there included the first U.S. surveyor-general for New Mexico, a secretary of the territory, an attorney-general, a bank president, a chief justice of the state supreme court, and Santa Fe's notorious defrocked priest, Padre José Manuel Gallegos.

■ 208 Grant Avenue

The **First Presbyterian Church** is the oldest Protestant church in New Mexico. It was built as a Baptist mission in 1854 but was abandoned and later bought by the Presbyterians, who remodeled it in 1867 by adding a square, crenellated tower and Gothic windows.

Bergere house. *Photograph by Richard Harris.*

First Presbyterian
Church, 1880.
*Photograph by
Ben Wittick, cour-
tesy Museum of
New Mexico, neg.
15855*

First Presbyterian Church, 1912. *Photograph by Jesse L. Nusbaum, courtesy Museum of New Mexico, neg. 61360.*

First Presbyterian Church today. *Photograph by Richard Harris.*

Another renovation in 1912 added a sloped roof and a stenciled exterior, intended to make the adobe look like red brick. Most recently, John Gaw Meem supervised a complete transformation of the church to the Spanish Pueblo Revival building that is still in use today. The exterior bears a strong resemblance to mission churches built throughout New Mexico by the Franciscans during the colonial era.

LINCOLN AVENUE

■ 116 Lincoln Avenue

The **McFie house**, attached to the Museum of Fine Arts by walls and court-yards, was originally one of six officers' residences attached to the Fort Marcy army compound adjoining the Palace of the Governors. It was converted to a private residence for John R. McFie, an associate justice of the New Mexico Territorial Supreme Court. Frank

Springer, a regent of the Museum of New Mexico, bought the property during the construction of the Museum of Fine Arts, had it remodeled in Spanish Pueblo Revival style to harmonize with the new art museum, and donated it to the museum as a residence for director Edgar Hewitt. It was subsequently used as the museum system's headquarters until 1972 and still houses museum offices. The free-flowing organic curves of the rooflines and walls, together with hand-crafted exterior woodwork, make this an exceptional early example of Spanish Pueblo Revival style in a residence.

■ 130 Lincoln Avenue

The **Old Sears Building** was built by Sears, Roebuck & Company in 1948 in the rather plain, functional variant of Territorial Revival style typically used for commercial and office buildings at the time. It stands on a site previously occupied by several Fort Marcy officers' resi-

McFie house. *Photograph by Richard Harris.*

Renovated Old Sears Building. *Photograph by Richard Harris.*

dences. In 1987, when the Sears store moved out to Villa Linda Mall on the west edge of the city, a renovation gutted the former department store building completely except for the escalator— the only one in the entire city, and it only goes up. The ground floor was converted into shops and the second floor to restaurants, one of which—the ultra-chic Café Escalera—takes its name from the Spanish word for escalator. The central area of the facade was demolished, exposing the escalator to the street, and the central part of the roof was transformed into a glass atrium to create a sunny second-floor courtyardlike area.

200 Lincoln Avenue
The **Santa Fe City Hall,** designed by John Gaw Meem in a modified Spanish Pueblo Revival style and built between 1951 and 1953, contains the city council chambers and the offices of the mayor, the city manager, and most municipal agencies. Some purists object to the building's architecture because the big office windows do not conform to the city's own regulations for recent Santa Fe style, while other critics feel that it would have been more appropriate to conform city hall and the neighboring Sweeney Convention Center to the Territorial Revival style used in state government buildings (not to mention the former city hall, now the public library). The centerpiece of the landscaped grounds in front of city hall is a bronze statue of Saint Francis, the city's patron saint.

WASHINGTON AVENUE

120 Washington Avenue
The **Fray Angélico Chávez History Library** was originally built as a library in 1905 by the Woman's Board of Trade and Library Association. Its collection totaled 2000 books, and its operating budget was less than $200 a year. The exterior was remodeled in Territorial Revival style by architect John Gaw Meem in the early 1930s; in 1934, artist Olive Rush was commissioned by the WPA to paint the mural that can still be seen in the front entrance stairwell. The building served as the main Santa Fe Public Library until 1987, when the library moved across the street to its present location. After the old library building was abandoned, the Museum of New Mexico persuaded the state legisla-

ture to buy it, but it sat empty for eight years as funds were raised from public and private sources for a $1,650,000 renovation. It was opened in November 1996. The history library contains collections of thousands of rare books, manuscripts, and maps as well as more than 500,000 historical photographs, a sampling of which appears in this book. Its namesake, the late Fray Angélico Chávez, a, writer, painter, and Franciscan priest at Peña Blanca on the Cochiti Pueblo Grant, is considered northern New Mexico's greatest twentieth-century historian. His 22 books range from short-story collections dating to the 1930s and 1940s to the masterpieces of his later years— *Missions of New Mexico: 1776* (1973), *Origins of New Mexico Families in the Spanish Colonial Period* (1973) and *My Penitente Land* (1974).

145 Washington Avenue
The **Santa Fe Public Library** was a reconstruction of a design by John Gaw Meem, the city's leading architect, in 1936. Called the Berardinelli Building, it served as the city hall for a time and then as a fire station, police headquarters, and jail. It is a classical example of the Territorial Revival style, a two-story building with classic Palladian projecting side wings.

150 Washington Avenue
Built in 1982–1984, the **First Interstate Plaza** is still referred to in Santa Fe as "the Ugly Building," a nickname bestowed on it by local news feature writers at that time. It is the quintessential example of an attempt to conform a large office building to the letter (although not the spirit) of the Santa Fe historic district ordinance standards for recent Santa Fe style design. Limitations on door and window area and the percentage of the exterior area that must be stuccoed were met simply by making the entire three-story north side of the building windowless and doorless, creating an appearance that some critics have likened to the

Santa Fe City Hall. *Photograph by Richard Harris.*

Santa Fe Public Library. *Photograph by Richard Harris.*

Woman's Board of Trade Library, 1912. *Photograph by Jesse L. Nusbaum, courtesy Museum of New Mexico, neg. 56603*

Fray Angélico Chávez Library today. *Photograph by Richard Harris.*

First Interstate Plaza. *Photograph by Richard Harris.*

world's largest cardboard box. The building houses the Wells Fargo Bank's lobby and offices, law firms, stockbrokers, and the Internal Revenue Service.

■ 215 Washington Avenue

The **Territorial Inn** was built between 1898 and 1902 by businessman George Schoch, a newcomer from Philadelphia. Incorporating a pitched roof and set back from the street to accommodate a grass lawn, the house seems out of place in the core area of the Santa Fe historic district. The house was built on a stone foundation with red brick walls that were later covered in stucco. In the 1920s it became the home of banker Levi Hughes, who is remembered for financing the La Fonda hotel and for throwing elegant high-society parties. Today, it serves as a 10-room bed-and-breakfast inn. Nonguests can view the living room and other common areas.

■ 227–237 Washington Avenue

The **Padre Gallegos house** was built in 1857 as the residence of José Manuel Gallegos, one of the best-known and most controversial figures in nineteenth-century New Mexico. A parish priest in Taos when New Mexico became U.S. territory, Gallegos was believed to have helped organize the 1847 Taos Revolt and the assassination of New Mexico's first U.S. territorial governor. He was defrocked by Archbish-op Lamy, in 1851, ostensibly for gambling and womanizing, but more likely as part of Lamy's campaign to dehispanicize the church. After leaving the clergy, Gallegos moved to Santa Fe, built this residence, continued his political activities, and served as Speaker of the House in the New Mexico Territorial Legislature, as Superintendant of Indian Affairs, and as New Mexico's delegate to the U.S. Congress until his death in 1875. The Territorial-style architecture of the part of the adobe house fronting on the street looks much as it did when Gallegos built it, with its typical dentilated brick coping, white-painted Greek Revival window and door frames, and square portal posts with Doric-like capitals instead of

Territorial Inn. *Photograph by Richard Harris.*

Padre Gallegos house courtyard. *Photograph by Richard Harris.*

the more traditional corbels. The other sections of the building surrounding the interior courtyard were added over the years, as the house became an Episcopal church, a boardinghouse, and an apartment compound where Sheldon Parsons, one of Santa Fe's first resident artists, lived. Today it contains offices and the Santacafé restaurant. The courtyard is open to the public.

FEDERAL PLACE

▦ South Federal Place
The **Federal Courthouse,** a two-story stone Greek Revival building set on a broad expanse of shaded lawn at Federal Place and Washington Street, is perhaps the only pre-twentieth-century public building in Santa Fe that stands in its original form without renovation or alteration. It was originally designed to be the New Mexico territorial capitol. Construction began in 1850, using stone quarried at Hyde Park in the Sangre de Cristo Mountains above Santa Fe and near Cerrillos south of the city. Appropriations from the U.S. Congress were far to small to complete the building, and construction was halted for

lack of funds in 1855, leaving only a roofless first story, while the Palace of the Governors continued to serve as the territorial capitol. In 1883, a floor and roof were added to the long-abandoned structure for a railroad-sponsored Tertio-Centennial Celebration (the celebration, marking Santa Fe's 333rd anniversary, was actually 59 years too early, but the arithmetic error was not noticed until too late to change the name), during which the building was used as a dormitory for Indian participants and a race-track was built around it. Even today, the rounded corners of the streets surrounding the Federal Courthouse and U.S. Post Office complex follow the original horse racecourse. The stone pylon monument to Kit Carson, which stands in front of the courthouse, was erected the following year, and the building itself was finished in 1886. It never served as the territorial capitol, however, since a new capitol building was already under construction. It initially housed the U.S. Land Office and Court of Private Land Claims. Today, it contains a circuit branch of the U.S. District Court for New Mexico, which is based in Albuquerque, as well as other federal offices.

Unfinished Territorial Capitol, now the Federal Courthouse, 1870. *Photograph by Nicholas Brown, courtesy Museum of New Mexico, neg. 10242.*

Federal Courthouse today. *Photograph by Richard Harris.*

PASEO DE PERALTA

▨ 463 Paseo de Peralta

The **Scottish Rite Temple,** located on the northwest corner of Washington and Paseo de Peralta, was built in 1910. Its Moorish design was created by Trinidad, Colorado, architect Isaac Hamilton Rapp based on a portion of the Alhambra in Spain. Notable features include a Mediterranean tile roof, a crenelated square tower, filligree metal lanterns, and horseshoe arch windows and entrances. Located just outside the boundary of the Santa Fe historic district, the building's distinctive pink color sets it apart from the earthtone hues required by ordinance within the historic district and makes it a handy landmark for offering directions.

▨ 924 Paseo de Peralta

The **Jean Morrison Rapp house** was built by the widow of architect Isaac Hamilton Rapp, originator of the Spanish Pueblo Revival style, when she returned to Santa Fe after his death in Trinidad, Colorado, in 1933. Mrs. Rapp, who had owned the property since 1912, based the design of the house on plans that she found in the files of the Rapp architecture firm and added details of her own invention. The house was unique among Santa Fe–style buildings of the time in that sections were staggered to allow for windows in at least two walls of every room. Mrs. Rapp, a watercolor artist and prominent figure in the local arts community, used the front section of the house as a studio and lived in the two-story back section. Converted to apartments after her death in 1941, the house retains its original exterior appearance except that the *vigas* that originally protruded along the front have been sawed off and stuccoed over.

View from Scottish Rite Temple tower, 1912. *Photograph by Jesse L. Nusbaum, courtesy Museum of New Mexico, neg. 61382.*

SANTA FE'S RELIGIOUS HERITAGE

Appropriately enough in a city whose name translates as "Holy Faith," five Catholic churches—San Miguel Mission (c. 1625/rebuilt 1710), Santuario de Guadalupe (c. 1781), Loretto Chapel (c. 1873), St. Francis Cathedral (c. 1884), and Cristo Rey Church (c. 1940)—rank high among Santa Fe's most visited tourist sights. They offer readily accessible glimpses into northern New Mexico's traditional Spanish culture, where religion has always played a central role. In adobe and cut stone, the churches tell a story of dramatic cultural clash and eventual compromise that goes to the essence of Santa Fe's character.

Passionately devout as it was, the religious life of Spanish colonial settlers in Nuevo Mexico appears to have diverged from orthodox Catholicism from the beginning. There is substantial evidence that the seventeenth-century Spanish pioneers included an unknown number of *conversos,* Sephardic Jews from Spain who converted to Catholicism to avoid exile or execution at the hands of the Inquisition, then emigrated to the most remote corners of the Spanish Empire to avoid scrutiny of their religious practices. The muster rolls of the Oñate expedition, which founded Nuevo Mexico, listed the family names of numerous conversos, as well as several persons who were wanted for heresy by the Inquisitors in Spain. How many early *converso* settlers were "crypto-Jews" (Jews posing as Catholics) or "Judaizers" (relapsed converts) is unknown because survival required absolute secrecy. Modern scholars continue to find Jewish customs and symbols in use among northern New Mexico Catholics, and since the 1970s growing num-

La Parroquía, drawing c. 1850. *Photograph courtesy Museum of New Mexico, neg. 21257.*

bers of New Mexicans have been rediscovering their Jewish roots. There is a widespread, although not academically accepted, belief that settlers whose names ended with the letter "z" came from Jewish *converso* backgrounds; among those early settlers identified as Jewish were the Gómez and López families, and the late Fray Angélico Chávez, New Mexico's leading twentieth-century Catholic scholar, freely acknowledged Jews among his direct ancestors. Although historians argue endlessly about the subject, there can be little doubt that religious freedom was one of the motivations that drove settlers to join expeditions to remote Nuevo Mexico.

Throughout the sixteenth and seventeenth centuries, New Mexico was primarily a mission area under the custody of Franciscan monks, whose first duty was to convert the local Indians to Catholicism. From 1617 on, the clergy was under the direction of the Bishop of Durango, Mexico, which lay 1000 miles away, beyond the vast Chihuahuan Desert. Chronic shortages of priests and supplies meant that the same Franciscans were also called upon to minister to the Spanish colonial villagers.

Fray Alonzo de Benavides, the bishop's appointee to supervise the New Mexican missions, arrived in Santa Fe to find that the capital city had no church except for a small chapel in the Palace of the Governors. He built the first *parroquía* on the site where St. Francis Cathedral stands today. Although Benavides was officially appointed as the agent of the Spanish Inquisition in New Mexico, there is no evidence that he exercised his power against heretics, witches, or unbelievers. Instead, he confronted the civil government in repeated disputes over legal jurisdiction, setting up ecclesiastical courts that claimed the power to override decisions of the governor in civil disputes. The governor and the missionaries also argued over who had the right to extort tribute from the Indians in the form of labor. As the Franciscans consolidated scattered indigenous villages into larger pueblos around the missions, enabling the priests to provide religious training more efficiently and organize larger communal farming efforts, the owners of large land grants objected that the Franciscans were "stealing" their Indians. The conflict between governor and priests was near the breaking point by 1680, when ancient spirits came in a vision to Popé, a Tewa shaman at San Juan Pueblo, and told him that his people must revolt and all Spaniards must be expelled or slain. Following the Pueblo Revolt, the Indians reverted to the old religion and utterly destroyed the Spanish missions.

As the Spanish fled Nuevo Mexico, they took with them a 26-inch-tall willow-wood statue of Mary. When they returned 12 years later, bringing the statue with them, it was the only Catholic religious artifact that remained from before the revolt. The statue, which was renamed La Conquistadora ("The Conqueress") for "leading" the reconquest of New Mexico, was given a chapel in the rebuilt *parroquía* and has been venerated ever since. When the rest of the church was demolished during the construction of St. Francis Cathedral,

La Conquistadora, 1951. *Photograph by Tyler Dingee, courtesy Museum of New Mexico, neg. 73832.*

La Conquistadora's chapel was left intact. Today, many worshippers visit La Conquistadora each day. A *cofradía* of women sees to such daily devotions as brushing her hair and dressing her in one of more than a thousand regal garments that have been donated to her over the centuries. She is carried on an annual pilgrimage to Rosario Chapel, at Santa Fe's main cemetery, where she stays for several days in remembrance of the hardships faced by the Spanish during the first desperate winter of the Spanish reconquest.

The Franciscans restored their missions in Nuevo Mexico after the reconquest, but they did not thrive. The success of the Pueblo Revolt had convinced many Indians that the priests' God was inferior to those of the old religion. The uneasy truce between Indians and Spaniards meant a separate-but-equal policy that protected indigenous people from unwanted evangelism, and friction between the Vatican and Franciscans in Europe undermined the missionaries' authority among the Spanish population. No bishop visited Nuevo Mexico after 1760.

Most missionaries had withdrawn from the region by the time Mexico became an independent nation in 1821. Mexico's new government saw the Catholic church as one of the forces that had been oppressing its people. Everyone who had been born in Spain was banished, and the clergy was subjected to restrictions so severe that although Nuevo Mexico continued to be an official part of the Diocese of Durango, not a single ordained clergyman remained in the state.

The local *norteños* were left in the care of a lay penitente sect known as *la cofradía de la luz*, The Brotherhood of the Light, which had come to Nuevo Mexico with the original settlers. Don Juan de Oñate, the colony's first governor, had himself belonged to the Mexican penitente brotherhood called the Third Order of St. Francis, which practiced self-whipping and ritual crucifixion and inspired the New Mexico's penitentes. As New Mexico became U.S. territory in 1848, church authorities severed Santa Fe's ties with the Durango diocese and created a new Diocese of Santa Fe under the care of Jean Baptiste Lamy, a French-born bishop from Ohio. Lamy's tacit assignment was to restore New Mexico's faithful to mainstream Catholicism.

Upon his arrival in Santa Fe in 1851, Bishop Lamy proceeded to dismantle and rebuild the Catholic church. He demolished the old chapel known as La Castrense, located along San Francisco Street on the south side of the Plaza, and brought stonemasons from Europe to wall up the city's main church, La Parroquía, inside a cocoon of neo-Gothic masonry, then demolish the old church, hauling it out piece by piece through the front doors of the new **St. Francis Cathedral.** He appointed a subordinate to remodel the old adobe **Chapel of Our Lady of Guadalupe** in neo-Gothic style. He brought teachers

Opposite: Drawing of St. Francis Cathedral, showing planned spires. *Illustration from* Aztlan *by William G. Ritch, 1885, courtesy Museum of New Mexico, neg. 10005.*

Construction of the "New Cathedral." *Illustration from* Harper's New Monthly Magazine, *April 1880, courtesy Museum of New Mexico, neg. 74486.*

from the Sisters of Loretto and the Franciscan Brothers to create Santa Fe's first school system. Lamy's network of Catholic parochial schools continues today and is attended by a large percentage of Santa Fe's schoolchildren, including many non-Catholics whose parents prefer them to the poorly funded public schools. Lamy's most beautiful creation, the small, neo-Gothic **Chapel of Our Lady of Light** (Loretto Chapel), served the nuns and students at the Loretto Academy girls' school. The first of Lamy's new churches to be completed, it immediately became the subject of a legend about a miraculous appearance by Saint Joseph.

Lamy did not get along with the 15 Spanish-speaking priests left in New Mexico. The vicar of Santa Fe refused to recognize Lamy as bishop because although Lamy had a letter of authority from the Pope, he had none from the Archbishop of Durango. Lamy responded by defrocking Padre José Manuel Gallegos of Taos, who was rumored to have been involved in the Taos Rebellion several years earlier. The ex-priest immediately moved to Santa Fe, where he became one of the most popular political figures in the territory. Other Spanish-speaking priests lodged formal complaints with the Vatican. Lamy was called to Rome to answer the charges but sent a representative instead. No action was taken on the case. Lamy continued to govern the church in New Mexico for another 37 years and was raised to the rank of archbishop when Santa Fe was declared an archdiocese in 1875.

The Catholic church continued to play a vital community role in Santa Fe after Lamy's death in 1888, establishing the city's first civilian hospital, orphanage, tuberculosis sanatorium, and school system. **Cristo Rey Church,** which symbolizes the healing of the rift between local people and the mainstream church, was built in 1940 at the upper end of Canyon Road. Inside is a magnificent stone *reredos,* or stone altarpiece, which graced colonial La Castrense on the Plaza a century before.

Today, about 50 percent of Santa Feans attend the city's Catholic churches. Forty-two other Christian denominations also have church services. The city has two Jewish temples, with a regular attendance of about 1200, and a Zen Buddhist center. Nearby are a sizable Moslem community in Abiquiu and the western hemisphere's largest Sikh center in Española.

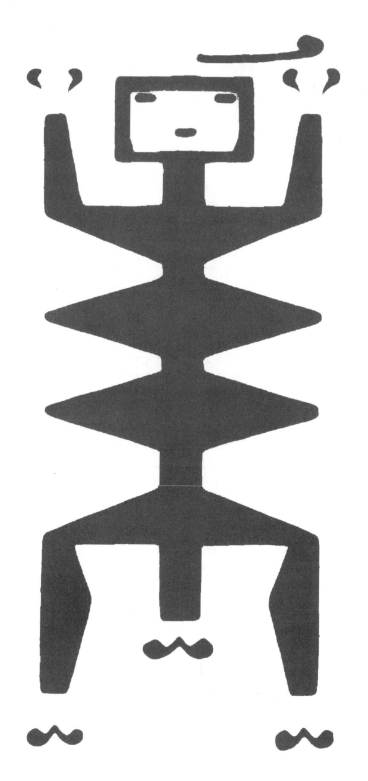

4

Canyon Road Area

Called El Camino de Cañón from colonial times until 1950, Canyon Road was the original route between Santa Fe and the Indian pueblo and eighteenth-century Franciscan mission at Pecos, about 20 miles to the southeast. The road almost certainly traced a footpath that had linked Indian villages along the Santa Fe River since the thirteenth century, following the river up through Santa Fe Canyon to its source and then crossing the northern ridgeline of Glorieta Baldy and descending into the Pecos River Valley and Pecos Pueblo, one of the most important trade centers of the southwest in pre-Columbian times. The route is no longer in use beyond the city limits. Santa Fe Canyon has long been closed to the public to protect the municipal watershed. The portion of the road that made its way over Glorieta Baldy still exists, although it is only passable on foot or by mountain bike on the west side and by four-wheel-drive vehicle on the east side.

The first homesteads were built in the Canyon Road area during the eighteenth century, when it was rural in character. Diverted by means of *acequias*, or irrigation ditches, the river provided irrigation for cornfields that covered most of the land here. The exact provenance of most early structures in the Canyon Road neighborhood is unknown because records are lacking. There were no official surveys, and most homesteads were merely possessory, held by the same families for generations without legal deeds. In the rare instances

Opposite: Masking wall detail, Wheelright Museum of the American Indian. *National Register of Historic Places.*

101

when deeds were filed, legal descriptions were so vague, often based on land-marks that are unknown today, that they are almost meaningless to present-day historians.

Despite the shortage of information about them, there can be no doubt that many of the residences in the Canyon Road area—far more, in fact, than downtown—are among the city's oldest structures. Thick adobe walls and portals along the sides and backs of houses were characteristic of home-steads built during the Mexican era (1821–1848). Examination of founda-tions, walls, and *vigas* shows that many Canyon Road buildings in use today incorporate smaller structures dating back to that era. Most houses fronting on Canyon Road at that time were built on long, narrow plots of land that extended back to the *acequia madre*, the main community irrigation ditch, with vegetable gardens filling the space between the house and the acequia.

For the most part, the neighborhood remained rural until the early years of the twentieth century, when Sunmount Sanitarium was established at the end of the road now called Camino del Monte Sol, making Canyon Road an axis between the downtown area and the tuberculosis treatment center on the city's outskirts. By the early 1920s, the artists and writers who were flock-ing to join the city's burgeoning creative community had settled the Canyon Road–Acequia Madre–Camino del Monte Sol area as the place to buy small lots inexpensively and build their own adobe homes and studios. So many small residences were built from the 1920s to the 1940s that virtually all the garden plots behind older houses on the street were transformed into hap-hazard compounds of dwellings that were often separated by only a few feet.

Although the first art gallery was opened on Canyon Road in 1935, gal-leries proliferated in the 1960s. Today, hardly any residences front on the street in Canyon Road's five-block gallery district. Even though many are quite small and rustic, the homes in the compounds behind the galleries and on nearby back streets have risen in value so much that, ironically, few work-ing artists can afford to live there. Canyon Road has been transformed into an art collector's fantasy and, for those who know a little local history, an intriguing open-air museum of the origins of Santa Fe's artistic and literary life.

TOURING CANYON ROAD

The lower end of Canyon Road meets Paseo de Peralta southeast of down-town Santa Fe; it is the first road junction south of the river. The narrow, ¾-mile-long segment of the road that is lined with art galleries and historic buildings runs one-way, uphill, and makes for an easy, pleasant walk despite the intermittent lack of sidewalks. The parallel parking along the road is much too limited to accommodate the numbers of people who visit on a typ-

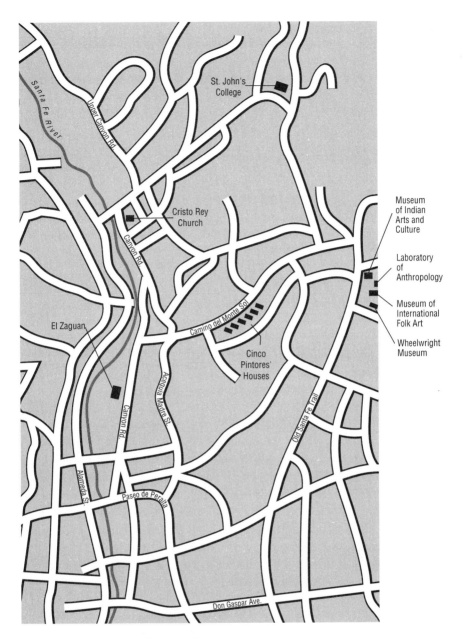

CANYON ROAD AREA

ical day in tourist season. There is a municipal parking lot at the intersection of Canyon Road and Camino del Monte Sol, at the upper end of the art gallery area. (Or look for free parking just off the lower end of Canyon Road on either of two side streets, Garcia and Delgado, or park along the nameless unpaved road that runs east from Delgado Street along the south bank of the Santa Fe River. It is also close enough to walk up Canyon Road from the Plaza area.)

A stroll along Canyon Road is fairly self-explanatory. Except for a few historic buildings such as **El Zaguán** and the **Quaker Meetinghouse,** virtually every doorway that fronts along the one-way stretch of Canyon Road leads into an art gallery. Dozens of private residences with Canyon Road addresses are set back in small compounds behind the galleries. In addition, there are a number of exclusive, locked-gate condominium complexes just off Canyon Road, along with a few off-street groups of galleries, ranging from the hidden cluster of exotica that includes Project Tibet (a nonprofit gallery that helps sponsor Santa Fe's sizable Tibetan refugee community) and a sculpture garden in the 400 block to Gypsy Alley, and an assemblage of modest studios and folk-art shops in the 700 block. Restaurants cluster around the intersection of Canyon Road and Camino del Monte Sol, at the upper end of the gallery district.

Shopping aside, the one must-see place along Canyon Road is El Zaguán, on the north side of the road in the 500 block. Most visitors pause to peer over the low picket fence at the lush flower gardens, unaware that the public is welcome to enter, stroll through the gardens, and rest on the benches shaded by tall cottonwood trees.

If you started from the municipal parking at the upper end of the gallery district, you can add variety to your walk by turning right on Delgado Street and continuing for one block to a nameless dirt road that runs along the south bank of the Santa Fe River. A shady foot trail parallels the road. Camino Escondido will return you to Canyon Road near the center of the gallery district. From there, you can continue for about a block to Gormley Lane, a tiny alleyway beside the old Gormley's Grocery (now Canyon Trading Post, though the facade still bears the Gormley's name), which will take you one block south to **Acequia Madre** to see some of the neighborhood's more historic homes, such as the **Mary Austin** and **Lynn Riggs houses** and **El Torreón** on the little side street called Caminito (which means "little road"). Incidentally, the 2-mile loop formed by Canyon Road and Acequia Madre is the route followed each Christmas Eve on Santa Fe's traditional *farolito* walk. For this high point of the holiday season, *farolitos* ("little lanterns"), the popular outdoor Christmas decoration consisting of altar candles inside brown paper bags weighted with sand, line the sidewalks, walls, and rooflines as locals and visitors by the thousands walk through the snowy streets, ducking into art galleries for steaming cups of cider and pausing at corner bonfires to chase away the night chill and join in Christmas carols.

From the municipal parking lot the upper end of the gallery district, there are several other scenic routes worth taking. The **Cinco Pintores'** and other artists' homes along **Camino del Monte Sol** are within easy walking distance, though driving (or better yet, bicycling) may be preferable because this route combines well with a visit to the **New Mexico Museum of Indian**

Arts and Culture, International Folk Art Museum, and **Wheelwright Museum of the American Indian** on Camino Lejo, just across Old Santa Fe Trail from the far end of Camino del Monte Sol. (From here it is possible to trace a segment of the original **Santa Fe Trail** by following the road of the same name east past the **National Park Service Southwest Office** and along the base of Sun and Moon Mountains, an exclusive area of widely dispersed Santa Fe–style custom homes. After about 8 miles, the road crests a low pass over a row of hills called the Cerros Negros, affording an impressive view, and soon deteriorates into a maze of unpaved ranch roads. Although unmarked, the route of the original Santa Fe Trail follows the last paved road to the south, joining into Old Las Vegas Highway, which parallels Interstate 25, near Seton Village.)

Cristo Rey Church, uphill from the gallery district at the intersection of Canyon Road and Alameda (which changes its name to Camino Cabra at this point) is also within easy walking distance but worth driving if you want to visit the **Randall Davey Audubon Center** on Upper Canyon Road, reached by taking a one-block jog to the south (right) on Alameda. If you drive or bike up Upper Canyon Road, a scenic return route is to turn off where the pavement ends on Upper Canyon and follow unpaved **Cerro Gordo Road** back downhill to Palace Avenue, bringing you out just a couple of blocks from the Canyon Road municipal parking lot. Cerro Gordo ("Fat Hill") is one of Santa Fe's most unique neighborhoods. In the 1960s, when the road was little more than a Jeep trail and public utility service was limited, it became the successor to Canyon Road and Camino del Monte Sol as a place where people could buy inexpensive land and build their own houses by hand. Today, like all places with good views on the city's east side, Cerro Gordo property is very expensive, and skyrocketing values have enabled many residents to expand their original modest adobes, dome homes, and converted garages into palatial residences, then sell them for small fortunes. The resulting mixed neighborhood is full of character, including the Schramm house, the pretty little picnic area at Cerro Gordo Park, and a Tibetan Buddhist center and stupa.

Although the Randall Davey Audubon Center on Upper Canyon Road is surrounded by wild, undeveloped land, it is not a good starting point for long hikes because the Talaya Hill Grant, which lies behind the center, contains such a maze of arroyos that no road or foot trail penetrates it, making it possible to get seriously lost in the wilderness within a few miles of downtown Santa Fe. The most popular local hike is Atalaya Trail, a steep and spectacular 3-mile climb from the trailhead by St. John's College to a 9121-foot summit on the city's western skyline. The same trailhead also provides access to Arroyo Chamiso, a large dry wash that leads to an area of natural chamisa-covered meadows at the foot of Sun and Moon Mountains that is said to have once been considered sacred by Indians in the area and is now reserved for future city park development. Behind the college, a short but intermittently steep trail climbs 500 feet to the top of Sun Mountain. **St. John's College** can be reached by following Camino Cabra uphill from Cristo Rey Church. Near the college, the main road merges into Camino de Cruz Blanca and loops around to bring you out near the intersection of Camino del Monte Sol and Old Santa Fe Trail.

■ 724 Canyon Road

The **Borrego house** (now the restaurant Geronimo) started as a farmhouse sometime before 1753, when the first deed conveying legal title to the property was recorded. Named for the Rafael Borrego family, which owned it through most of the nineteenth century, renovated it in Territorial style and expanded it to its present size, the house was gradually subdivided into self-contained apartments as portions of the house were distributed among successive generations of heirs. The practice of dividing property among children was widespread in Santa Fe in the nineteenth century and is still common in rural northern New Mexico today. Like other venerable Canyon Road properties, the Borrego house was purchased piecemeal from its multiple owners between 1928 and 1939 by preservationist Margretta S. Dietrich, who sponsored an award-winning restoration of the building by her sister, Dorothy Stewart. It passed through several private owners until, in 1961, the Old Santa Fe Association raised $20,000 in charitable donations toward an attempt to save the condemned Simon Nusbaum house downtown. The attempt failed, and when the Nusbaum house was demolished, they applied the funds as a down payment on the Borrego house instead. The association later resold it under a deed containing restrictive covenants that require present and future owners to preserve its historic character. The Borrego house is now Geronimo, one of several fine restaurants around the intersection of Canyon and Camino del Monte Sol.

Borrego house, 1925. *Photograph courtesy Museum of New Mexico, neg. 29086.*

630 Canyon Road

The **Society of Friends Meetinghouse** was the home and studio of Olive Rush, the first woman painter in Santa Fe's art colony, who moved into this structure upon moving to the city in 1920. It had previously been a small hacienda owned in turn by two prominent Santa Fe families, the Senas and the Rodriguezes, and probably dates back to the 1820s. Ms. Rush preserved the house as it was when she first moved in and willed it to the Quakers, who continue to maintain it without major alterations. The meetinghouse is open to the public.

553 Canyon Road

The **Fremont Ellis Studio/Gallery** was renovated and expanded from a small adobe of uncertain origin by artist/architect William Penhallow Henderson in 1923 for his daughter, Alice, and son-in-law John Evans, who was the son of Taos art patroness Mabel Dodge Luhán. It was occupied by Fremont Ellis, a member of the early Santa Fe artists' cooperative known as Los Cinco Pintores, from 1956 until his death in 1985. The home, which remains in the Ellis family, now serves as a gallery for Ellis's estate. It is open by appointment only.

545 Canyon Road

El Zaguán is best known as the home of Swiss archaeologist Adolph Bandelier, who inhabited it in the 1880s and created the beautiful formal garden on the west side of the house. Virtually nothing is known about the origin of the stately old hacienda, a portion of which was already old in 1849, when it was purchased by James Johnson, a pioneering trader who had helped open the Santa Fe Trail and opened the city's largest mercantile store on the plaza location where the Catron Building now stands. Renovating it in Territorial style, Johnson gradually expanded the house from three rooms to 24, including a private chapel and the largest library in New Mexico at the time. The oldest adobe walls are 4 feet thick, and those added by Johnson are 3 feet thick. The name comes from the unusual *zaguán* ("hallway" or "vestibule"), an enclosed portal that runs the length of the back of the house. Today, El Zaguán is owned by the Historic Santa Fe Foundation, which rents out the interior as residential apartments

Olive Rush house, 1965. *Photograph by Karl Kernberger, courtesy Museum of New Mexico, neg. 43321.*

El Zaguán. *Photograph by Richard Harris.*

but maintains the exterior and gardens as they appeared in Bandelier's time. The gardens are open to the public.

■ 519 Canyon Road

The **Juan Prada house** is believed to date back to the 1760s or earlier, based on structural evidence and early maps. The earliest record relating to the home is in 1860, when owner Juan José Prada subdivided it and sold the east half. The deed contained a condition requiring that the hallway separating the two halves of the house be kept open at all times to provide access to a dance hall, no longer in existence, which Prada ran in the rear of the home. The two halves were rejoined around 1930, when the Prada House became the residence of Margretta S. Dietrich, an early leader in the movement to preserve historic homes along Canyon Road. A shed on the property is one of the finest remaining examples of *jacal,* a type of vertical log cabin construction commonly used for outbuildings in colonial times. The Prada house is a private residence.

■ 400 Canyon Road

The red brick **First Ward School,** built in 1906 on the site of a former dance hall, was the work of Carlos Digneo, a European stonemason brought to Santa Fe by Archbishop Lamy to build St. Francis Cathedral. The first public school in Santa Fe, it competed for students with the series of parochial schools that had been established by the Catholic church under Lamy. Built just a few years before the Santa Fe–style revival began, the school was seen as a symbol of progress because it was the first public building in the city to be made entirely of kilned red brick. It was used as a school until 1928, when it was sold by the school district to private owners. Since then it has served such varied functions as antique store, art film theater, and animal shelter. In recent times it became well known as the home and gallery of Linda Durham, a prominent contemporary art dealer. It now houses the Ventana Fine Art gallery.

■ 408 Delgado Street

The **Stevenson house** was a six-room farm homestead built sometime before

Prada house. *Photograph by Richard Harris.*

First Ward School. *Photograph by Richard Harris.*

1848 and expanded room by room by the Rafael García family throughout the second half of the nineteenth century. In 1920 the Garcías sold it to Kate Chapman, the wife of archaeological artist Kenneth Chapman of the School of American Anthropology and Museum of New Mexico. Mrs. Chapman restored the old hacienda in partnership with Dorothy Stewart, the sister of Canyon Road preservationist Margretta Dietrich. In 1930, Mrs. Chapman sold the property to Philip Stevenson, a writer most remembered in New Mexico for his play *Sure Fire: Episodes in the Life of Billy the Kid*. Stevenson lived in the house until 1939, when he left Santa Fe to work as a screenwriter in Hollywood, where he was subsequently blacklisted for alleged communist sympathies. He died in the Soviet Union in 1965.

Delgado Street Bridge

One block north of Canyon Road, the modest concrete **Delgado Street Bridge** over the Santa Fe River has unique historical curiosity value: It was the rendezvous spot where a British researcher at Los Alamos National Laboratories leaked atomic bomb plans to a Soviet agent in 1945, touching off the Cold War.

533 Garcia Street

The **Garcia homestead,** built sometime between 1880 and 1912 by the family for whom the street is named, was the only true Territorial-style residence in the neighborhood surrounding lower Canyon Road. Although it has the characteristic Greek Revival pedimented window frames, the house does not conform to present-day conceptions of Territorial style as defined by the historic styles act because it has a sloping hipped roof, probably original, rather than the flat roofs used in most adobe construction in Santa Fe. It is a private residence.

569 Garcia Street

The **Garcia Street Club,** an L-shaped Territorial Revival home built in the

1920s, was converted into a neighborhood teen center in the late 1940s by Amelia White, a wealthy Santa Fe art patron. The original design was preserved both inside and out. It still serves as a community center.

660 East Garcia Street

The **School of American Research,** which was originally called the School of American Archaeology, occupied parts of the Palace of the Governors and adjacent buildings for 65 years before benefactress Amelia White left her big, rambling Spanish Pueblo Revival home to the school in 1972. The School of American Research is open to the public only on Friday afternoons, when tours are available by advance reservation (982-3584), allowing visitors to view the best of its collection of more than 10,000 Indian artifacts.

506 Acequia Madre

The **B. B. Dunne house** was designed and built in the early 1920s by the owner. A journalist by profession, Dunne became one of those self-reliant Renaissance men who seemed to proliferate in Santa Fe's art colony. Besides his own gracefully curved and buttressed Spanish Pueblo Revival home, he built two other neighboring houses at 508 Acequia Madre and 501 Garcia Street. All are private residences.

614 Acequia Madre

The **Curtin house** was designed and built in 1925 by a mother and daughter team, Eva Scott Fenyes and Leonora Musse Curtin, without the help of an architect. It is considered one of the purest examples of Territorial Revival architecture in the area — except for the Spanish Pueblo–style corbels on the porch posts. The house is also referred to as the Paloheimo house after its most prominent resident, a Finnish honorary consul who served as spokesperson for Scandinavian citizens throughout the southwest and restored El Rancho de las

Golondrinas, the Spanish Colonial open-air museum on Santa Fe's western outskirts. The house is a private residence.

740 Acequia Madre

The **Old Mill house** was built sometime before 1912 as a corn grinding mill, powered by the flow of water through a diversion of the *acequia madre*. Architect Irving Parsons renovated it into a Spanish Pueblo Revival–style house in 1933, although the millstone remains as a reminder of its earlier purpose. It is a private residence.

770 Acequia Madre

The **Lynn Riggs house,** a small Spanish Pueblo Revival residence, was built sometime in the early 1920s. Riggs came to Santa Fe as the personal secretary of poet Witter Bynner, one of the region's most prominent literary figures, and later turned her hand to playwrighting. Her 1931 play *Green Grow the Lilacs* was later adapted into the Rodgers and Hammerstein musical *Oklahoma!*.

805 El Caminito

The **Galt house,** an old adobe residence of uncertain origin, was the first restoration project undertaken by novice architect John Gaw Meem, who would become the leading proponent of Santa Fe style. Features added by Meem, including exposed *vigas, canales,* and fluid lines, are characteristic of the Spanish Pueblo Revival style. The house is a private residence.

830 El Caminito

El Torreón ("the tower") was one of the most unusual experiments in the Spanish Pueblo revival of the 1920s. Created by Frank Applegate, one of several artists and writers who worked as self-taught architects and builders in the Camino del Monte Sol neighborhood at the time, El Torreón was modeled after the round watchtowers that had been built in colonial times to defend outlying communities from Indian raids. Although similar towers have been incorporated in a few

El Torreón. *Photograph by Richard Harris.*

custom homes of more recent vintage, the two-story tower was unique in Santa Fe at the time it was built. It is part of a private residence.

831 El Caminito

The **De la Pena house** was probably the first homestead built along El Caminito and one of the first in the Camino del Monte Sol area. The oldest recorded deed to the farmhouse and land was recorded in 1845. Frank Applegate bought the four-room adobe in 1925 and expanded and renovated it in Spanish Pueblo Revival style. It remains a private residence.

324 Camino del Monte Sol

The **Rios wood lot,** one of the last vestiges of Canyon Road's pretourism days, has operated as a family business since the days of Los Cinco Pintores. A coyote fence of juniper poles encloses giant heaps of curing firewood, and the homes of several generations of the Rios family surround the compound. Canyon Road merchants have been lodging intermittent protests against the wood lot for decades, complaining that it is an "industrial" use inappropriate to such a high-toned neighborhood (most firewood

sold in Santa Fe comes from the outlying village of Pecos, where woodcutting is the principal occupation), and investors have offered the Rios family literally millions of dollars for the prime location at the corner of Canyon and Monte Sol, but the family and their wood lot endure.

409 Camino del Monte Sol

The **Laura Gilpin house,** built as a homestead sometime before the first map of the neighborhood was made in 1912, was acquired in the early 1930s by photographer Laura Gilpin, whose southwestern work is collected in books including *Rio Grande: River of Destiny, The Pueblos: A Camera Chronicle,* and *Enduring Navaho.* The original part of the house, at the rear, has a corrugated iron gable roof of the type common in northern New Mexico mountain villages; the Pueblo Revival front portion of the house is a relatively recent addition.

439 Camino del Monte Sol

The **Mary Austin house** (Gerald Peters Gallery), which bears the name Casa Querida ("Darling House"), is a simple, owner-built Pueblo Revival residence built in 1925. Austin was one of Santa

Rios wood lot. *Photograph by Richard Harris.*

Fe's major literary figures between 1924 and 1934; her books include *Land of Journey's Ending, Earth Horizon: An Autobiography, Indian Pottery of the Rio Grande,* and *One Smoke Stories.* Fellow photographer Ansel Adams shared the house while the two collaborated on books, and author Willa Cather wrote much of *Death Comes for the Archbishop,* her fictionalized portrait of Santa Fe's Archbishop Lamy, in the library of the house. Austin planned and supervised construction of the house with advice from her neighbor, artist–writer–architect Frank Applegate, whose writings she edited, and from budding architect John Gaw Meem. Today, the house serves as the art gallery of Gerald Peters, the most prominent landlord and business owner in the Santa Fe historic district today. The gallery carries works by most early artists of the Camino del Monte Sol group, as well as those of New Mexico's most famous painter, Georgia O'Keeffe.

■ 503–507 Camino del Monte Sol

The **Alice Clark Myers house,** hidden behind a high adobe wall at 503 Camino del Monte Sol, was the masterwork of Alice Clark Myers, the third woman to receive a degree in architecture in the United States, and her husband, artist Datus Myers. When it was completed in the late 1920s, it was the second-largest Spanish Pueblo Revival residence in Santa Fe; only the Carlos Vierra house was larger. While building the house, the couple lived in the small adobe home-stead on the property—originally a sin-gle room, though several more were added later—that is now the **Datus Ensign Meyers house** at 507 Camino del Monte Sol. After completing the big house, Alice Myers never designed another building but turned her attention to pottery and ceramic tilemaking. Datus Meyers became the coordinator of Indian artists and other New Mexico

artists for the Depression-era Public Works of Art Project.

■ 544 Camino del Monte Sol

The **Dasburg house** may have been designed and built by Frank Applegate in 1920–1921. It was sold in 1921 to Andrew Dasburg, a French-born cubist painter who had moved to Santa Fe the previous year. Dasburg occupied the house with his wife and son for ten years, keeping his studio in the nearby *jacal* log cabin at 520 Camino del Monte Sol, which he expanded, adding a Pueblo Revival "pen tile" addition with the help of young architect John Gaw Meem. In 1930, Dasburg moved to Taos, where he was a prominent figure in the Taos Society of Artists until his death in 1979.

■ 555 Camino del Monte Sol

The **William Penhallow Henderson house** was a small, old adobe home-stead when Chicago artist Henderson and his wife, poet Alice Corbin, bought it after leaving Sunmount Sanitarium, far-ther up the road, where Corbin had been undergoing tuberculosis treatment. With the inspiration of the sanitarium's then-unique Spanish Pueblo Revival architec-ture designed by Isaac Hamilton Rapp, Henderson used adobe bricks, which he made by hand, to add rooms on the sides and rear, with a new inset portal. When completed, the house appeared as it does today. He then turned his atten-tion to building his studio at 557 Camino del Monte Sol, which he later expanded into the headquarters of his construction enterprises, Pueblo Building Supply (later the Spanish Pueblo Building Company). The first Anglo homeowner in the neighborhood, Henderson per-suaded the city council to change the road's name from from Telephone Road to Camino del Monte Sol ("Road of Sun Mountain"; Sun Mountain is the round-topped 8000-foot mountain immediately behind St. John's College).

▪ 538, 542, 550, 558, 566, 580, and 586 Camino del Monte Sol

The **Cinco Pintores houses** and their builders—Will Shuster, Fremont Ellis, Willard Nash, Walter Mruk, and Josef Bakos—epitomize the spirit of the early Santa Fe artist colony. Unlike earlier painters such as Henderson, Cassidy, Parsons, Dasburg, Sloan, Davey, and Henri, all of whom had formal art school training and substantial professional reputations before coming to Santa Fe, the five young men arrived while still in their twenties, at the beginning of their careers. Hoping to learn under the mentorship of the older artists, the five found their way to Santa Fe individually and banded together in 1921 under the name Los Cinco Pintores ("the five painters") for the first of their annual exhibitions at the Museum of Fine Arts. Nearly penniless, they pooled their meager financial resources and building skills to cooperate in the construction of a row of small, plain adobe houses. Despite early disasters—Shuster's and Ellis's walls fell down before the first houses were finished—the painters not only completed their homes but in some cases went on to build additional houses, selling their earlier ones for living expenses. All of the houses are still standing and have been enlarged and extensively renovated in Spanish Pueblo Revival style.

The **Willard Nash houses** were at 538 and 566 Camino del Monte Sol; it is unclear whether Nash built 538 first and lived there during construction of 566, or whether he lived in 566 from the start and built 538 to sell. In any case, he lived in 566 until he moved away from Santa Fe in 1936.

The **Will Shuster houses** were at 542 and 580 Camino del Monte Sol. Number 542, the first one built, flanked the larger home of his mentor, William Penhallow Henderson, while 580 stood next to Henderson's studio. In the 1930s, Shuster moved to a third house, number 550, on the other side of Henderson's home; this house is believed to have been built in the early 1920s by Frank Applegate.

The **Walter Mruk house** at 558 Camino del Monte Sol is the most distinctive of the original Cinco Pintores houses, with its inset entryway New Mexico Mission–style second-floor balcony. Mruk moved away after five years, and the house was bought by Boy Scouts of America executive Benjamin Hyde, for whom Hyde Memorial State Park west of Santa Fe is named.

The **Joseph Bakos house** at 576 Camino del Monte Sol is distinguished by well-crafted doors and other wood details, such as the twisted rope scroll below the garage lintel. Bakos, the only Cinco Pintores member with previous construction experience, supported his passion for painting by working as a carpenter and furniture maker.

Will Shuster house detail. *Photograph by Richard Harris.*

Will Shuster house detail. *Photograph by Richard Harris.*

Joseph Bakos house. *Photograph by Richard Harris.*

The **Fremont Ellis house** at 586 Camino del Monte Sol is the most complex of the Cinco Pintores homes. Ellis saw many possibilities in the new Spanish Pueblo Revival style and experimented with setbacks, indentations, curved lines, and buttresses. The artist's original concept was marred by the later addition of an awkwardly boxlike second story. Ellis lived in the house until 1956, when he moved to the Fremont Ellis house on Canyon Road. The last survivor of the original Cinco Pintores, he continued to live in Santa Fe until his death in 1985.

■ 704 Camino Lejo

The **Wheelwright Museum of the American Indian,** the only major Santa Fe museum that is not government owned, was built in 1937 to preserve aspects of Navajo ceremonies and traditions that then appeared in danger of being forgotten. Then known as the Museum of Navaho Ceremonial Art, it was the creation of legendary Navajo shaman Hosteen Klah and Boston heiress Mary Cabot Wheelwright, who had moved west in 1920, at the age of 40, to experience life among the Indians. The two collaborated for two decades to build the museum's collection, although they could not speak each other's languages. The building was one of the major architectural accomplishments of William Penhallow Henderson, a well-known artist from Chicago who came to Santa Fe in 1916, developed an enthusiasm for the concepts of Santa Fe style, and started his own construction, restoration, and furniture-making business. The exterior and main floor of the museum are in the shape of an eight-sided *hoogan* with the entrance facing north, as Navajo ceremonial tradition requires. (There is a replica of an actual *hoogan* down the hill behind the museum.) The subterranean lower level, pat-

Wheelwright Museum. *Photograph by Richard Harris.*

terned after the interior of an old-fashioned Navajo Reservation trading post, right down to the creaking floorboards, serves as a gift shop. The museum's changing exhibits of American Indian art are open to the public by donation.

■ 706 Camino Lejo

What the **New Mexico Museum of International Folk Art,** a huge, windowless, boxlike structure built in 1953, may lack in terms of historical or architectural interest, it makes up for through sheer novelty. It is the most popular unit of the Museum of New Mexico, primarily because of the vast Girard Collection, containing more than 100,000 handmade toys and dolls from around the world arranged in elaborate dioramas. Visitors will find insights to the cultural context of Spanish Colonial New Mexico in the museum's recently opened Hispanic Heritage Wing.

■ 708 Camino Lejo

The design for the **Laboratory of Anthropology,** built in 1930–1931, began as John Gaw Meem's entry in a contest sponsored by John D. Rockefeller, Jr., and judged by a blue-ribbon panel of archaeologists, anthropologists, and architects, including Sylvanus Morley, Frank Mera, Kenneth Chapman, Amelia White, Mary Cabot Wheelwright, and John van Pelt. A classic example of Spanish Pueblo Mission Revival style, the building consists of three distinct, carefully balanced segments—a churchlike two-story hall (referred to as "the lounge"), a gallery area beyond the main entrance portal, and a squat, irregular mass that houses offices and an extensive library—each with its own height, fenestration, and pattern of protruding *vigas.* Massive, sculptured buttresses around the exterior of the lounge pay tribute to the widely painted and photographed rear elevation of the nineteenth-century San Francisco de Asís Church at Ranchos de Taos. (Such buttresses were used to prop up weak or sagging walls of adobe churches; in the case

Laboratory of Anthropology. *Photograph by Richard Harris.*

of the Laboratory of Anthropology, however, they are hollow constructions of red brick covered with stucco and serve a purely decorative function.) The Laboratory of Anthropology incorporates only a small portion of the winning design originally submitted by Meem, a vast complex that included 36 other buildings, which were never built. A division of the Museum of New Mexico, the laboratory contains storage space for more than 50,000 pre-Columbian Indian artifacts. Only a few are exhibited in the display cases near the entrance; more extensive exhibitions from the state collection are shown next door at the Museum of Indian Arts and Culture.

710 Camino Lejo

The **Museum of Indian Arts and Culture,** the newest unit of the Museum of New Mexico, was opened in 1987 to provide display space for rotating exhibits from the Laboratory of Anthropology's Indian artifact collection. Other changing displays cover various aspects of indigenous arts and traditions from pre-Columbian times to the present day. Designed with the participation of advisors from New Mexico's Indian tribes, the architecturally unique museum features a high glass south wall for passive solar heat, an open central atrium for craft demonstrations, classrooms, and an outdoor ceremonial dance plaza.

908 Old Santa Fe Trail

The **Bronson M. Cutting house,** built in 1910 by Colorado Springs architect Thomas McLaren, represents one of several peculiar experiments during that period that involved reviving architectural elements borrowed from other Hispanic regions of the world. The fancifully curvilinear roofline and arched windows and doorways derived from the Mission Revival style then in vogue in California, which had no antecedent in New Mexico architecture of any era, was thought to be appropriate as a broadly stylized evocation of Latin American heritage. Cuttings, the publisher of the *Santa Fe New Mexican* newspaper and later U.S. Senator from New Mexico, lived in the house until his premature death in a 1935 plane crash. It later served as a Catholic orphanage and today is a private residence once more.

▣ 1100 Old Santa Fe Trail

The **National Park Service Southwest Office Building** is the largest all-adobe office building in the United States and one of the largest secular adobe structures. More than 200,000 adobe bricks were used in construction, and the building covers more than an acre of ground. Designed by National Park Service architect Cecil J. Doty and built by the Public Works Administration and the Civilian Conservation Corps, it was completed in 1939. The walls are 4 feet 9 inches thick at the base and are supported by massive buttresses. Two stories high on the east side and one story on the other three sides, the building surrounds a beautifully landscaped courtyard with offices that open off a sheltering portal. The courtyard's dominant feature is a large fountain and goldfish pond. A National Historic Landmark, the building houses the administrative and public affairs offices for all national parks in New Mexico and Arizona. Other National Park Service departments have moved the Piñon Building on St. Francis Drive.

▣ Mount Carmel Road

The **Immaculate Heart of Mary Seminary,** located on a little road off Camino del Monte Sol just north of Old Santa Fe Trail, was the site of Sunmount Sanitarium. Established in 1903 as a municipally operated tent city for tuberculosis patients, Sunmount failed to attract much business until 1914, when a permanent facility was built. Leading figures in Santa Fe's early artists' and writers' colony, including poet Alice Corbin, photographer Carlos Vierra, painter Sheldon Parsons, and architect John Gaw Meem, originally came for treatment at the sanatorium, and their fascination with the early Santa Fe style design by Isaac H. Rapp spurred the architectural creativity of the 1920s. A second main sanatorium building, also designed by Rapp, was built in 1920 and today serves as the seminary's administration building. The tuberculosis epidemic that had plagued the United States since the 1880s subsided by the early 1930s, and in 1938 the complex was converted into a resort hotel called the Santa Fe Inn. But as fuel shortages put a

National Park Service courtyard. *Photograph by Richard Harris.*

Mural at Immaculate Heart of Mary Seminary (formerly Sunmount Sanitorium). *Photograph by Richard Harris.*

stop to tourism during World War II, the inn suffered financial hardship, and the Archdiocese of Santa Fe bought the property in 1946. Operated by the Carmelite Order of nuns, the seminary offers religious education to a student body of about 40 prospective priests, who simultaneously take academic courses at the College of Santa Fe.

■ 924 Canyon Road

The **Gerald Cassidy house,** one of the oldest houses in the residential neighborhood uphill on Canyon beyond Camino del Monte Sol, was built sometime before 1915, when painter Gerald Cassidy bought the property. Over the next 19 years, he renovated the house, expanded it, and added *vigas*, corbels, and other Spanish Pueblo Revival fea-

tures. Cassidy was the first artist to take up residence in the Canyon Road–Camino del Monte Sol area. Sheldon Parsons and his daughter were sharing the house with the Cassidy family in 1916 when Parsons's old friend, William P. Henderson, arrived in Santa Fe and was persuaded to build his own house a short distance away.

■ 1002½ Canyon Road

The **Van Dresser house,** a small house in a secluded compound across from Patrick Smith Park, is the "oldest continuously operating solar house in America" according to local historian John Sherman. It was built around 1940, and the solar heating panels were added in the late 1960s. Since then, solar greenhouses and collector panels have become common in

Santa Fe, where the sun shines, on the average, 350 days a year.

▦ 1120 Canyon Road

Cristo Rey Church has an authentically Spanish colonial feel even though it is of recent vintage. Designed by architect John Gaw Meem on commission from the Society for the Preservation and Restoration of New Mexico Mission Churches, it was built to house a giant stone *reredos*, or altar screen, made in 1760 by artists brought from Mexico using stone quarried in northern Santa Fe County. The *reredos* had once graced La Castrense, a military chapel on the south side of the Plaza (a commemorative plaque at 58 East San Francisco Street marks the chapel's site), but had been in storage behind the altar of St. Francis Cathedral since the 1880s, hidden due to Archbishop Lamy's distaste for local religious art. The church was completed in 1940 and dedicated on the 400th anniversary of Coronado's expedition into New Mexico. Built from more than 150,000 adobe bricks, all of which were made from the soil on site in the traditional manner before construction began, Cristo Rey Church incorporates design elements inspired by several historic mission churches of New Mexico—a tower similar to the ones at the Acoma Pueblo mission (c. 1642), a transverse clerestory like the one at Santa Ana Pueblo (c. 1692), transepts like those of the old Santa Fe Parroquía (c. 1717), and a balconied facade like the one at Las Trampas (c. 1763). It has been in use as a parish church continuously since 1940 and is open to the public.

▦ 1800 Upper Canyon Road

The **Randall Davey Audubon Center** was built in 1847 at the mouth of Santa Fe Canyon as the city's first industrial sawmill. Using timber cut in the canyon and waterwheel power from the Santa Fe River, it supplied lumber for military buildings at Fort Marcy. When the fort was finished and the mill was shut down in 1856, the stone building was converted into a residence, probably one of the most secluded dwellings in the Santa Fe area at the time. It passed through several hands before Randall Davey, a well-

Cristo Rey Church. *Photograph by Richard Harris.*

Reredos hidden in old Parroquía section of St. Francis Cathedral, 1890. *Photograph by Charles F. Lummis, courtesy Museum of New Mexico, neg. 10023.*

known painter of horse race scenes who had just moved to town. He made it his home and studio until his death in 1964. Davey left the home and 135-acre estate to the National Audubon Society, which operates it as a wildlife sanctuary and uses the house and studio as a headquarters. The natural foothills environment of the hillside estate attracts more than 100 bird species throughout the year. It also harbors rabbits, coyotes, and raccoons. Deer, bobcats, black bears, and mountain lions have sometimes been known to wander out of the wilderness of nearby Santa Fe Canyon, a critical watershed that has been closed to human visitors for decades. The sanctuary is open to the public by donation, and tours of the Davey home and studio are offered on an irregular schedule.

▧ 1371 Cerro Gordo Road

The **Schramm house,** the first of numerous marvelously creative owner-built homes along Cerro Gordo Road and still the most impressive from a distance, perches high on the hillside. It was built little by little in the 1940s and 1950s by

watchmaker Curt Schramm, using only salvaged building materials. The residence still belongs to the Schramm family.

▧ 1160 Camino de Cruz Blanca

St. John's College blends old and new in an unusual way that fits the spirit of Santa Fe perfectly. Founded in 1696 in Annapolis, Maryland, under the name King William's School, the college is the third-oldest in the country; only the College of William and Mary and Harvard University are older. During World War II, the U.S. Naval Academy at Annapolis tried to annex the St. John's College buildings there, and although the attempt failed, St. John's board of regents began thinking about opening a second campus in the western United States. The idea was not acted upon until 1960, when the president of the college began a serious search for the location of the second campus. He had narrowed the list of possibilities to three California towns when his wife had a self-described "mystical experience" that inspired her to urge her husband to consider Santa Fe. Within weeks, meetings

Randall Davey house, 1921. *Photograph courtesy Museum of New Mexico, neg. 10518.*

Mural, Mrs. Davey's dressing room, Randall Davey house. *Photograph by T. Harmon Parkhurst, courtesy Museum of New Mexico, neg. 32104.*

St. John's College. *Photograph by Richard Harris.*

with a group of Santa Feans who had been working for several years to attract a private liberal arts college to the city resulted in a commitment to build the second campus in Santa Fe. Architect John Gaw Meem donated 214 acres that he and his wife owned at the foot of Sun Mountain and presented a design for the college's stately Territorial Revival–style buildings. The campus opened in 1964 and graduated its first class in 1968. St. John's College is unique among American colleges today in that it has no elective courses; all students follow the same curriculum, based on 100 "great books." Students are free to transfer between the Annapolis and Santa Fe campuses whenever they wish. Many guest lectures at the college are open to the public, and free performances of Shakespeare's plays in the school's central courtyard are a cultural highlight of Santa Fe's summer season.

124

THE SANTA FE ARTS COMMUNITY

The history of the Canyon Road and Camino del Monte Sol district in the twentieth century is interwoven with Santa Fe's art community. Still a semirural area on the outskirts of town, the neighborhood saw the development of semicommunal artists' compounds consisting of small adobe houses and studios, often built by the artists' own hands. In recent years, a seven-block segment of Canyon Road has been transformed into one of the Santa Fe's two main gallery zones, boasting more than 60 of the roughly 200 visual arts galleries in the city. City planners adapted the zoning ordinances to accommodate Canyon Road's unique character by creating a new classification: "residential arts and crafts zone." The neighborhood is part of the original Santa Fe historic district, which also takes in the downtown area.

Santa Fe and its smaller northern rival, Taos, first caught the attention of artists in 1883, when famed western documentary painter Joseph Sharpe passed through on a sketching expedition. His pictures of the region, with its exotic people, enchanted landscapes, and the "quality of the light" (a reason cited by virtually every painter who has moved to Santa Fe since), inspired other traveling artists to include New Mexico in their itineraries.

The first to take up residence in Santa Fe was George Stanley, who rented an apartment and studio on Palace Avenue west of the present-day site of the Museum of Fine Arts in 1896 and exhibited his watercolors and sketches in an empty room of the decrepit Old Palace (now called the Palace of the Governors). There is no evidence that Stanley sold a single painting during his year's stay in Santa Fe, but his exhibit provided a precedent in support of the movement to transform the Old Palace into a museum 12 years later.

The first artist to move to Santa Fe permanently was Carlos Vierra, a photographer and painter who came from California in 1904 for treatment of lung problems and opened a photography studio on the Plaza. He traveled extensively throughout northern New Mexico and in 1908 became the staff photographer for the School of American Archaeology. Although he had no formal training in architecture, his photographs of traditional Indian and Spanish buildings around the state provided much of the basis for the restoration of the Palace of the Governors, the design of the Museum of Fine Arts, and the early development of Santa Fe style. Three of the large mural panels in the art museum's St. Francis Auditorium, which depict Franciscan friars' roles in the Spanish conquest of the New World, were painted by Vierra. (The figure of Christopher Columbus is actually Vierra's self-portrait.)

Donald Beauregard, a young artist from the faculty of the University of Utah who was known for his paintings of Pueblo Indians, briefly became Santa Fe's second resident artist. He was hired by Museum of New Mexico patron Frank Springer to paint a series of canvas murals for the New Mexico Building which Isaac H. Rapp was designing for the Panama Pacific Exposition in San

Santa Fe artists, La Fonda Hotel art gallery, 1933; left to right: Carlos Vierra, Datus Myers, Sheldon Parsons, Theodore Van Soelen, Gerald Cassidy, and Will Shuster. *Photograph courtesy Museum of New Mexico, neg. 20787.*

Diego's Balboa Park. The theme of the murals was to be the Franciscan Order, from the life of St. Francis of Asissi to the work of missionaries among the Indians in New Mexico. Springer sent Beauregard on an extended trip to Europe. He fell ill in Switzerland and was forced to return to the United States, where he was given a studio in the Palace of the Governors to work on the murals. After a few months in residence during 1913, he became too ill to go on with the project and went to a hospital in Denver, where he was diagnosed with incurable cancer. He died less than a month later at his family home in Utah. Carlos Vierra painted other murals for the San Diego Exposition; later, he and Kenneth Chapman completed Beauregard's murals and installed them in St. Francis Auditorium in the Museum of Fine Arts, where they can still be seen.

Although the artists' colony 70 miles away in Taos was already gaining an international reputation, when Sheldon Parsons arrived in Santa Fe in 1913 he found himself the only painter in the city except Vierra, who had become a full-time employee of the museum. Parsons, a well-known painter from New York, had recently lost his wife to tuberculosis and traveled west with his 12-year-old daughter Sara. Bound for San Francisco, the Parsons got as far as Denver before he collapsed from tuberculosis himself. Changing their plans, they headed south to Santa Fe because the city was becoming known as having a climate favorable to recovery from TB. Museum of New Mexico supporters, who were eager to build a regional art collection for the museum, bought several of Parsons's landscape paintings and helped him find living quarters in the Padre Gallegos house downtown. The artist's health declined rapidly, and at one point his doctor—who was exchanging daily medical care for some of Parsons's paintings—declared that he was dying. He recovered, though, and lived and painted in Santa Fe for the next 30 years. In 1919 his daughter married Victor Higgins of the Taos Society of Artists and moved to Taos, where she would achieve prominence as an artist in her own right under the name Sara Mack.

When Gerald Cassidy and his wife, magazine correspondent Ina Cassidy, came from New York to Santa Fe in 1915, he had already cultivated a fascination with painting the Indians of the southwest. Twenty-five years before, at age 21, during a year-long recovery from pneumonia at an Albuquerque sanatorium, Cassidy had visited nearby Indian pueblos, and thereafter he had continued to make painting trips to the west. On moving to Santa Fe, the Cassidys bought an old adobe on Canyon Road, becoming the first artist and writer to take up residence in what would soon become the heart of the Santa Fe art colony. They quickly made friends with Sheldon Parsons and his daughter, who became their housesitters when the Cassidys took extended trips to the east coast and Europe for exhibitions. Like Parsons, Cassidy continued to live in Santa Fe until 1934, when he died in his studio of carbon monoxide poisoning from one of the first natural gas furnaces in Santa Fe, installed a few weeks earlier.

The person most often credited with founding the Canyon Road art colony, William Penhallow Henderson moved to Santa Fe from Chicago in 1916 in the company of his wife, poet Alice Corbin, who came for treatment of tuberculosis at Sunmount Sanitarium. Henderson's credentials as a painter —postgraduate studies at the Boston Museum of Fine Arts and an assistant professorship at the Chicago Academy of Fine Arts—were impressive enough to establish him as one of the art scene's leading figures. Henderson embraced the rising enthusiasm for a Santa Fe–style revival. Beginning in 1917 with a small, isolated adobe on Camino del Monte Sol, he expanded the structure over a period of several years into a large Spanish Pueblo Revival residence, learning the building trades as the project progressed. In 1925, Henderson established the Pueblo Spanish Building Company. Self-taught in skills as diverse as architectural design, construction contracting, and furniture making, he restored Sena Plaza and designed and built the Fremont Ellis house on Canyon Road and the hogan-shaped Wheelwright Museum. He also dabbled in playwrighting and acting and illustrated his wife's now-classic book on the penitentes of northern New Mexico, *Brothers of Light*.

In 1917, Henderson served a short tour of duty at the San Francisco Naval Shipyards, where he and other artists were put to work painting camouflage on battleships. There he ran into Swedish painter B. J. O. Nordfeldt, whom he persuaded to return to Santa Fe with him for a visit. Nordfeldt, too, liked Santa Fe so much that he stayed for the next 20 years and persuaded other painters, including Chicago artist Gustave Baumann, to join the fledgling artists' colony.

Around the same time, with the new Museum of Fine Arts under construction, museum director Edgar L. Hewett was pursuing a separate campaign to interest artists in Santa Fe. Hewett's idea was to develop a museum collection that would focus exclusively on New Mexico subjects and artists. Foremost among the nationally known painters he brought to visit Santa Fe were a group of revolutionary artists, including Robert Henri, John Sloan, George Bellows, Paul Burlin, and Leon Kroll, collectively known for a series of controversial New York exhibitions that had inspired critics to dub them the "Ashcan School." Although none of them were moved to relinquish New York City for life on the frontier, Sloan and Henri made repeated painting trips to Santa Fe and became as well known as any resident painter for their depictions of New Mexico's land and its people.

Unlike the artists who had come before them, Santa Fe's most legendary painters, Los Cinco Pintores ("the Five Painters")—Will Shuster, Fremont Ellis, Willard Nash, Walter Mruk, and Josef Bakos—came to Santa Fe at the beginning of their careers to live cheaply, study with more established artists such as Henderson, Cassidy, and Parsons, and explore the possibilities of New Mexico subject matter, which was enjoying a wave of nationwide interest. Shuster, the oldest of the group, arrived in 1921 at age 28 from Philadelphia; he had been trained as an electrical engineer, but when ill health forced him to move west, he was drawn to Santa Fe by the budding art

Artist John Sloan at work, 1926. *Photograph by T. Harmon Parkhurst, courtesy Museum of New Mexico, neg. 28835.*

scene and decided to pursue his interest in painting. Ellis, who came in 1919 at the age of 22, was born in Montana and traveled widely and visited art museums around the country but had little formal artistic training; self-taught, he spent a year as an art teacher in El Paso, Texas, before coming to Santa Fe. Nash was studying art in Detroit, Michigan, when he won a commission to paint a New Mexico landscape mural for a building there; after visiting in 1920 for research purposes, he moved to Santa Fe permanently the following year, at age 22. Mruk and Bakos had grown up together in Buffalo, New York, and went to art school together in New York and Denver. Mruk moved to Santa Fe in 1920 and worked for the U.S. Forest Service to support himself while painting. Bakos, an art instructor at the University of Colorado, paid a visit to Mruk while the university was closed down by an influenza epidemic and decided to move to Santa Fe the following year.

The Cinco Pintores banded together to present annual shows at the Museum of Fine Arts, proclaiming themselves the southwest's artistic avante garde and pledging "to take art to the people and not to surrender to commercialism." They lived in neighboring home-built houses on Camino del Monte Sol, across the street from Henderson's house, sharing their meager resources in an informal cooperative arrangement. The Cinco Pintores alliance lasted for five years. By then their artistic visions were diverging, several members of the group had married, and artistic poverty was losing its appeal. Mruk moved back to New York in 1926; Bakos increasingly devoted his energy to furniture making; Nash developed a fascination with cubism and painted in Santa Fe for 10 more years before he, too, moved away; Shuster became a local character, known as much for a wide assortment of none-too-practical inventions as for painting and is best remembered today as the man who invented Zozobra and revitalized the Santa Fe fiesta; and Ellis continued to paint at his Canyon Road studio, becoming the grand old man of the Santa Fe art scene long before his death in 1985 at the age of 88.

In the early days, the Museum of New Mexico actively sponsored the fledgling artist community. There was not a single art gallery in Santa Fe before 1935, and while most local artists sent their work to galleries back east, the ground-floor galleries in the Museum of Fine Arts provided exhibition space for Santa Fe and Taos artists to show and sell their work. The basement of the museum contained a workshop where artists could stretch their own canvases and frame their work. Free monthly banquets were provided for artists in the museum's upstairs hall. In 1920, there were 15 resident artists in Santa Fe. By 1930, the number had grown to 68, including a new generation of aspiring young painters that included Gina Knee, Charles Barrows, Cady Wells, and Jim Morris. By 1935, the Great Depression had dried up art investment funds from private collectors throughout the country, and the federal government saw the plight of New Mexico's artists as particularly urgent. In October of that year, the New Mexico Art Project came into being. A total of 206 artists in Santa Fe, Taos, and elsewhere were paid to "paint without restraint." Their canvases were distributed to public institutions, and their murals and sculptures can still be seen in many public buildings around the state.

Over the years, the artists' colony has also included a number of leading American photographers, including Edward Curtis, Ansel Adams, Elliot Porter, and Paul Caponigro, as well as retired New York Museum of Modern Art photography curator Beaumont Newhall. The annual Santa Fe Photographic Workshops are rated as some of the finest in the country, rivaled only by the Maine Photographic Workshops.

The visual arts have grown unabated in Santa Fe. As of the 1990 census, more than 1200 city and county residents listed "artist" as their primary occupation. Besides the nearly 250 art galleries in town, many artists sell their work at weekend open-air art shows held at several downtown locations during the summer tourist season. Because of the highly competitive art market, many Santa Fe artists today have gone back to the practice of earlier decades, sending their works to galleries in other cities, particularly in Texas and California. In the 1970s, a local journalist described Santa Fe as "the third-largest art market in the United States"; although this often-repeated bit of local mythology is almost certainly not accurate, there can be no doubt that art is fundamental to Santa Fe's economy, rivaled only by state government and the hospitality industry.

American Indian art, which makes up an important part of the art market in Santa Fe today, developed independent of the Anglo artists' community. Pueblo Indians, who had been making decorated pottery, textiles, and turquoise jewelry for at least 1000 years, shared their knowledge of these crafts with their Navajo allies following the Pueblo Revolt of 1680 and the subsequent Spanish Reconquest, when many Pueblo people fled the Rio Grande Valley to live among the Navajo. By the mid-1880s, Anglo traders had begun exchanging food and clothing for Indian craft items to be shipped east for sale to private collectors. At the same time, the traders persuaded the Indians to adapt their traditional crafts to appeal to non-Indian buyers, resulting in new styles of Navajo wool rugs and silver jewelry as well as many creative variations on Pueblo pottery. The market for these items grew much larger with the arrival of tourism in the early years of the twentieth century. During the 1920s, the federal government implemented policies aimed at eradicating indigenous culture to eliminate Indian reservations and assimilate tribal people into the American mainstream. The belief that Indian traditions were vanishing spurred museum curators and private collectors to rush to buy Indian craft items at what then seemed like inflated prices. Sadly, the benefit of the increasing value of Indian crafts went into the pockets of non-Indian traders, as the Pueblo and Navajo people continued to suffer some of the worst poverty conditions in the country. Attempts to correct this situation

Wheelright Museum of the Ameridan Indian.   *National Register of Historic Places.*

began in 1922 with the First Annual Southwest Indian Fair, held in connection with the Santa Fe fiesta. The event offered Indians a chance to deal directly with tourists and collectors in large numbers. It evolved into today's Santa Fe Indian Market, the largest Indian arts and crafts market in the United States, which features more than 1200 vendors from 80 tribes and attracts more than 100,000 buyers.

The roots of contemporary Indian art, a term that usually signifies modern or stylized painting and sculpture, can be traced back to 1920. Kenneth Chapman of the Museum of New Mexico, who had been working with other anthropologists to preserve a record of San Ildefonso Pueblo at a time when its tribe seemed to be in danger of dying out from disease, had been providing crayons and watercolor paints to young Indians at the pueblo, encouraging them to express themselves on paper. The museum mounted an exhibit of 30 Indian drawings and paintings which met with enthusiastic critical appreciation and became a continuing tradition. For the most part, however, in the 1920s Indians were usually subjects, not artists.

In 1931, inspired by the museum shows, the Santa Fe Indian School decided to include art in its curriculum. The school hired Dorothy Dunn as the teacher, and with Canyon Road artist Olive Rush she organized what

Masking wall, Wheelright Museum of the Ameridan Indian. *National Register of Historic Places.*

became known as The Studio and helped classes of about 20 Indian students per year to develop a distinctive style of tempera painting and fresco murals that is still in use today. Walt Disney was so impressed by the color work he saw at The Studio that he hired a team of graduating Navajo artists to work on his first color animation features. As the federal Indian Agency began to realize that fine arts, as well as crafts, could provide a significant source of income for native people, The Studio was expanded into a separate school, the Institute of American Indian Arts (IAIA), which the most talented art students from all U.S. tribes could attend free of charge. Students at the IAIA learn not only composition and technique but also marketing. Several Indian-owned galleries now operate in Santa Fe, and many other galleries specialize in contemporary Indian art. A high percentage of IAIA students choose to stay in the Santa Fe area after graduation.

Spanish residents of the region are also known for their traditional arts and crafts, especially handwoven wool textiles, wood carving, ornamental tin and wrought iron work, furniture, and *colcha* embroidery, all that date back to colonial times. Many early Anglo artists collected *bultos*, carved wooden religious statues, and incorporated them in their paintings. Lacking both the formal art education available to Indians and the professional mentorship of the Anglo artists' colony, however, Hispanic artisans have been slow to find a wide market for their work, until recently. The Spanish Colonial Arts Society has sponsored the annual Traditional Spanish Market on the Plaza since 1925 and subsequently added a Contemporary Spanish Market and, beginning in 1989, a Winter Spanish Market, although none of these events has achieved nearly the popularity of the Indian Market. A growing number of Hispanic contemporary painters and sculptors have established a presence in Santa Fe galleries.

Since 1978, when renowned architect and fabric designer Alexander Girard and his wife Susan endowed the New Mexico Museum of International Folk Art with their 106,000-piece collection of handmade toys and naive art from all parts of the world, it has become increasingly apparent that collectors who come to Santa Fe bring an interest in folk art that goes well beyond traditional Indian and Spanish crafts. Today, there are local galleries specializing in everything from Afghani rugs to Balinese jade and Japanese handpainted silk, not to mention the world's largest Mexican import store (Jackalope Pottery— "Folk Art by the Truckload!"). Many freelance folk art importers consider Trader Jack's Flea Market, north of town near the Santa Fe Opera, the best place in the country to sell moderately priced folk art and artifacts brought back from Guatemala, Namibia, India, and a host of other exotic lands.

Santa Fe's literary community was born somewhat earlier than the painters' colony but grew more slowly. Although "dime novels" about the Wild West were set in New Mexico as early as 1851, there is little to indicate that their authors actually visited the territory. The first Santa Fe resident to have a book published was retired U.S. Army general Lew Wallace, who served as territorial governor from 1878 to 1881. Already known for his first novel, a historical romance about Mexico at the time of the Spanish Conquest called *The Fair God; or The Last of the 'Tzins* (1873), Wallace finished his masterpiece, *Ben Hur: A Tale of the Christ* (1880), during his term as governor. The novel became the biggest bestseller of its era and lives on today in print and on film. His wife, Susan, recorded her impressions of territorial New Mexico in a series of travel essays for *The Atlantic* magazine, which were later reprinted in book form under the title *The Land of the Pueblos* (1888).

Archaeologist Adolph Bandelier also found a wide readership for his novel, *The Delight Makers* (1890), an imaginary romance that attempted to bring to life the ancient Puebloans in the area now known as Bandelier National Monument, where he devoted 34 years of his life to excavating ruins. Bandelier's novel, too, is still in print, although more for its connection to the national monument than for literary merit. He also wrote several historical works about the region, notably *The Journey of Alvar Nuñez Cabeza de Vaca and His Companions from Florida to the Pacific, 1528–1536* (1905).

Journalist Charles Lummis first came to Santa Fe in 1885 while walking westward across the United States and writing accounts of his travels for the *Los Angeles Times*. After completing his trek, Lummis returned to Santa Fe, where he spent several years as Adolph Bandelier's protégé and friend; a canyon in Bandelier National Monument is named after him. He wrote five volumes of essays about New Mexico and collected Pueblo folk tales. His best-known work, and the only one that is in print today, is *The Land of Poco Tiempo* (1893).

First among the literary figures who helped establish Santa Fe as a widely known writers' colony was Alice Corbin, who came in 1916 for tuberculosis treatment at Sunmount Sanitorium. The wife of artist William Penhallow Henderson, Corbin had already achieved some renown in four years as associate editor of *Poetry: A Magazine of Modern Verse*, where she had worked with many leading poets of the day. While in the sanatorium, she wrote travel essays extolling the beauty of New Mexico for such magazines as *House Beautiful* and *Sunset*. Meanwhile, she invited such poets as Carl Sandburg, Ezra Pound, Vachel Lindsay, and Witter Bynner to visit Santa Fe, stay at the Henderson home on Camino del Monte Sol, and present readings at Sunmount. In 1917 she joined with Sandburg and others in a special issue of *Poetry* magazine devoted to poetry inspired by American Indian chants of New Mexico. She would continue to reign as the queen of Santa Fe's literary community for many years. Her books include *Red Earth* (1920; poetry) and *Brothers of Light: The Penitentes of the Southwest* (1937; nonfiction), but she is most remembered as the editor of an anthology, *The Turquoise Trail* (1928), containing poems about New Mexico by 37 writers who had been guests at the Henderson–Corbin home over the years, including Paul Horgan, D. H. Lawrence, Sinclair Lewis, Lynn Riggs, Marsden Hartley, John Galsworthy, Vachel Lindsay, Carl Sandburg, and Edgar Lee Masters.

Mary Austin, a prominent novelist and playwright from Carmel, California, first arrived in Santa Fe two years after Corbin came. She helped the Santa Fe Women's Club establish the city's first community theater, using amateur actors and enlisting the services local artists for set construction. Austin divided her time between New Mexico and California for several years and finally became a full-time Santa Fe resident in 1924. She wrote a number of fiction and nonfiction books about New Mexico over the next 10 years,

Masking wall, Wheelright Museum of the Ameridan Indian. *National Register of Historic Places.*

including an autobiography, a collection of Indian legends, and the definitive work, *Indian Pottery of the Rio Grande* (1934).

Witter Bynner, the third major luminary of Santa Fe's Roaring Twenties literary scene, arrived in 1922 to visit old friend Alice Corbin and immediately decided to make New Mexico his new home. Then 41 years old, Bynner had grown bitter over the lack of acceptance of his poetry, particularly after poems that he wrote under a pseudonym as part of an elaborate literary hoax garnered both critical acclaim and a wider readership than those he presented as his own. He also hoped to find in New Mexico a haven from the homophobic intolerance that faced him in more "civilized" regions of the country. Of the seven published poetry collections that Bynner produced during the 46 years he lived in Santa Fe, none is in print today; but his contacts brought several other key players into the Santa Fe literary community —his secretary and friend, Walter "Spud" Johnson, publisher of the *Laughing Horse Review,* New Mexico's first literary magazine; his protégé, playwright Lynn Riggs; and his old Harvard classmate, English professor Haniel Long— and his leadership provided the impetus for the city's first writers' group and book publisher. The writers' group, formed in 1925 as the Rabelais Club and immediately shortened to "The Rabble," consisted of Bynner, Johnson, Riggs, Long, and Alice Corbin and met first at Henderson's studio on Camino del Monte Sol and later at Bynner's new home on Buena Vista Street. The publisher, Rydal Press, was brought to Santa Fe from Pennsylvania in 1932 with the encouragement and financial support of Bynner, Haniel Long, Alice Corbin, and Peggy Pond Church. It operated for many years as a self-publishing authors' cooperative. Bynner is remembered today mainly for having endowed the Witter Bynner Foundation, a private nonprofit organization that provides grants for local and visiting poets.

Several members and associates of the Santa Fe literary community achieved national reputations in the 1930s. Several Lynn Riggs plays were produced on Broadway (one of them would later be adapted into the Rogers and Hammerstein musical *Oklahoma!*). Mary Austin's friend Willa Cather, who often spent summers in Santa Fe, received critical acclaim and popular success with her 1927 novel *Death Comes for the Archbishop,* based on the career of Archbishop Lamy. Ernest Thompson Seton, a Santa Fe resident, naturalist, and cofounder of the Boy Scouts, wrote several books of animal stories, one of which would become the basis for the Walt Disney film *Bambi.* Santa Fe's two Pulitzer Prize–winning novelist–historians, Oliver La Farge (*Laughing Boy,* 1929) and Paul Horgan (*The Great River,* 1954), also began their careers during this period.

In the end, however, the literary community of the 1920s and 1930s proved unable to rise above the personalities that had given it life. A long-standing rivalry between the Santa Fe group and Taos arts-and-letters maven Mabel Dodge Luhán culminated in her luring Spud Johnson, Witter Bynner's

Carlos Vierra was the first artist to move to Santa Fe. His house, 1002 Old Pecos Trail, built over 1918-1924, was based on his extensive photographic surveys of Indian pueblos and Spanish colonial villages and inspred many other builders in the Santa Fe style. Wesley Bradfield, November 19, 1921. *Museum of New Mexico, neg. 51927.*

personal assistant and longtime friend, away from Santa Fe to work for her in Taos, touching off a vicious campaign of insults (for instance, Luhán publically accused Bynner of "bringing homosexuality to New Mexico") that the camaraderie of the early years gradually deteriorated. The writers' community failed to match the rapid growth rate of the artists' colony, and on the national level literary critics seemed to take no notice at all of Santa Fe writers. Fifty years after the publication of *Ben Hur,* no other Santa Fe author had come close to matching that book's success. The belief grew widespread that, unlike artists, writers could thrive only in New York City.

The frustration of Santa Fe's writers reached rock-bottom in 1935, when Rydal Press invited Pulitzer Prize recipient Robert Frost to present a reading in Santa Fe. Witter Bynner, who had been Frost's classmate at Harvard, failed to show up in time to introduce the poet at the reading. The following day, the two poets got into an argument over the merits of a volume of poetry that included homosexual imagery which culminated in Bynner's pouring a glass of beer over Frost's head. As word of the incident spread, Santa Fe's literary colony became a subject for jokes and disdain. A few good writers moved to town each year, and Bynner, Corbin, and other old-timers kept working, but the state's major journals—the Museum of New Mexico's *El Palacio,* the University of New Mexico's *New Mexico Quarterly*, and the state-run *New Mexico* magazine, as well as the *Santa Fe New Mexican* newspaper—stopped touting Santa Fe's literary community and turned their focus to the visual arts instead.

The written word did not become a vital part of Santa Fe's character until 1969, when John Muir (a distant relative of the naturalist and Sierra Club founder), a former California aerospace engineer who had dropped out to join the hippie migration to New Mexico, wrote *How to Keep Your Volkswagen Alive*. After the manuscript was rejected by 17 publishers, Muir decided to publish the book himself in Santa Fe. Promoted through the *Whole Earth Catalog*, it became a 1960s classic, selling 2 million copies and establishing John Muir Publications, the first nonsubsidized publisher in Santa Fe. Muir died at home of a brain tumor in 1979. His company, which has undergone several changes of ownership and management since then, remains in Santa Fe and publishes about 90 new titles and revisions per year, specializing in travel guides and children's books.

John Muir Publications touched off a publishing renaissance in Santa Fe by proving that publishing could be not only feasible but profitable in New Mexico. At the same time, it attracted a steady flow of editors, illustrators, typesetters, art directors, and other publishing professionals into the local economy. Today, book and magazine publishing is Santa Fe's fastest-growing industry. John Muir Publications is still the largest book publisher, and there are some 80 others, ranging from long-established, nationally recognized independent publishers to tiny one- or two-book self-publishers. About a dozen national and regional magazines are also headquartered in Santa Fe, the largest being *Outside*. Due to a peculiarity in New Mexico's tax laws, most Santa Fe publishers use out-of-state writers, and most local writers are published outside New Mexico.

About 700 full-time professional writers live in Santa Fe today. There is a preponderance of travel writers and, as in the early days, poets. A sizable number of novelists who write genre fiction have also chosen to make their homes in Santa Fe, among them thriller writers Sarah Lovett, David Morrell, Douglas Preston, and science fiction writers George R. R. Martin and the late Roger Zelazny.

Even though the Santa Fe colony of the 1920s and 1930s played host to a number of famous composers, including Igor Stravinsky and Aaron Copeland, the performing arts came to Santa Fe much later than painting and literature. Well into the second half of the twentieth century, a shortage of suitable stage venues limited drama and dance to occasional amateur productions by the community theater. Outside investors were wary of trying to establish live theater organizations in Santa Fe because of the unfortunate experience of a group called the Cultural Centre of the Southwest in 1926. Their vision was of a Chautauqua-style center that would bring a full summer season of lectures, plays, and dance performances to town each year. Developed by the Southwestern Federation of Women's Clubs, the project had the enthusiastic support of the Museum of New Mexico, the Santa Fe Chamber of Commerce, and the Santa Fe Railroad, and the city offered land behind Sunmount Sanitarium at a nominal price. Then, apparently without warning, the Santa Fe artists' and writers' colony rose up in angry protest.

Rumors circulated that the project's backers were from Texas, rekindling a long-standing animosity between the two states. Within six weeks after the proposal for the center was announced, a Canyon Road group led by novelists Mary Austin and Sinclair Lewis had rallied organizations as diverse as the Kiwanis and Rotary Clubs, the Santa Fe Women's Club, the Women's Board of Trade, La Union Protectiva, and El Centro de Cultura against what they called "The Texas Ladies' Chautauqua." Taken aback by the furious, unexpected opposition, planners beat a swift retreat. After that, nothing that sounded even remotely similar was proposed for more than a generation.

The situation changed in 1956, when philanthropist John Crosby, who knew northern New Mexico from his years as a student at the Los Alamos Ranch School before World War II, announced plans to organize an opera company in Santa Fe using top European talent. Although the idea initially met with ridicule (one critic wrote, "'How can you sell an opera to people who have never heard one?'"), Crosby stood firm in his conviction that an opera season would suit the growing number of art connoisseurs among the city's summer visitors. He invested $200,000 in buying a tract of land among the piñon-covered hills north of the city and building a 470-seat wooden opera house there. By the opera's fourth season, in 1960, it was playing to capacity crowds. The opera house burned to the ground in 1967, forcing the company to finish its eleventh season in the Santa Fe High School gymnasium, but Crosby built a new 1889-seat open-air theater on the site in time for the next season.

The Santa Fe Opera has gained an international reputation because of its world-class talent, lavish costumes and sets, and two exceptionally innovative programs. Its apprentice program brings the finest young performers from around the United States to understudy the starring singers and musicians, and several apprentices have gone on to join leading opera companies elsewhere. The SFO is also known for premiering contemporary operas by young American composers, which alternate with more familiar classical operas throughout the six-week, five-program season. The opera season reflects Santa Fe's unique cultural diversity in several ways. Although tickets for most performances sell out months in advance at prices starting in the $75 range, locals line up a few hours before each performance for standing-room tickets that cost about the same as going to a movie. It has become traditional on opening nights for formally dressed opera-goers to host "tailgate parties" in the parking lot, with lavish sunset dinners often catered by the city's finest restaurants. The parties take their name from the fact that perfect etiquette calls for the gourmet meals to be served on the tailgates of pickup trucks, although folding card tables are also acceptable. The major drawback of the open-air opera is that when he picked the location, during a severe two-year drought, Crosby did not realize that the July–August opera season would coincide with New Mexico's "monsoon season," when roughly three-fourths of

Santa Fe's precipitation for the entire year falls, turning a night at the opera into a game of chance. After years of drenched tuxedos and divas drowned out by thunder crashes, plans have been announced to construct a roof over the seating area in 1997; the sides of the opera house will remain open.

While the opera continues to be the central cultural event of the summer season, other annual classical music programs have ridden its coattails to varying heights of success. Foremost among them is the Santa Fe Chamber Music Festival, held in St. Francis Auditorium and featuring about 30 world-renowned string musicians each year, as well as a composer-in-residence who is commissioned to write a new work to premier at the festival. Other groups include the Santa Fe Desert Chorale, the Orchestra of Santa Fe, the Santa Fe Symphony, and the Santa Fe Women's Ensemble. Theater and dance companies come and go; visitors at any time of year can choose from four to eight live stage performances, but with the exception of the long-established Santa Fe Community Theater, the companies are rarely the same from one year to the next. Dance in Santa Fe is virtually synonymous with Estampa Flamenco, the performance company of Taos native María Benítez, North America's greatest flamenco dancer.

The sculpture garden at Project Tibet exemplifies the electric character of the Canyon Road art district today. *Photograph by Richard Harris.*

5

Capital, Don Gaspar, and Westside–Guadalupe Districts

In 1880, when the first train pulled in, Santa Fe had a population of 5000. Although it would be considered a small town by modern standards, it was the largest city in the southwest at that time. The south edge of town was Montezuma Avenue, which continued through what is now the capital district, following what is now East De Vargas Street. The west edge was Guadalupe Street, then called Jefferson Street north of the river. Federal Place, then known as Capitol Avenue, marked the northern perimeter, and the eastern extent of the city was marked not by any street but by a broad expanse of Catholic church property, including St. Francis Cathedral and the old St. Vincent's Hospital. Then, as now, rugged landscapes hindered expansion to the north and east; the impetus of development lay toward the southwest, in the quadrant between the old Camino Real and Santa Fe Trail routes. Almost everyone in the city lived within 15 minutes' walk of the Plaza.

The three areas covered in this chapter developed between 1880 and 1912, when New Mexico became a state. Oddly enough, although a temporary population boom accompanied the railroad's arrival, the city's population in 1912 was almost exactly the same as in 1880. The expansion during the railroad era was neither economic nor demographic, but cultural.

Opposite: Lamy Building (detail). *Photograph by Richard Harris.*

143

Hispanics, then as in modern-day Mexico, made their homes in tight-knit communities and went to work on the outskirts of town. Anglos craved their own mini-estates, complete with lawns and trees, and preferred to work downtown but live in the "suburbs," although still within walking distance of the Plaza. Cultural and economic segregation seem to have shaped the patterns of development in the railroad-to-statehood period. Most homes in the middle-class Don Gaspar district were originally built for Anglo owners (using the term in its New Mexico sense to mean non-Hispanic groups, including German-Jewish and Italian immigrant families), while the poorer Westside–Guadalupe *barrio* was almost entirely Hispanic.

The most recent of the three areas covered in this chapter, the Capital Complex is included within the boundaries of the Santa Fe historic district, although all but two of the government buildings it contains are of twentieth-century vintage. It was an agricultural area of pastures, orchards, and cornfields sandwiched between the campuses of St. Michael's College and the New West Academy until 1900, when it was selected as the site for the new state capitol (now the Bataan Memorial Building). Since then the complex has developed in two major construction and renovation periods, the first in 1950–1951 accompanying the remodeling of the capitol building and the second in 1965–1969 accompanying the building of the present capitol building. Limited parking space has prevented new construction since then, and today many government offices are located in other parts of the city, primarily the South Capital Complex near St. Francis Drive and Cordova Road.

The Don Gaspar historic district is located south of the state Capitol complex, separated by Paseo de Peralta. Along with the somewhat more recent residential area extending to Cordova Road, the Don Gaspar district has traditionally been known as the south Capitol neighborhood. Today, the South Capitol Complex is the name given to the state office buildings near the intersection of Cordova and St. Francis Drive, near the southwest corner of the South Capitol neighborhood.

Although most buildings in the Don Gaspar historic district were built between 1890 and 1930, the main roads that bound the district—Old Santa Fe Trail on the east and Galisteo Street on the west—were already major approaches to the city in much earlier times, both already shown on the oldest surviving map of Santa Fe in 1766. The district contains well-preserved examples of most New Mexican architectural styles, predominantly Spanish Pueblo Revival style but also such styles as Italianate Bracketed, Mission Revival, Territorial Revival, Prairie, and Bungalow.

The Guadalupe–Westside historic district is roughly bounded by Guadalupe Street on the east, St. Francis Drive on the west, and the U-shaped Paseo de Peralta on both the north and south. Exempted from the official boundaries of the district is the railroad yards. Although some of the neighborhood's landmark buildings stand in the railroad yards and are individually protected as historic structures, local government has been reluctant to impose blanket restrictions on the railroad yards because, as the last remaining vacant space in the downtown area, its future use is controversial and uncertain.

Separating the Westside–Guadalupe district and the railroad yards from the capital and Don Gaspar districts is an architectural no-man's-land of mixed residential and commercial buildings called the historic transition district. Since the mid-1980s, these three areas—the Westside–Guadalupe historic district, the historic transition district, and the railroad yards—have shared in a wave of restoration and gentrification that makes it easiest to survey them as a single historic district regardless of political boundaries.

The most striking characteristics of the former warehouse zone revived in the 1980s as a shopping and restaurant area are several muraled buildings and a predominance of California Mission Revival architecture, which has no historic precedent in Santa Fe but spread from two structures that form its axis, the Atchison, Topeka & Santa Fe Railroad Station and the often-remodeled Santuario de Guadalupe.

Also included in the historic district is part of the residential neighborhood west of the railroad tracks, commonly referred to as "the barrio." Although economically mixed today, it was the poor part of town until recent years and, as a result, contains many small adobe homes built by hand in a

East side of Gildersleeve, Don Gaspar historic district. Ellen Threinen, 1982, National Register of Historic Places.

traditional Mexican style that is quite distinct from the experimental revival styles of eastside adobe homes. The other residential style characteristic of this neighborhood is known as the Santa Fe Vernacular style. This peaked-roof style is characterized by foundations and porch pillars built of river rocks and mortar.

CAPITAL–DON GASPAR WALKING TOUR

This exploration route starts at the Lamy Building on the Old Santa Fe Trail. You can follow it as an extension of the downtown Santa Fe walking tour described in Chapter 3—the Lamy Building is next door to San Miguel Mission—or as a separate tour, parking in the visitors' lot of the New Mexico Division of Tourism Information Center. The parking lot behind and to the south of the **Lamy Building** is also flanked by the **Lew Wallace Building** and the **PERA Building**. Walk to the corner of Paseo de Peralta and, crossing the Old Santa Fe Trail, stroll the broad, landscaped walkway to the State Capitol Building. Free 90-minute tours of the capitol are available most week-day afternoons, or you can explore most parts of the Roundhouse on your own.

Leaving the Capital through the entrance opposite the one where you came in, walk north, toward the downtown, and you will come to the **New Mexico State Library,** then the **Supreme Court Building,** its broad, neatly manicured lawn sloping down toward the Santa Fe River. Crossing Don Gaspar Avenue, walk back in the direction you came, passing the **State Education Building** and perhaps wandering into the labyrinth of the **Bataan Memorial Building,** the first New Mexico state capitol building. If you go out the door on the far side, you will see the **Villagra Building** across the street.

Returning to Don Gaspar Avenue, continue south past **New Mexico's Eternal Flame** to the intersection with Paseo de Peralta. The **Digneo–Valdez, Digneo–Moore,** and **A. M. Digneo houses** are in the next block east, on the other side of the paseo. The **Salmon-Greer house** stands diagonally across the intersection, and next to it is the **E. A. Fiske house.**

The Don Gaspar historic district originally was entirely residential, although many residences in the district, especially toward the north end, have now been converted to office use and are occupied by private schools, publishers, law firms, insurance brokers, and the like. Although as early as 1886 a few scattered structures stood along the Old Santa Fe Trail and Galisteo Street, both old roads dating back to Spanish colonial times, the district was mainly open grazing land until around 1910, and most houses were built between then and 1937. The area displays a wider diversity of historic styles than in any other Santa Fe neighborhood, ranging from traditional Territorial style adobe homes through imported styles, including Italianate, Mansard, Queen Anne, and Bungalow homes to the Spanish Pueblo Revival style of the 1920s. A number of homes retain their original appearance, whereas many others have been stuccoed and otherwise "disguised" in Santa Fe style. Among the many examples of these varied styles are the **Danleavy–Berry house** left on east Santa Fe, the side street one block south of the paseo and the Frank Andrews house in the next block of Don Gaspar.

To extend your walk by about an hour, continue down pleasant, shady Don Gaspar Avenue for about a mile before reaching Cordova Road, the next busy street. Along the way you will pass the Unitarian Church; on the Galisteo Street side of the church grounds stands the old **powder house.** Taking Cordova east several blocks to the Old Pecos Trail, at the corner is the **Carlos Vierra house** and a short distance to the south is the **Armory for the Arts,** home of the **Bataan Memorial Military Museum** and the **Santa Fe Children's Museum.** It is another mile's walk back. Along the way, set back from Buena Vista Street along the Old Pecos Trail, is the **Witter Bynner house.** The Old Pecos Trail joins the Old Santa Fe Trail and returns you to the Lamy Building parking lot, where this hike started.

Don Gaspar historic district, 247 Anita. Ellen Threinen, 1982. *National Register of Historic Places.*

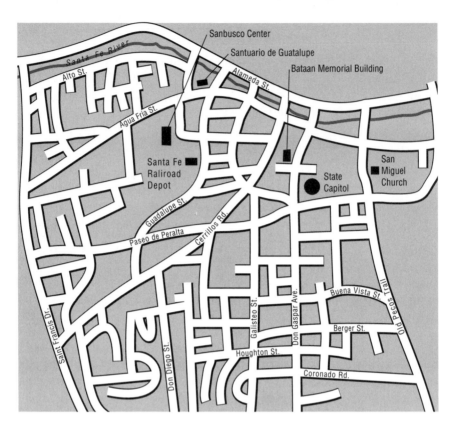

Capital, Don Gaspar, and Westside–Guadalupe Districts

STATE CAPITAL DISTRICT

■ Old Santa Fe Trail at Paseo de Peralta

The **New Mexico State Capitol,** which Santa Feans invariably refer to as the "Roundhouse," is one of the newest state capitol buildings in America. Designed by architect W. C. Kruger, it was completed in 1966 at a cost of $4,676,860. After only 22 years it was closed for "renovation" to remove asbestos insulation, a process that involved tearing out all interior walls and rebuilding them. During the four-year renovation, the governor's offices were temporarily relocated to another state office building and legislative sessions were held in the former state capitol, the Bataan Building. The Roundhouse was reopened in 1992 after expenditures of $24,982,000, nearly six times the original construction cost.

Designed in the Territorial Revival style of all state buildings in the capital complex, the Roundhouse is a domeless, flat-roofed rotunda with square projections in the four compass directions, intended to resemble the Zia sun symbol of the state flag and seal. The overall concept of the building was inspired by the great kivas built in the eleventh to thirteenth centuries by Anasazi ancestors of the Pueblo Indians. It is set into the side of a low ridge, so that the entrance doors on the east side are at street level, while those on the west side are at the top of a double flight of steps. The entrances at ground level (which is called the second floor) open into a ceremonial rotunda 49 feet in diameter, which rises 60 feet to a turquoise- and coral-colored stained-glass ceiling. Flags of the state's 33 counties hang over the rotunda from the third-floor walkway. The great seal of the state

148

New Mexico State Capitol. *Photograph by Richard Harris.*

of New Mexico is inlaid in turquoise and brass in the center of the polished terrazo floor. The walls of the rotunda are of gold-hued travertine marble that was quarried south of Albuquerque. All construction materials used in the building came from New Mexico except the cherry wood used for paneling in the legislative chambers and doors and trim in the office areas, which was imported from Pennsylvania. The trees, shrubs, and flowers used in landscaping the capitol grounds, whether native to New Mexico or introduced from elsewhere, all grow wild in various parts of the state.

Doorways from the rotunda lead to the visitors' galleries overlooking the Senate chambers on the north side of the building and the House chambers on the south side. The windowless legislative chambers are sunken 20 feet below ground level on what is referred to as the first floor (perhaps because it would be unseemly to convene the legislature in the basement). There is no access to the chambers from ground level; legislatures enter and exit through doorways that lead to private underground parking lots.

The upper levels of the Roundhouse contain offices and committee rooms that open off walkways around the rotunda. There are 10 legislative committee rooms on the third floor, along with offices of committee chairpersons and legislative council staff. The fourth floor contains the offices of the governor, lieutenant governor, and secretary of state, along with more committee rooms. The more than 90 paintings, photographs, and sculptures, all by New Mexico artists, on exhibit in the Roundhouse hallways are from the permanent collection of the Capitol Art Foundation. Changing New Mexican art exhibitions are shown in the Governor's Gallery, located off the reception area for the governor's office. The capitol is open to the public and free guided tours are offered. During legislative sessions, the House and Senate visitors galleries seat 281 and 206 spectators, respectively, and fill up around 8:00 A.M.; sessions start at 10:00 A.M., following early-morning committee meetings.

■ 491 Old Santa Fe Trail

The **Lamy Building,** one of the oldest structures in the state government complex, houses the New Mexico Division of Tourism Information Center and other government offices, including the State Board of Examiners for Architects. It was built by the Christian Brothers in 1878 as part of St. Michael's College (now the College of Santa Fe, located on St. Michaels Drive in the southern part of the city). The tallest building in Santa Fe when it was built, it originally had a third story and a mansard roof. Classrooms and a community room filled the lower floors, while the third floor served as a dormitory. The third floor was destroyed by fire in 1926, and heroic firefighting efforts by the resident students saved the rest of the building from going up in flames. Today, the part of the building that faces the Old Santa Fe Trail stands two stories high and has an ornate concrete and sandstone front doorway that is no longer used. In the rear, a single-story wing flanks a brick patio with a fountain. Although it is now government property, the building is still attached to the neighboring San Miguel Mission by a shared portal.

■ 495 Old Santa Fe Trail

The **Lew Wallace Building,** located behind the Lamy Building, is named after the only New Mexico governor to write a bestselling novel while in office (*Ben-Hur: A Tale of the Christ,* 1880). The building contained the state government printing facilities for many years and, just as appropriately, now houses the offices of the state-published *New Mexico Magazine.* Like the Lamy building, it was constructed of red brick in 1887 as part of the St. Michael's College campus. After extensive remodeling in 1969 to harmonize its appearance with other capital district buildings by removing the sloped roof in favor of a flat one, and adding stucco and simple Territorial Revival features, the only original features still visible are the sandstone window ledges and a ceramic tile image of the Virgin of Guadalupe, a religious touch that is

Lamy Building. *Photograph by Richard Harris.*

Lew Wallace Building. *Photograph by Richard Harris.*

unusual for a government building. It is attached to the addition on the south side of San Miguel Mission by a nonstructural wall.

▪ 1120 Paseo de Peralta

The **Public Employees Retirement Association Building** (invariably called the PERA Building), located across the parking lot from the Lamy and Lew Wallace buildings, was constructed in 1966–1967 as a centerpiece of the ambitious Capitol Buildings Improvement Project during the administrations of Governors Jack Campbell and David Cargo. The U-shaped three-story Territorial Revival office building has a two-story-high portico supported by 18-foot double columns and surrounds a broad brick patio often used for public demonstrations when the legislature is in session.

▪ 325 Don Gaspar Avenue

The **New Mexico State Library,** also designed by W. C. Kruger, was completed in 1966. It contains reference books and periodicals on a wide variety of subjects,

collected for use by lawmakers and others in state government. They are also available for general public use.

▪ 237 Don Gaspar Avenue

The **Supreme Court Building,** designed by Gordon F. Street and built in 1936–1937, is stuccoed and uncharacteristically painted white, with classically Territorial styling details such as red brick parapets, an entryway portal supported by square, white-painted columns, and pediments over side door entrances. It was one of the first large public buildings to be designed in Territorial Revival style. The exposed wood beam lintel over the window above the front portal is a nod to Spanish Pueblo Revival styling. Besides the chambers and courtrooms of New Mexico Court of Appeals judges and Supreme Court justices, the three-story building houses the state law library, which is open to the public.

▪ 300 Don Gaspar Avenue

The **State Education Building** was designed by architect W. C. Kruger and

PERA Building. *Photograph by Richard Harris.*

State Library. *Photograph by Richard Harris.*

Supreme Court Building. *Photograph by Richard Harris.*

built in 1950. The Territorial Revival exterior matches that of the Bataan Memorial Building next door, which was remodeled at the same time. The lobby features striking pink-and-gray polished marble walls and a terrazo floor inlaid with Indian petroglyph motifs.

■ 407 Galisteo Street

The **Bataan Memorial Building,** designed by architect Isaac Hamilton Rapp as the New Mexico territorial capitol, was completed in 1900 on the site of an earlier capitol building that burned in 1892, just three years after its completion. (Arson was suspected but never proven.) After New Mexico became a state in 1912, the building served as the state capitol until 1966, when the present capitol was completed. In 1951, the dome that had crowned the capitol was removed, as were the pillars that had graced its stately facade. In an ambitious three-year renovation, the building was redone in the Territorial Revival style that characterizes all state government buildings in the Capital District today, and a portal running the length of the building and a five-story-high observation tower, one of the tallest structures in town, were added. A Governor's Mansion stood in what is now the open, landscaped area

Bataan Memorial Building. *Photograph by Richard Harris.*

just north of the capitol from 1907 to 1955, when the present Governor's Mansion was built north of the city. The Bataan Memorial Building now houses various government offices, including those of the attorney general and the Department of Finance and Administration. It is named in memory of the victims and survivors of the 1941 Bataan Death March in the Philippines during World War II, among whom were disproportionate numbers of New Mexicans who had belonged to the state's National Guard unit when it was activated and assigned to the 200th and 515th Coast Artillery Anti-aircraft Regiments in the Philippines. Largely as a result of Bataan, New Mexico suffered the highest casualty rate of any state during World War II. At the southwest corner of the Bataan Memorial Building grounds, **New Mexico's Eternal Flame** burns above a large marker that originally identified the 200th Coast Artillery Headquarters at Fort Bliss, Texas, where New Mexico's National Guard trained. The marker, a concrete artillery emblem

topped by two red-and-yellow Zia sun symbols, was handmade by the guardsmen before they shipped out for the Philippines.

■ 408 Galisteo Street

The **Villagra Building,** across Galisteo Street from the west side of the Bataan Memorial Building, was originally built in 1934 as the New Mexico Public Welfare Building. Remodeled in 1969 with Territorial Revival features designed by the Western Association of Collaborative Architects, it now houses the New Mexico Departments of Game and Wildlife, Parks and Recreation, and Energy and Minerals.

DON GASPAR HISTORIC DISTRICT

■ 1227, 1231, and 1233 Paseo de Peralta

Three brick houses across Paseo de Peralta from the state capitol were built by the family of Carlo Digneo, an Italian stonemason who was brought to Santa Fe by Archbishop Lamy in 1880 to work on

New Mexico's Eternal Flame. *Photograph by Richard Harris.*

Digneo–Moore House. *Photograph by Richard Harris.*

St. Francis Cathedral. The first of the three, the **Digneo–Valdés house** at 1231 Paseo de Peralta, was built of hand-molded red brick by Carlo Digneo in 1889. The house, with its large bay window, cross-gabled roof, and Eastlake porch, reflects the architectural tastes prevalent in the last years of the nineteenth century. In 1911, Digneo deeded the house to his niece, who married the son of Santa Fe mayor Manuel Valdés, and moved into a larger house that he built five years earlier next door at 1233 Paseo de Peralta. Now known as the **Digneo–Moore house,** it is perhaps the best example in Santa Fe of the Italianate Bracketed style, character-ized by quoins of cut granite on the exteri-or corners. After Carlo Digneo's death, the house was sold to E. P. Moore, who owned and operated Santa Fe's finest men's cloth-ing store on the Plaza. A third Digneo resi-dence at 1227 Paseo de Peralta, a hip-

roofed red brick house with inset porch that is now known as the **A. M. Digneo house,** was built sometime before 1912 by Carlo Digneo's nephew, a house paint-ing and wallpapering contractor. A. M. Digneo's wife was the sister of municipal judge Joe Berardinelli, the patriarch of Santa Fe's other prominent Italian immi-grant family. The interiors of the Digneo houses have been converted to commer-cial office space.

▪ 505 Don Gaspar Street

The **Salmon–Greer house,** located directly across Paseo de Peralta from the state capitol, was built in 1909 by Nathan Salmon, a leading Santa Fe merchant; it was later occupied by Salmon's daughter and her husband, John Greer. Although constructed of red brick, the house incor-porated elements of the California Mission Revival style, exemplifying the

Salmon–Greer House. *Photograph by Richard Harris.*

trend of the times toward using architectural elements identified with Spanish colonialism in various parts of the world even though they were not characteristic of New Mexico. The large, arcaded front porch is distinctively Californian, while the surrounding wall with its unusual semicircular cutouts barred with wrought-iron arabesques was inspired by a similar wall that Salmon had seen in Mexico City. Before the brick masonry was stuccoed, painted white, and renovated to enhance its California Mission Revival look, the mansion looked much like the E. A. Fiske house next door. The flat-roofed two-story addition to the rear of the house was added in recent years when the building was converted to office space. The house now contains title company offices.

515 Don Gaspar Street

The **E. A. Fiske house,** one of the best-preserved turn-of-the-century brick homes in the district, was built between 1905 and 1912 by hardware and building supply merchant L. B. Vickeroy, which accounts for the exceptional quality of its materials and workmanship. The tan brick two-story home with full basement features a bay window, parapet, and

metal roofing made to resemble a Mediterranean tile roof; the interior woodwork and hand-carved fireplace are original. The home was never lived in by its namesake, E. A. Fiske, the U.S. Attorney for New Mexico Territory and later the president of the New Mexico Bar Association. It was bought after Fiske's death by his widow and should more properly be called the "Mrs. E. A. Fiske house." In the 1980s it served as temporary state government offices and later as St. Elizabeth Shelter for the homeless before being converted to magazine offices in 1988.

121 East Santa Fe

The **Danleavy–Berry house** is one of the best remaining examples of the Bungalow-style houses that predominated in this neighborhood. While various bungalows incorporated elements of different architectural styles, this one was built in late Victorian style with a bay window and an upstairs dormer. It was built in 1912 for local attorney Melvin Danleavy and later sold to Ferdinand Berry, manager of a lumber company.

614 Don Gaspar Street

The **Frank Andrews house** is the best

example of Spanish Pueblo Revival architecture in the neighborhood. Built of adobe in 1920, it features battered walls, a set-back second story, and an undulating parapet. Andrews, the original owner of the house, was a grocer who later became mayor of Santa Fe.

■ Galisteo Street at Barcelona Road

The stone **powder house,** which stands along Galisteo Street on the grounds of the Unitarian Church of Santa Fe, is the oldest structure in the neighborhood. In 1880, when it was built, it stood well beyond the

Fiske house. *Photograph by Richard Harris.*

Powder house. *Photograph by Richard Harris.*

edge of town. Originally used by the Hazard Powder Company to store blasting powder for use in the short-lived silver mines at Bonanza Hill, southwest of the city, the Powder house has 18-inch-thick stone walls and a wooden door reinforced with sheet iron. It was used by various owners for more than 60 years to store explosives, and abandoned only when residential development began to surround it in the 1940s.

1002 Old Pecos Trail

The **Carlos Vierra house** was designed and built by Carlos Vierra, Santa Fe's first artist and the staff photographer for the School of American Archaeology and later the Museum of New Mexico. Prominent local attorney Frank Springer, a regent of the museum and first president of the School of American Research, gave Vierra and his wife a life estate in the land on which the house now stands in appreciation for his years of service, with the condition that both the land and the house Vierra built on it would revert to the Springer family upon their deaths. Vierra's design for the Spanish Pueblo–style house won second place in a Santa Fe style competition in 1917. He began building the house himself the following year and completed it within the next three years. Among the distinctive features are the hand-carved exposed beams and the cutaway wall around the second-floor terrace, giving the roofline a look suggestive of an old pueblo ruin. The west-facing portal helped keep the interior of the house cool. Less practical were the large, north-facing upstairs windows, which

The arched gateway of the Carlos Vierra House echoes the distant Sangre de Cristo skyline. *Photograph by Wesley Bradfield, courtesy Museum of New Mexico, neg. 51924.*

provided the best possible light for Vierra's second-floor studio but caused serious heat loss in the winter. Vierra died in 1937 and his wife continued to live in the house for five more years. When she moved to Kansas, the house and land reverted to the Springer family. It remains a private residence today.

1050 Old Pecos Trail

The Spanish Pueblo Revival–style **Armory for the Arts** served as the local armory of the New Mexico National Guard beginning in the mid-1930s. It replaced an earlier armory downtown on Washington Street adjacent to the Palace of the Governors, which was converted into the Museum of New Mexico History Library and Archives. A new armory was built southwest of the city in the 1960s, and this building was turned into a theater and art exhibit space. In a fit of patriotic fervor following the Gulf War and coincidental financial problems within the theater organization, the front portion was converted into the **Bataan Memorial Military Museum,** with historical displays and a collection of antiaircraft artillery and other vintage army equipment. Another building in the old armory complex became the new home of the **Santa Fe Children's Museum,** with scientific, artistic, and cultural hands-on exhibits designed for preschool and grade school–age kids.

342 East Buena Vista

The **Witter Bynner house** was the home of a leading figure in the Santa Fe literary community from 1922 to 1968. It served as the meeting place for the Rabelais Club (commonly known as "The Rabble"), the city's first writers' organization. Here, too, Bynner hosted dozens of nationally known authors of the time, including Robert Frost, Carl Sandburg, John Galsworthy, and Edna St. Vincent Millay. At the core of the present house are two small rural farmhouses built toward the end of the nineteenth century. Before Bynner bought them, the two houses belonged to painters Andrew Dasburg and Paul Burlin. Today, the Witter Bynner house is operated as a bed and breakfast establishment, the Inn of the Turquoise Bear. By sheer coincidence, one of the innkeepers is named Robert Frost.

Armory for the Arts. *Photograph by Richard Harris.*

WESTSIDE–GUADALUPE DISTRICT
WALKING TOUR

The commercial area of the Guadalupe district is compact and easy to stroll. Numerous restaurants make it a good lunchtime destination. Parallel parking is difficult along busy Guadalupe Street, so the best bet is to park in one of the parking lots off Montezuma Street beside or across from Sanbusco Market Center.

From Sanbusco, walk north along Montezuma Street for one long block to Agua Fria and turn right to go around the big Guadalupe Church. The much older Santuario de Nuestra Señora de Guadalupe is on the other side of the block at the corner of Agua Fria and Guadalupe. After seeing the santuario, simply follow Guadalupe Street south. You will pass the Stone Warehouse, the Zia Diner, and the New Mexico State Records Center and Archives, along with several other retail buildings of modern construction with contemporary renditions of California Mission–style motifs. Across the street, more shops and restaurants are housed in rather plain adobe buildings dating back to about 1900 and resembling what most of downtown Santa Fe looked like in the days of the Santa Fe Trail. The showpiece building on the east side of the street is the tall, mansard-roofed University Plaza.

Continuing south for another block will bring you to the railroad yards, where the most striking buildings are the Spanish Mission Revival–style Santa Fe Railroad Depot and the Gross Kelly Almacen, the first Pueblo Revival–style building in Santa Fe. From the railroad yards, all you have to do is follow the tracks north to the end and you'll be within sight of the parking lots on Montezuma Street.

Touring the residential part of the Westside–Guadalupe District on foot is more confusing and not necessarily safe. You can see a sample of the Westside barrio by driving along Agua Fria Street (see the driving tour Chapter 6).

WESTSIDE–GUADALUPE HISTORIC DISTRICT

■ 500 Montezuma Avenue

Sanbusco Market Center, a retail mall and restaurant complex located one block west of Guadalupe Street, is a floor-to-ceiling renovation of what was originally the warehouse of the Santa Fe Builders Supply Company (nicknamed SanBuSCo). The company's owner, C. W. Dudrow, a popular local figure as well as a prominent one, was elected sheriff of Santa Fe County twice—without running for the office—and declined both times. The company was the main importer of factory-made building materials from the east, which made the proliferation of architectural styles in the late nineteenth and early twentieth centuries possible. The brick building was constructed in 1880 in the Railroad Commercial style, with a wooden false front and a pitched roof. Two-and-a-half acres of sheds and docks were cleared away during the renovation to make a parking lot.

Sanbusco Center. *Photograph by Richard Harris.*

▓ 100 South Guadalupe Street

The **Santuario de Nuestra Señora de Guadalupe** (Guadalupe Chapel), for which Guadalupe Street was named, is often dated to 1781; the date is uncertain, however, since the license authorizing its construction was not issued by the Archbishop of Durango, Mexico, until 1795, and some historians contend that it was not completed until 1807. In any case, it is almost certainly the oldest shrine in the United States dedicated to the Virgin of Guadalupe, the brown-skinned madonna revered in Mexico. The site of the chapel was the official endpoint of El Camino Real, the 1064-mile-long "Royal Road" (actually mere wagon ruts) that connected Santa Fe with Mexico City. The original chapel built on the site by Franciscan missionaries was a simple, flat-roofed cross-shaped adobe structure with a bell tower. The interior was 90 feet long and had a dirt floor. With Mexico's independence from Spain, the Franciscans withdrew from New Mexico and the church was rarely used. It gradually deteriorated into ruin. In 1880, Archbishop Lamy declared the old chapel a parish church and appointed Father De Fouri, a French Franciscan monk, as parish priest in charge of

restoring the building. De Fouri redesigned the church, with its 5-foot-thick adobe walls, in Gothic style. A steeple towered above the entrance, rising from a steeply peaked roof. Windows with pointed arches lit the interior. *Vigas,* corbels, and the choir loft from La Castrense, the downtown military chapel that was being dismantled at the same time, were used in the rebuilding. The adobe Gothic church was used until 1922, when it was destroyed by fire. In the spirit of the Santa Fe style movement of the 1920s, the new Archbishop decided to rebuild in California Mission Revival style, with a tile roof and curvilinear parapet. In 1961 the church was replaced by a larger modern church, situated directly behind the old church. Opposing a plan by the archdiocese to tear down the old church, the nonprofit Guadalupe Historic Foundation formed and obtained a grant from the American Bicentennial Administration to restore the Santuario de Guadalupe to its original Spanish Colonial design for use as a museum. The historic church showcases "Nuestra Señora de Guadalupe," a large oil-on-canvas *reredos,* or altar screen, done in 1783 by classical Mexican painter José de Alzibar, and a collection of colonial New Mexican *bultos,* or

Santuario de Guadalupe ruin, 1880. *Photograph by Ben Wittick, courtesy Museum of New Mexico, neg. 15847.*

carved wood statues depicting saints, along with several Italian Renaissance paintings. The Santa Fe Desert Chorale is among several arts groups that use the Santuario de Guadalupe as a performance space. La Tertulia, a restaurant behind the *santuario* and church complex, was originally a convent associated with Guadalupe Chapel. Also part of the church complex was the Guadalupe Parish Grade School, renovated in the 1970s to become the Mercado Hispano del Norte, which houses several shops and galleries.

316 South Guadalupe Street

The **Stone Warehouse** built of rough stone by merchant Frederick Schnepple in 1885 is said to be the oldest stone commercial building in the city. The front windows and brick and sandstone facade were added during later renovations. It served as a beer distributor's storehouse, a Coca-Cola bottling plant, and an art gallery before becoming part of a large kitchenware store that also occupies two other adjacent buildings.

326 South Guadalupe Street

The **Zia Diner** was built of red brick in 1880 as a warehouse for the H.B. Cartwright & Brother Company, which operated grocery and hardware stores. In 1920 it was remodeled and the California Mission Revival curvilinear facade, inspired by the nearby AT&SF train station, was added. Other buildings along the west side of Guadalupe Street, including the Santuario de Guadalupe itself, were later remodeled in the same style, and recent buildings in the area have been designed in contemporary renditions of the same curvilinear motif. Before being transformed into the Zia Diner in the mid-1980s, the building housed an auto body shop for many years.

404 Montezuma Avenue

The **New Mexico State Records Center and Archives,** a windowless stucco building that houses millions of pages of state government documents, is notable mainly for the elaborate mural evoking New Mexico's multicultural heritage, which covers the entire Guadalupe Street side of the building. The mural, a cooperative effort by a group of local artists including Cassandra Harris, Zara Kriegstein, Rose Mary Stearns, and Frederico Vigil, was completed in 1980. It set a precedent for other grand-scale murals in and around the Guadalupe historic district.

Santuario de Guadalupe, 1900. *Photograph courtesy Museum of New Mexico, neg. 10032.*

Stone Warehouse. *Photograph by Richard Harris.*

Zia Diner. *Photograph by Richard Harris.*

Records and Archives mural. *Photograph by Richard Harris.*

■ 330 Garfield Street

University Plaza, at the corner of Guadalupe and Garfield streets, was originally built in the 1880s as the Protestant Christian University of New Mexico (not affiliated with the state-owned University of New Mexico), a college for "moral education" operated by evangelist missionaries who came to Santa Fe in the hope of converting Hispanic Catholics to their own fundamentalist faith. Their efforts were not received enthusiastically, and the school failed within a few years. The building later housed another private school, called the New West Academy, and then became the Franciscan Hotel. Constructed of red fired brick, the building originally had a mansard roof, which was removed when a third story was added; a new roof replicating the original one was installed in 1977 in an effort to recapture the building's historic character. University Plaza is now an office building.

Railroad Yards

The **Santa Fe Railroad Depot** was built in 1910 by the Atchison, Topeka & Santa Fe Railroad. The station was built in California Mission style, a company trademark symbolizing the westward expansion of the railroad; all A.T. & S.F. stations of the era west of the Mississippi were constructed in the same standard design and style, with archways, pitched red tile roofs, a curvilinear parapet, and a covered outdoor waiting area. The Atchison, Topeka & Santa Fe Railroad arrived in New Mexico in 1880, but despite its name, it bypassed Santa Fe because landowners wanted too much money for rights-of-way through the narrow pass below Glorieta where Interstate 25 now runs. Instead, the railroad veered its tracks southward to the smaller town of Albuquerque. Archbishop Lamy intervened and persuaded the railroad to extend a 20-mile spur line into Santa Fe. (The village that grew at the junction between the spur and the main

line is named after Lamy.) A spur of the Denver and Rio Grande Railway known as the Chili Line followed the Río Grande south from Colorado, reaching the Santa Fe railroad yards in 1884 by way of the route that is now Buckman Road. Not long after New Mexico became a state, both railroads discontinued passenger service and later regular freight service to Santa Fe. The tracks are now used only by a sightseeing excursion train and by special-purpose charter trains such as the ones sometimes used as temporary headquarters for motion picture production companies. Designed by Isaac Hamilton Rapp and completed in 1914, the **Gross Kelly Almacen** claims the distinction of being the oldest Spanish Pueblo Revival–style commercial building in the United States. It stands in the railroad yards south of the old train station and Tomasita's restaurant. Almacen means warehouse; Gross Kelly and Co., one of the largest wholesalers in the state, had earlier employed Rapp to design another, more conventional-looking warehouse in the city of Las Vegas, New Mexico. The Gross Kelly Almecen in Santa Fe was Rapp's second attempt to design a large building in what is now recognized as Spanish Pueblo Revival style. The first, which was almost identical to this one, was a Colorado Supply Company warehouse in Morley, Colorado. Rapp would use the same elements in more refined form over the next two years for Sunmount Sanitarium, the New Mexico Building at the Panama–California Exposition in San Diego, and the New Mexico Museum of Fine Arts. Some elements seem excessive, such as the closely spaced vigas that protrude from all four sides of the roofline. The building also contains hints of the California Mission Revival style, such as the curvilinear parapets on the squat towers that flank the building entrance portal; Rapp had employed the California style in earlier buildings with-

University Plaza. *Photograph by Richard Harris.*

Santa Fe Railroad depot. *Photograph by Richard Harris*

out notable success and, after this warehouse, abandoned it completely. Today, the Gross Kelly Almacen houses artists' studios, art supply wholesalers, and book publishers' offices. The railroad yards contain 17 other buildings, ranging from a plumbing supply wholesaler to the recently built headquarters of *Outside* magazine. With the exception of *Outside*, the building owners lease the land beneath them from the city, which now owns the railroad yards. The railroad yards extend south beyond Paseo de Peralta to Cerrillos Road. Most of this southern portion is vacant land inhabited by a prairie dog colony and sometimes by the homeless. As the last sizable undeveloped space near downtown, the appropriate use for the railroad yards has been a controversial topic for more than a decade. Proposals put forth by various factions include a convention center, a public park, a "publishers' row," an affordable housing project and luxury condominiums.

POLITICS — SANTA FE STYLE

The great seal of the state of New Mexico, which is reproduced in the middle of the multihued terazzo floor of the state capitol rotunda in Santa Fe, is in the shape of a Zia sun sign—as is the capitol building itself. The symbol is sacred to most Pueblo Indian groups and appears in petroglyphs more than 1000 years old. The New Mexico state flag and seal were inspired by a sun design on a water pot made at Zia Pueblo in the late nineteenth century, and the sun sign itself—a circle with a set of four parallel lines radiating outward in each of the four directions—came to be known as a zia. To the Pueblo people, the number four is sacred because it embodies everything on earth: north, east, south, and west; spring, summer, fall, and winter; sunrise, noon, sunset, and midnight; infancy, youth, adulthood, and old age; and the four sacred obligations—a strong body, a clear mind, a pure spirit, and a devotion to the welfare of the people. The four aspects are bound together in a circle of life and love, without beginning, without end.

In the center of the great seal, above the motto "crescit eundo" ("It grows as it goes"), stand twin eagles—the bald eagle of the United States clasping three arrows in its talons, side by side with the harpy eagle, Mexico's national symbol, on a cactus with a serpent in its beak. The state seal was adopted in 1912. The territorial seal, dating back to 1851, had lacked the zia sign; it had depicted the U.S. bald eagle with its wings wrapped protectively around the smaller, weaker Mexican eagle, a paternalistic bit of symbolism designed to show who was boss in a nice way.

In the last 14 years before the adoption of the 1851 seal, New Mexicans had killed two territorial governors—one representing Mexico, the other from the United States—during armed uprisings against each of the two governments in turn. Violent revolt always posed a threat to be reckoned with. For decades after the United States took control of New Mexico Territory, there were fewer Anglos than Indians in New Mexico, and both groups were outnumbered by the Spanish population.

Gross Kelly Warehouse. *Photograph by Richard Harris*

As military rule gave way to a constitutional civilian government, with the Mexican War still a recent and vivid memory, some federal politicians believed that establishing a democratically elected government in a territory where Hispanic voters were in the majority could only lead to long-term problems. In 1858 the U.S. Congress authorized the first donation land claims, the forerunner of the Homestead Act, in southern New Mexico. The law allowed U.S. citizens to claim 160 acres of land by occupying it, cultivating it, and building a home on it. The plan was intended to populate New Mexico with pioneer farm families; its drawback was that most of the semiarid land opened to homesteaders was climatically incapable of supporting crops.

Throughout the sparsely inhabited eastern and southern parts of the territory, farming communities sprang up only to be abandoned in a few years as families lost their land to bank foreclosure or sold it for pennies an acre to wheeler-dealer ranching barons, who used the failed farms to establish water rights that gave them control over vast areas of grazing land, establishing beef empires that are now entire counties, spanning millions of acres.

One of the most powerful of these land tycoons was Santa Fe lawyer Thomas B. "Boss" Catron, a director and major shareholder in cattle corporations that owned the southern half of Santa Fe County as well as most of what is now Catron County in the western part of the state. Catron was reputed to be a leader of a notorious political machine known as the Santa Fe Ring, along with his law partner, Stephen "Smooth Steve" Elkins,

Boss Catron. *Photograph by Wesley Bradfield, courtesy Museum of New Mexico, neg. 13309.*

and territorial Supreme Court Justice Joseph G. Palen. According to opponents led by the editor of the Las Vegas Weekly Mail newspaper, no other lawyer could try a case successfully against Boss Catron and Smooth Steve, enabling the pair and their pocket judge to amass huge fortunes through extortion, trumped-up litigation, and fraudulent land claims. Although the men certainly grew rich through tactics that would be illegal today, modern historians doubt that the "conspiracy" was anything more than the kind of sharp practice that was widespread in the American West during the "robber baron" era.

Although Catron and his cronies were Republicans, the Santa Fe Ring spread its political power by coopting potential opponents and came to be made up of both Republicans and Democrats, Anglos and Hispanos. One historian, Kenneth Owens, has described politics in territorial New Mexico as a "no-party system," in which Boss Catron and his cronies wielded absolute control over both political parties. Forging alliances with the Territorial Cattlemen's Association and the New Mexico Militia, the ring solidified its influence throughout the territory. The *Santa Fe New Mexican* newspaper, under the management of Colonel Max Frost, became the official spokesman for the Republican Party and the unofficial voice of the Santa Fe Ring. The purchase of votes for small amounts of money, or even liquor, became common practice.

The first real opposition to the Santa Fe Ring and the ruthless cattle empires it represented came out of the small southern New Mexico ranching town of Lincoln, where the owners of the the largest ranch and the only general store were allegedly involved with the Santa Fe Ring in a complex scheme of fraudulent government contracts, in 1876–1878. Texas cattleman John Chisum, an enemy of the cattlemen's association, financed John Tunstall, a newcomer from Scotland, in setting up a competing cattle ranch and store. The naively optomistic Tunstall wrote home to his father, "Everything in New Mexico that pays at all is worked by a 'ring.' To do any good it is necessary to either get into a ring or make one for yourself. I am working at present making a ring." Toward this end, he hired a team of private security guards known as "regulators" to protect his enterprises against both cattle rustlers and the Lincoln County sheriff's posse, who nevertheless quickly assassinated Tunstall. The regulators persuaded the U.S. Marshall's office to deputize them by mail to arrest Tunstall's killers. But in attempting to do so, the regulators' leader was killed, too,, leaving the small makeshift federal posse under the command of 19-year-old William Bonney—better known as Billy the Kid.

Bonney's brief, violent life is certainly the most familiar legend in New Mexico history, and the most enigmatic. His three-year criminal career has been the subject of more than a dozen Hollywood westerns, which together with dime novels and newspaper reports of the time as well as the many letters he wrote trying to resolve his legal problems in an essentially lawless land present a portrait that is equal parts Robin Hood of the Old West and psycho killer. Bonney and his gang killed every posse member who had taken part in Tunstell's assassination, and that was only the beginning. Freelance gunfighters from all over the West came to join one side or the other, and before the end of the year the feud had escalated into the Lincoln County War, in which more than 200 people were shot to death before the end of the year. The "war" shocked newspaper readers all over the United States. President Rutherford B. Hayes fired the territorial governor, replacing him with retired U.S. Army General Lew Wallace, an outsider untainted by New Mexico politics, who carried explicit orders to end the Lincoln County War and disband the Santa Fe Ring.

By the time Lew Wallace took office, every key figure on both sides of the Lincoln County War had been killed. The governor met privately with Bonney and persuaded him to accept amnesty in exchange for court testimony. Bonney took the witness stand against the last surviving instigators of the range war but returned to Lincoln County to find that the governor's pardon did not carry much weight. Charged again with murder from the Lincoln County War, he took to the empty hills and went into business as a cattle rustler, for which he was gunned down by Sheriff Pat Garrett two years later at the age of 22.

Wallace was still governor when Billy the Kid died. He spent much of his time traveling around the territory observing quaint customs. Meanwhile, in the territory's far-flung ranching empires, gun violence continued to be the norm. An outlaw band known as the Dodge City Gang, led by a local justice of the peace, took over the town of Las Vegas, 50 miles east of Santa Fe, for six months in 1879–1880. After they were driven out by the New Mexico Militia, saloonkeeper Vincente Silva and his Cuarenta Bandidos ("forty

New Mexico State Constitutional Convention, 1910. *Photograph by William R. Walton, courtesy Museum of New Mexico, neg. 8119.*

thieves") seized control of the town, murdering dozens of rivals and inform-
ers—among them his own wife and brother-in-law—before he himself was
assassinated by one of his henchmen. In 1881, Wallace sent the state militia
to Doña Ana County against another 40-man gang of cattle rustlers who were
terrorizing the local population. At the height of the turmoil, fellow Civil War
general William T. Sherman advised Governor Wallace, "The United States
ought to declare war on Mexico and make it take back New Mexico."

At the end of his term in office, Wallace was content to relinquish state
government back to the Santa Fe political machine. When Grover Cleveland
became president two years later, however, he decided to present a more
direct challenge to the ring's control of the territory by appointing Edmund
G. Ross as territorial governor. Ross, a former Republican who had been banished from the party as a traitor after casting the deciding vote against
removal of Democratic President Andrew Johnson in impeachment proceed-
ings 17 years earlier, was known as an idealistic and incorruptible, if cantan-
kerous, reformer who owed political favors to no one.

Ross's first problem was that his predecessor had appointed a new territorial treasurer, attorney general, and district attorney just before leaving
office, mindful of a territorial court ruling that appointees could not be
removed without cause for two years. These officials blocked Ross's actions
at every turn. In an attempt to get rid of them, he began a series of corruption hearings charging them and other public officials with "drunkenness,
licentiousness, gambling, and misfeasance, malfeasance and nonfeasance in
office." The scandals got out of hand when Ross's chief ally, territorial
surveyor George Julian, reported to Washington that 90 percent of all land
conveyances in New Mexico Territory were fraudulent. Although modern historians agree that this figure was probably accurate, the implications for
every person of means in the territory were so sweeping that it brought the
New Mexico economy to a standstill. In the second year of Ross's term, the
territorial legislature was taken over by candidates who had campaigned
with promises to disregard past land frauds. Having alienated both the Old
Guard and reformers in both political parties, Ross finished out his term
completely powerless. His successor as governor was L. Bradford Prince, a
key figure in the Santa Fe Ring.

The plunderers of the territorial era had mellowed into an entrenched
and rather sedate Old Guard by the time New Mexico was granted statehood
in 1912. Boss Catron, fresh from a term as mayor of Santa Fe, was elected as
one of the new state's first U.S. Senators. The other was Albert B. Fall, who
would later be sent to federal prison in the Teapot Dome Scandal.

The New Mexico Constitutional Convention was made up of a broad
cross section of New Mexicans, Spanish as well as Anglo. (Women and
Indians were not represented, since by law they could not vote.) The resulting constitution was 20,000 words in length, three times as long as the U.S.

Old Territorial Capitol, 1900. *Photograph by Christian G. Kaadt, courtesy Museum of New Mexico,* neg. *10392.*

Constitution, and designed to protect both the interests of the wealthy and politically powerful and the rights of Hispanics. Although it appears easily amendable—a mere majority of legislators can submit a constitutional amendment to a vote of the people—a requirement that amendments to most sections be approved by a majority of voters in each county of the state has made changing the constitution virtually impossible. Unlike most other western states, New Mexico's constitution has no provision for voter recall of politicians and no initiative or referendum procedure to let voters propose or pass new laws. It provides for the popular election of many more public officials than in other states. For instance, the attorney general is elected instead of appointed by the governor and as often as not comes from the opposing political party, pitting the two offices against each other and paralyzing the executive branch.

The most extraordinary provisions of the constitution are those relating to language and culture. New Mexico is the only U.S. state that recognizes both English and Spanish as its "official languages," requiring that all laws, regulations, and government publications be issued in both languages. Schools are required to be bilingual, and separate schools for Anglo and Hispanic children are prohibited. It guarantees that no distinction can be made in jury duty or holding public office on account of the inability to

Old State Capitol. *Photograph by T. Harmon Parkhurst, courtesy Museum of New Mexico, neg. 10385.*

speak or understand English. There can be no language or literacy requirement for voting, and voters have the right to bring another person into the
voting booth to help them mark their ballots. This last provision, essential to
protect civil rights in the early years of the century when a large percentage
of the population could not read English, was quickly turned to the advan-
tage of political bosses who would round up large numbers of illiterate people and "help" them vote; this practice became rampant after 1948, when
Indians won the right to vote and thousands of Navajo people who spoke
neither English nor Spanish became pawns of a powerful political machine
in the northwestern counties of New Mexico. Oddly, the framers of the state
constitution had not mentioned Indians once.

New Mexico's legislature is made up of 42 senators, who are elected for
four-year terms, and 70 representatives, who serve two-year terms. The state
constitution provides that legislative districts may be redrawn for each election. Today, because of federal legal requirements, both senate and house
districts are apportioned by population, but this was not always the case.
Until the mid-1960s, each county had one state senator. For example, in 1960,
Harding County, with a population of 1800, had the same Senate representa-
tion as Bernalillo County (Albuquerque), population 262,000. With mandato-
ry reapportionment, the legislature increased the number of senators from 32
to 42 so that each county could keep at least one. In recent years, however, as
Albuquerque and Las Cruces have continued to grow rapidly while 17 rural
counties have experienced drastic population declines, Bernalillo County
elects 16 senators and Harding County shares a single senator with four other
neighboring counties. Santa Fe County elects four senators (of which two
represent districts that cross county lines) and four representatives.

As of 1996, Hispanic legislators make up 31 percent of the house of representatives and 38 percent of the senate. Women make up 21 percent of the
house and 19 percent of the senate. There are two Pueblo Indian representatives and two Navajo senators. Since 1933, the Democrats have controlled
both chambers of the legislature continuously except for 1953–1954, when
the Republicans briefly controlled the house. New Mexico had only one
Spanish governor during the territorial era—Miguel Otero, appointed to finish assassinated Governor Charles Bent's term in 1847—and since statehood
four of the 22 people who have served as governor have been Hispanic.
None has been a woman or an Indian. The governor's office has been occupied by Democrats two-thirds of the time.

The legislature convenes on the third Tuesday in January each year, for a
30-day session in even-numbered years and a 60-day session in odd-num-
bered years. State senators and representatives receive no salaries, only a $75
per diem during the session and a mileage allowance for travel from their
homes to the Santa Fe. It may seem strange that although bills to authorize

Old Governors Mansion, 1952. *Photograph by T. Harmon Parkhurst, courtesy Museum of New Mexico, neg. 14010.*

salaries for legislators are often introduced, they are always voted down by a large margin. The simple truth is that unsalaried legislators provide "casework service" to wealthy campaign contributors and depend on well-financed lobbyists—most notoriously the horse-racing, liquor and cattlemen's lobbies—to make resources available, and all these backers like the system just the way it is. In recent years, other special-interest groups, ranging from environmental activists to religious fundamentalists, have also learned to play the lobbying game effectively. Since the Roundhouse was designed to minimize contact between legislators and the public, it has become traditional for lobbyists to state their cases at the Bull Ring restaurant and bar, 414 Old Santa Fe Trail, just down the block from the capitol. Three-margarita lunches there are such an institution that it has recently become fashionable for senators and representatives to pledge publicly that they will not show up inebriated at afternoon sessions.

The city of Santa Fe is run by an elected mayor and city council through a city manager appointed by the mayor. There is no two-party system in local government; officials run for election without official party affiliation. This arrangement means that any resident who can collect enough petition signatures can run for mayor, and every four years at least a dozen do. In a recent mayoral election, candidates included an art gallery owner, a channeler running on behalf of a deceased artist, a philosopher gas station attendant, and a private investigator; all lost to Debbie Jaramillo, an outspoken and sometimes outrageous activist for the interests of native Santa Feans and against growth and development. The city council, too, mirrors the extreme diversity of Santa Fe's population. At this writing it included a construction contractor, a member of an old Spanish family that has wielded political clout for more than two centuries, a community activist who was the first openly gay woman ever elected to the council, a ponytailed scientist from the Santa Fe Institute who was the first Green Party candidate ever elected to office in

Demolition of Governors Mansion, 1952. *Photograph by Mugatt, courtesy Museum of New Mexico, neg. 56414.*

New Mexico (17 percent of Santa Fe voters cast their ballots for at least one Green in the last election), and the same private investigator who unexpectedly lost the mayoral election. It is rare to see the city's policymakers agree on anything. The issues they must decide a little at a time, week by week, are first and foremost whether Santa Fe should grow or not and whether the city should do things the way things are done in Santa Fe—provincially, with homegrown style and a blind eye toward small faults—or the way other cities do them—professionally, promptly, and with maddening efficiency. The City Different approach always seems to win by a landslide.

6

Santa Fe Neighborhoods

S anta Fe is shaped like a comet radiating toward the southwest. At the center, all the areas that are now historic districts already existed when Santa Fe was a small town, one-eighth the size it is now. The tail is Cerrillos Road, the old main highway from the days before the interstate was built. This crowded commercial strip extends for six congested miles, making motors feel as if they are in a big city; but anywhere along the route they are within 5 minutes' drive of open country out past the edge of town. The less privileged neighborhoods lie close to Cerrillos Road and Agua Fria Street, the older route that parallels it. As you go farther north or south, residential lots become larger and homes more expensive. To the west, the Santa Fe National Forest boundary blocks development in the Sangre de Cristo Mountains, and a limited number of very expensive homes occupy the narrow strip of ponderosa pine forest between the national forest and the old part of the city.

Living on an unpaved road is a Santa Fe status symbol. Secluded enclaves throughout the city fight back all proposals to pave their streets, knowing that it would lower property values. Residents of the most exclusive subdivisions typically need four-wheel-drive vehicles to get home in bad weather. Santa Fe style tops the list of features that home buyers desire, so Territorial and Pueblo Revival architecture has spread far beyond the boundaries of the city's historic districts. Free from the legal restrictions of the historic styles act, custom-

Opposite: San Isidro Church. *Photograph by Richard Harris.*

home builders have come up with some highly imaginative variations on traditional themes. In less exclusive neighborhoods, residents create their own stylistic innovations in concrete blocks and stucco. In fact, except for the profusion of prefab buildings and electric plastic signs along Cerrillos Road, almost all the city's buildings incorporate the look, if not all the formal elements, of Santa Fe style.

Amazingly, in a city that thrives on tourism, there is not a single tourist attraction outside the historic districts in Santa Fe. There is plenty to see beyond the city limits, but with the exception of the Santa Fe Opera and the Hyde Park/Ski Basin Road—both outside the city—none of the areas described in this chapter is even mentioned in any other guidebook.

DRIVING TOURS OF THE CITY

NORTH

Guadalupe Street and St. Francis Drive merge at the edge of town to become U.S. Highway 84/285, the four-lane artery that links Santa Fe with Española, Taos, and other northern New Mexico communities. Along the north end of Paseo de Peralta between these two streets is **De Vargas Mall,** the city's major shopping mall before the construction of Villa Linda on the southwest side in the late 1980s.

On the east side of Guadalupe Street, across from the mall, is **Rosario Cemetery.** At the center of the cemetery is **Rosario Chapel,** one of Santa Fe's oldest and least-known churches. The chapel was built in 1806 on the site where, according to legend, Spanish governor Diego de Vargas had camped during the Spanish reconquest of Santa Fe 113 years before, following the Pueblo Revolt. La Conquistadora, the revered wooden figure of the Virgin Mary that accompanied the Spanish colonists during the reconquest, has been carried on a pilgrimage of thanksgiving from her chapel in the cathedral to the main altar of Rosario Chapel every year since it was built. After an addition to the chapel in 1914, the original chapel became the transept of the new, much larger one. The Catholic cemetery was started in the 1850s, when construction of St. Francis Cathedral engulfed the former cemetery on the site and put a halt to burials on church property near the old *parroquía*.

Located on a small road off Paseo de Peralta that runs behind Rosario Cemetery, **Saint Catherine Indian School** (801 Griffin Street), originally the Saint Catherine Indian Industrial School for Boys, dates back to 1887. It was founded by Benedictine monks and then operated for a short time by the nuns of the Loretto Academy for Girls. In 1893 the Sisters of the Blessed Sacrament took the school over. The newly formed, well-financed order, which organized schools for American Indians and African Americans in

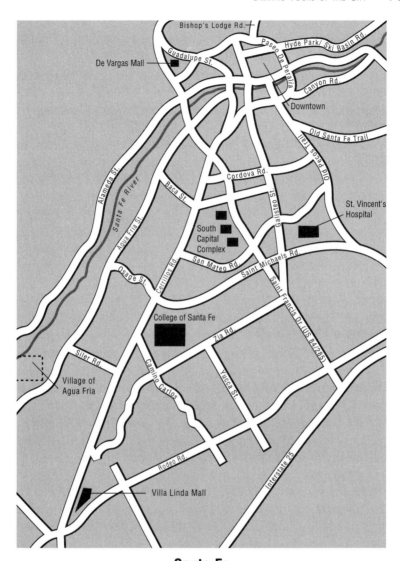

Santa Fe

many parts of the country, built most of the buildings and continues to operate the school today.

Immediately to the north of Rosario Cemetery is the **Santa Fe National Cemetery,** with its precise rows of identical white grave markers. One of a number of national cemeteries where soldiers who served in World War II are entitled to burial as a veterans' benefit, in recent years it has been expanding faster than more lawn can be planted to keep up with it.

Proceeding north along U.S. Highway 84/285, you will pass two left turns, the first for **La Tierra Road** and the second for **Tano Road.** Both are part of an exclusive area of custom homes and horse ranches nestled in a low piñon and juniper forest. Although the piñon trees do not reach more than 10 feet high, they grow extremely slowly, and many are up to 500 years old. Long-burning with a spicy smell that reminds New Mexicans of Christmas, piñon is the preferred firewood in Santa Fe. Juniper adapts to a wide range of growing conditions by mimicking other evergreen trees. When it shares an area with piñon trees, it grows to the same height and in the same roundish shape. Higher in the mountains, among the ponderosa pines, the junipers grow much taller. La Tierra Road eventually turns to dirt and becomes Buckman Road, the former railroad bed of the old Texas, Santa Fe & Northern Railroad, which linked Santa Fe with the Denver & Rio Grande's "Chile Line" in 1887. Buckman Road leads about 9 more miles to the Río Grande at the upper end of the otherwise inaccessible wilderness of White Rock Canyon. Lining Buckman Road is a series of large wells that yield the water necessary for growth; the aquifer has reached its productive capacity, meaning that any new well drilled now decreases the water from the other wells by as much as it produces.

Five miles north of the city, just south of the Tesuque Pueblo grant boundary, the **Santa Fe Opera** occupies a natural bowl in the hills west of the highway. Although the 1889-seat open-air theater is used only six weeks of the year, it is a centerpiece of Santa Fe's cultural scene during the peak tourist season. The opera presents major name singers along with talented newcomers in alternating performances of premieres by leading contemporary composers and classic works by Mozart, Verdi, and others. Although it has only been in existence since 1957, the Santa Fe Opera has presented more premieres of new operas than any other company in the country. With more than 500 singers, musicians, technicians, set and costume designers, and office personnel, the opera is one of the largest nongovernment employers in the greater Santa Fe area—but only in July and August.

Just north of the opera, **Trader Jack's Flea Market** is regarded by many as one of the best open-air markets in the country. Indian and frontier artifact dealers and importers of folk art from throughout the world exhibit their wares side by side with local chile growers, tarot readers, and massage therapists. The flea market operates on Fridays, Saturdays, and Sundays except in winter, when it is closed. The parking lot becomes the largest campground in the county on Thursday night, when hundreds of vendors camp there in order to vie for the best locations on Friday morning.

Past the flea market, Highway 84/285 continues north across the Tesuque Pueblo Grant. It is the only route from Santa Fe to northern communities such as Pojoaque, Española, Chimayo, Los Alamos, Taos, and several Indian pueblos.

Old Taos Highway starts from Paseo de Peralta north of downtown and follows a ridgeline for about 2 miles before joining U.S. 84/285, the present highway to Taos. A low, thick forest of piñon and juniper trees covers the surrounding hills, where custom homes are scattered along winding dirt roads. Close to downtown, the large, one-of-a-kind hillside homes are closer togeth-

Hayt-Wientge Mansion in background, 1890. *Photograph by Dana B. Chase, courtesy Museum of New Mexico neg. 89281.*

er, and a few of them are considerably older. The north side became the city's first exclusive town-and-country neighborhood soon after the railroad arrived.

Heading north from Paseo de Peralta on the Old Taos Highway, you can detour through the older part of the north side by taking the first left onto the Paseo de la Cuma. The pavement soon ends as the road winds to the top of the ridge. Partly hidden from the road by two houses of more recent construction, the **Hayt–Wientge Mansion** (620 Paseo de La Cuma) stands high on a hillside overlooking the city. In startling contrast to the surrounding free-form Spanish Pueblo Revival–style homes, the old Victorian home with its mansard roof was built around an older adobe house in 1882 by merchant Walter Hayt, a recent arrival from New York who ran a retail store on San Francisco Street and became Santa Fe's first bookseller. After living there for only six years, he sold the house to the wife of jeweler Frederick Wientge; the Wientge family occupied the house for the next 86 years. Meticulously restored, this private mansion is known for its elaborate Christmas Eve *farolito* display. Following the Paseo de la Cuma brings you to Reunion Road, where a right turn returns you to the Old Taos Highway.

Continue northward on the Old Taos Highway for a little less than 1 mile and turn right on Camino Estado. This unpaved road makes its way up to another ridgeline, known as Mansion Ridge because the **Governor's Mansion** is located at the summit. The mansion was opened in 1955, replacing a previous one that had stood next door to the old state capitol (now the Bataan Building). The grandeur of this low Territorial Revival mansion is not obvious from the road; its lush landscaping is secluded from view, although

183

the paved parking lot is impressive in size and hints at the hidden extent of the residence. The interior is not open to the public. As you drive past the mansion, the road becomes paved and wider, descending the other side of the ridge to Bishop's Lodge Road.

Bishop's Lodge Road is the extension of Washington Street north from Paseo de Peralta, passing the big municipal sports complex at **Fort Marcy Park** (once a military training field, not to be confused with Old Fort Marcy Park on the mesa west of downtown). Besides a year-round swimming pool and fitness center, the city park has a pretty creekside walkway and an intramural baseball stadium that is best known as the site where Zozobra, the effigy of "Old Man Gloom," is burned for a cheering crowd at the opening of the Santa Fe fiesta each September.

Bishop's Lodge Road winds north through the foothills toward the village of Tesuque (see Chapter 7). Just beyond the Santa Fe city limit, 3½ miles north of downtown, the road reaches **The Bishop's Lodge.** At the core of this luxury resort complex is Villa Pintoresca, the modest retreat that Archbishop Lamy created for himself and his guests in the early 1870s at the place where Tesuque Creek spills out of the mountains to irrigate the fruit orchards of the picturesque little valley known as Cajoncita de Tesuque, which he said reminded him of his native France. The archbishop rebuilt a small adobe house that had stood on the hillside overlooking a fruit orchard that dated back to the seventeenth century. He then added a small chapel where he prayed in private and held mass for visiting dignitaries. The chapel has high vaulted ceiling and painted-glass windows emulating the stained glass of French cathedrals. The property was bought by the Pulitzer publishing family, which built two summer homes on the property. In 1918 it was acquired by Denver mining tycoon James R. Thorpe, whose family still owns the property. Expanding the lodge compound and acquiring 1000 acres of adjoining land, the family created today's resort. Lamy's chapel, restored in 1928 with the help of Santa Fe artist Carlos Vierra, has been preserved in its original condition and is open to the public as part of the present lodge.

The shortest return route to town is back south on Bishop's Lodge Road. For a more scenic excursion, continue north to Shidoni Art Foundry and the village of Tesuque, where it meets a road that rejoins the U.S. Highway 84/285 in the vicinity of Tesuque Pueblo, Trader Jack's Flea Market, and the Santa Fe Opera.

EAST

Santa Fe's downtown district sits right at the foot of the hills that rise steadily into the high country of the Sangre de Cristo Mountains, and motorists can find themselves beside a stream in a cool evergreen forest within 10 minutes of leaving the Plaza. The only route into the mountains starts from Washington Avenue two blocks north or Paseo de Peralta as Artist Road (signs point the way to Hyde Park and the Ski Basin), so called because it leads to the mesa near Old Fort Marcy Park, a favorite painters' viewpoint. The 17-mile paved road changes its name to Hyde Park Road at the city limits and, upon passing Hyde Park, becomes Ski Basin Road.

For a scenic drive that offers grand vistas as well as a look at an exclusive eastside neighborhood before joining Hyde Park Road, follow West Palace Avenue from downtown. It curves around to the south and, just before crossing the Santa Fe River, intersects Alameda Street. Turn left on Alameda, go one block, and turn left again on Gonzales Road, a recently paved road that climbs a steep hill and then traverses the mesa through a neighborhood of large, newish custom homes with spectacular views of the city and the wild desert and mountains to the west. Gonzales meets Hyde Park Road about half a mile above downtown.

About a mile up Hyde Park Road on the left is the **Santa Fe Institute** (1399 Hyde Park Road), home of a private nonprofit "think tank" founded in 1984. Researchers and educators from around the world come here to spend days, weeks, or months working on collaborative, multidisciplinary projects in such fields as adaptive computation, theoretical immunology, and cultural evolution.

The road continues for about 4 miles past scattered, exclusive hillside subdivisions before reaching the national forest boundary. The highest and most prestigious of the custom home developments is **Hyde Park Estates.** Past there, an atmospheric Japanese bath and hot-tub spa called **Ten Thousand Waves** rambles up a mountain slope through tall pines, and the road enters the national forest.

Santa Fe National Forest covers more than 1.5 million acres and sprawls across parts of six counties, including both the southern end of the Sangre de Cristo Mountains above Santa Fe and a separate unit that encompasses the Jemez Mountains around Los Alamos and Bandelier National Monument. The 17-mile, paved Hyde Park/Ski Basin Road provides the only major road access in Santa Fe County to the high-country Sangre de Cristo range. Along the way are several popular hiking trails, including the relatively easy Chamisa Trail at Mile 5.5 and the Hyde Park Loop starting at the upper end of **Hyde Memorial State Park** (Mile 8). The state park also has picnic and camping facilities along a creek in the pine and aspen forest, as well as a restaurant in a log building that dates back to the 1930s.

Farther up the road, a parking area serves the **Aspen Vista Picnic Area,** where a road limited to hiking and mountain biking use only winds for 6 miles through the largest contiguous aspen forest in the world, ultimately reaching the broadcast towers atop 12,040-foot Lake Peak (often called Tesuque Peak), where there is a spectacular view of other 12,000-foot peaks and—far below surrounded by sheer cliffs—Santa Fe Lake, the headwaters of the Santa Fe River. Nearby, an unpaved side road twists through a canyon

Pathway to Ten Thousand Waves. *Photograph by Richard Harris.*

northward to **Aspen Meadows,** a primitive campground and picnic area operated by Tesuque Pueblo. Hyde Park/Ski Basin Road climbs to an altitude of 10,500 feet before dead-ending at the parking lot for the Santa Fe Ski Basin and the trailhead for the Pecos Wilderness.

Temperatures among the high mountain peaks run about 30 degrees lower than in Santa Fe. As a result, the high mountains receive several times more rainfall and snowfall than that received in the city. Winter temperatures usually stay low enough so that snow does not melt on north-facing slopes. Supplemental snow-making maintains an average 225-inch snow base for the downhill ski runs of the **Santa Fe Ski Basin.** There is no overnight ski lodge at the Ski Basin, only a cafeteria and equipment rental facility. In the summer, the chair lift carries visitors to the summit of Lake Peak for hiking and sight-seeing. Expansion of the ski area has been a controversial environmental issue in Santa Fe for several years.

At the north end of the Ski Basin parking lot is the main trailhead for the **Pecos Wilderness,** a vast, roadless area of granite crags, ancient fir forests, and alpine tundra that sprawls across parts of five counties and two national forests. Motorized or wheeled vehicles (including mountain bikes) are prohibited in the wilderness area. The network of more than 200 miles of trails is reserved for hiking, cross-country skiing, horseback riding, and llama trekking.

SOUTH

Santa Fe's south side has been the area of greatest development in the 1980s and early 1990s. This is the area where most new apartment complexes and midrange housing subdivisions are interspersed with considerable expanses of vacant fields. Paradoxically, it is also the least interesting area for sightseeing. Interstate 25 effectively puts a cap on suburban sprawl to the south, since no main thoroughfare continues across the interstate. The historic route south from the city, Galisteo Street, once ran all the way to the village of Galisteo following the route now used by the railroad spur from Lamy, but today the street fades into a maze of dead-end dirt roads long before it reaches the interstate. Today, the main traffic arteries to the south are the two streets that have on-ramps to the interstate: St. Francis Drive and Old Pecos Trail.

St. Francis Drive, the busiest north–south street in Santa Fe, bypasses the downtown area on the west and becomes U.S. Highway 84/285, the main route north to Pojoaque, Los Alamos, Española, and Taos and one of the busiest highways in the state. Mixed homes, apartment and office complexes, small commercial establishments, parks, and vacant lots line the six-lane divided street haphazardly except for the area surrounding the intersection with Coronado Road. In the 1950s, when this was the newest and largest suburban area in the city, **Coronado Center** was the main shopping mall, complete with a cafeteria, bowling alley, and movie theater. It was slipping toward oblivion by 1990, when the owners undertook a major renovation that transformed the Eisenhower-era look to Territorial Revival style. The shopping center's tenants are gradually adapting to the needs of the hundreds of people who work across St. Francis Drive in the **South Capital Complex,** a group of multi-story square concrete office buildings (painted adobe color, of course) that house as many state government offices as all the buildings in the downtown capitol district. Among the state buildings is the federal **Piñon Building,** containing national offices as well as the Intermountain Cultural Resource Center, the federal agency in charge of anthropology and archaeology.

Old Pecos Trail is the most scenic route between the interstate and the city, but also the most confusing. Heading away from the Plaza, the Old Santa Fe Trail veers off to the east several blocks north of downtown, inconspicuously except for small signs pointing to the museum. The main street changes its name to Old Pecos Trail. Except for a couple of restaurants and an exclusive racquet club, Old Pecos Trail is noncommercial, with a number of churches and many side streets, paved and unpaved, that turn off into quiet neighborhoods half-hidden by piñon trees and chamisa. The two-lane road goes past **St. Vincent's Hospital,** the only general hospital in the city, and the growing sprawl of medical office complexes surrounding it. Soon after, Old Pecos Trail comes to a T-intersection with a bigger, four-lane divided street. Turn left at this confusing junction and you're still on Old Pecos Trail; turn right and the same main street changes to St. Michaels Drive. Farther on, just before reaching the interstate, Old Pecos Trail forks, and the left fork becomes Old Las Vegas Highway, paralleling the interstate for about 10 miles and then joining it, while the right fork goes to the Interstate 25 on-ramps. If you cross the interstate, the road ends abruptly at an intersection with an aimless fragment of unpaved frontage road known as Old Agua Fria Road serving an area of custom homes widely scattered along the brink of a large arroyo. It's worth the trip to drive past the **Duke–Victor house** (53-D Old Agua Fria Road). Handbuilt of adobe by a local couple who travel the world as folk-art importers, the fanciful castle proves that the spirit of the 1920s do-it-yourself adobe architecture revival lives on today.

St. Vincent's Hospital. *Photograph by Richard Harris.*

Duke-Victor House. *Photograph by Richard Harris.*

Farther west along Old Las Vegas Highway, several roads cross the interstate and lead into a pine-covered foothills area of widely dispersed homes known as Sunlit Hills. One road, vaguely indicated by a historical marker on Old Las Vegas Highway, takes you to **Seton Village,** a cluster of 1920s-vintage Pueblo Revival houses built around the 45-room castle of author Ernest Seton, a naturalist, authority on Indian lore, founder and first chief scout of the Boy Scouts of America, who presided over a small writers' and artists' colony here until his death in 1946. Nothing at Seton Village is presently open to the public, although over the years, Seton's art collection, library, and Indian museum have sometimes been open to view by appointment.

The two major east–west thoroughfares on the south side are St. Michaels Drive and Rodeo Road. Both run west from Old Pecos Trail and intersect St. Francis Drive. **St. Michaels Drive** is a developed commercial area of small,

Granary from Michoacan on College of Santa Fe campus. *Photograph by Richard Harris.*

adjacent shopping malls and branch banks that curves northward and merges with the commercial zone along Cerrillos Road. The major landmark along the road is the **College of Santa Fe** (1600 St. Michaels Drive), a private college with an enrollment of about 1500. The college was formerly operated by the Catholic church as St. Michael's College and was originally located on Old Santa Fe Trail (then called College Avenue), in what are now the Lamy Building and Lew Wallace Building. The college is best known in the community today for its theater and its motion picture production facility, both gifts of the school's longtime patroness, the late Greer Garson.

    Rodeo Road, the city's most recent major thoroughfare, runs through an area of subdivisions so new that they are landscaped with saplings, allowing unobstructed views of the spectacular Sangre de Cristos. The road is named for the **Santa Fe Rodeo Grounds,** home of the Rodeo de Santa Fe, a weeklong competition of calf roping, bucking horse and bull riding, and bulldogging that takes place in July. The rodeo grounds are also used for the county fair and occasional outdoor concerts but are vacant much of the year. Farther west, Richards Avenue turns south off Rodeo Road and crosses open ranchland for about 2 miles before reaching **Santa Fe Community College.** The largest college-level school in the city, the community college now has an enrollment of 5400—twice as many students as St. John's College, the College of Santa Fe, UNM Graduate Studies, the University of Phoenix branch, and the Institute of American Indian Arts combined. Rodeo Road joins Cerrillos Road on the west edge of the city at **Villa Linda Mall,** Santa Fe's newest and largest all-weather shopping mall.

WEST

Two main roads run south from downtown Santa Fe, both on the south side of the river. **Agua Fria Street** was the original Camino Real, the trade route that followed the Río Grande south through New Mexico and continued to Chihuahua and Mexico City in Spanish colonial times. There were no bridges west of downtown Santa Fe in colonial times — and there are not many today — so El Camino Real never crossed the Río Santa Fe or Río Grande all the way to El Paso, 350 miles south. As a result, almost all development on Santa Fe's west side stayed south of the river. In the twentieth century, when the first automobile highways were being built, the main highway to Albuquerque bypassed the homes and farms that had grown to line much of Agua Fria Street and instead followed **Cerrillos Road,** the route that had served the mining districts southeast of town in the 1880s. The road was a natural because it entered Santa Fe from the southwest as a diagonal, thereby intersecting every major thoroughfare of the city, including both north–south and east–west streets.

Free of the restrictions that govern the downtown historic district, Cerrillos Road quickly developed into nearly 6 miles of congested, unsightly strip city. Santa Feans who live east of the railroad tracks insist that they never go there. Many visitors do, though, because the most affordable and available accommodations in town are the ma-and-pa motels that sprung up along this old highway in the days before the interstate bypassed Santa Fe and, farther out, a number of recently built motor inns.

Santa Fe style architecture is less evident along Cerrillos Road than any place else in the city because of uniform building designs required for many national franchise and chain locations. What local style does appear usually takes the form of stuccoing boxlike utilitarian buildings or at least painting them tan.

There are only a few places of historic or architectural significance along Cerrillos Road. On the northwest corner of the intersection of St. Francis Drive and Cerrillos stands the **James A. Little Theater,** an imposing Spanish Pueblo Revival–style stage theater on the campus of the **New Mexico School for the Deaf.** The theater itself, which is rented for various lectures and performances and is considered the best dance stage in the city, was built in 1982 and named for the school's superintendent at the time. The School for the Deaf itself dates back to 1887. The red brick buildings of the original school can still be seen at the west end of the campus. The big, cream-colored Spanish Pueblo Revival–style halls at the center of the school grounds were built with WPA funds and labor in 1935–1940, emulating the design that John Gaw Meem had used in the renovation of the nearby Santa Fe Indian School a few years earlier. The theater, which is the building most noticeable from the street, was designed by local architects to harmonize with the WPA buildings.

James A. Little Theatre. *Photograph by Richard Harris.*

Several blocks southwest on Cerrillos Road, on the same side as the
School for the Deaf and similar in architecture and color, is the **Santa Fe
Indian School.** The school was started in 1899 with a federal appropriation
of $31,000 to provide education for Pueblo, Navajo, and Apache children.
Tuition was free, but students were required to work in exchange for room and
board. The government originally saw Indian schools as a way to help (or
force) the assimilation of reservation Indians into mainstream American cul-
ture, and toward that end many Indian children, especially on the Navajo
reservation, were kidnapped and sent to boarding schools such as this one.
Today, the Santa Fe Indian School is operated by the 19 Indian pueblos of New
Mexico and has become a vehicle for keeping Indian culture alive. The central buildings of the Indian School were renovated in Pueblo Revival style by
John Gaw Meem in 1931. One of the most noteworthy features of the Indian
School campus, although a hard one to get a look at except during events, is
the Paolo Soleiri Amphitheater. This acoustically sophisticated outdoor bowl
with its upswept roof sheltering the stage and its ingenious arrangement of
backstage walkways is the major popular music concert venue in Santa Fe
and a major source of supplemental income for the Indian School. Paolo
Soleri, the Italian-born architect who designed it, was a disciple of Frank Lloyd
Wright. A resident of Scottsdale, Arizona, he is best known for Arcosanti, a single megastructure providing integrated work and living space for a population

of 5000, between Phoenix and Flagstaff and a pilot project for the imaginary Mesa City, a desert metropolis for 2 million people that Soleiri designed in 1959 and described 10 years later in his book, *Arcology: The City in the Image of Man.*

Two blocks south of Cerrillos Road on Second Street is **Second Street Studios,** an industrial-looking two-story complex of various-sized workspaces designed for artists. This is where the city's largest concentration of artists can be found. Other art-related businesses, from gemstone, granite, and marble dealers to sculptural welders (not to mention a microbrewery), occupy surrounding buildings. The **Cloud Cliff Bakery and Coffee Shop** in the studio complex is a popular artists' café scene.

At the end of the commercial district, where Cerrillos Road meets Rodeo Road, **Villa Linda Mall** is the city's largest indoor shopping center, with the lion's share of chain retailers. Still referred to as the "new mall," the mall changed the character of the downtown area when it opened in the late 1980s and lured several major department stores away from the historic district and De Vargas Mall (the "old mall"), among them Sears Roebuck, whose old store on Lincoln Street was soon transformed into a complex of upscale restaurants and designer clothing shops.

Past the mall, Cerrillos Road crosses Rodeo Road, continues to an on-ramp for Interstate 25 and then onward into the open ranchlands of southern Santa Fe County, where it passes the state penitentiary and goes on to the villages of Cerrillos and Madrid. As it crosses Cerrillos, Rodeo becomes Airport

Second Street's controversial "gargoyle." *Photograph by Richard Harris.*

Buddhist stupa. *Photograph by Richard Harris.*

Road and runs west for a mile or so, past fields, industrial lots, and the gleaming gold stupa that marks the entrance to the **KSK Tibetan Buddhist Center,** and ends at **Santa Fe Municipal Airport.** The airport, with its single 8300-foot runway, is classified as a commercial airport by the Federal Aviation Administration but offers only minimal passenger service and hardly justifies the grandiose boulevard that leads to it. Another wide, well-lit boulevard heads north near the Cerrillos–Interstate 25 junction only to end abruptly after a mile or so in an aimless maze of dirt roads. This is the first phase of a planned **Northwest Bypass** that is planned to skirt the city, connecting the interstate with U.S. Highway 84/285 northbound and relieving traffic congestion on St. Francis Drive.

Agua Fria Street, the original Spanish colonial highway, parallels Cerrillos Road a few blocks to the north. A drive down this narrow street provides a cross section of Santa Fe's soul, the part that few visitors ever see. It runs through the center of the westside barrio, where small adobe homes and apartment buildings date back to the railroad era, and large custom homes of imaginative design have begun to appear, as unexpected as UFOs. Here and there are neighborhood businesses: an old-fashioned grocery store, an in-home beauty parlor, even a hay and feed store. Agua Fria Street continues past **Frenchy's Field Park,** where a paved walking trail winds through a broad open field that looks like dry weeds in the winter but blossoms into a technicolor display of wildflowers in the summer. It was open country out past the edge of town not long ago. The road runs along the north side of the

Siler Road light industrial and warehouse district, also empty space until recently, and suddenly enters a fragment of rural New Mexico.

The **village of Agua Fria** was an independent community two hours' walk from Santa Fe when it was established in the early nineteenth century. Today, this area of old adobe houses and family farms is bounded by the city on three sides. In 1995, the County Commission declared Agua Fria a "traditional historic district," a status that precludes its annexation and urbanization by the city.

The centerpiece of Agua Fria village is **San Isidro Church** (Route 6, Box 111, Agua Fria Street), a classic white stuccoed adobe church built in 1835, beautifully preserved and still in use. Recalling earlier days when Agua Fria was an independent farming village, the church is dedicated to San Isidro the Ploughman, patron saint of farmers and protector of crops. According to legend, an angel came to plow San Isidro's fields so that he could spend more time in prayer. The Feast of San Isidro, May 15, commonly called "His Day of Goodwill," is an important religious observance in the village.

Agua Fria Street affords panoramic views across the Santa Fe River gulch to the scattered, semirural residential neighborhood in the northwest hills. The area can be reached via **Alameda Street,** which wanders west into a tangle of unpaved roads that do not go anywhere. Agua Fria Street seems to end out past the old village in the maze of trailer parks and dirt truck roads to industrial sites near the airport that mark the western outskirts of the city. With perseverence, detours, and preferably four-wheel-drive, however, it is possible to find the forest access road that traces the old Camino Real for 8 miles across uninhabited La Bajada Mesa to the place where old-time wagon trains made their steep switchback descent to the Río Grande almost four centuries ago.

SANTA FE'S FUTURE

A city that often seems obsessed by the past, Santa Fe's future has seemed a little murky ever since Albuquerque surpassed it as an economic center in the 1880s. Almost nothing about twentieth-century Santa Fe could have been foreseen by the city's residents of 100 years ago, who were busy talking about tearing down those unsightly old adobe buildings, such as the Palace of the Governors. From the present vantage, it is as challenging to imagine twenty-first-century Santa Fe as to know the mysterious Anasazi civilization of 1000 years ago. It doesn't require a psychic, however, to predict the course of development in terms of present trends.

The 1996 population of Santa Fe County was about 110,000, of which 70,000 live within the city limits. Over the past 25 years, the city-and-county population has grown at an average annual rate of 3.48 percent. This growth rate is 40 percent higher than New Mexico as a whole, although considerably less than the neighboring states of Arizona and Colorado. Population growth within the city limits during the same period was only 1.65 percent per year, and this rate has been declining. In other words, most population growth is taking place in outlying areas. Based on these demographic trends, city and county government analysts forecast that the county population may reach 150,000 or more by the year 2015, of which anywhere from 99,000 to 114,000 will live within the city limits.

The main flaw in this projection is the water supply. In 1996, a drought year because almost no snow fell in the southern Sangre de Cristos during the previous winter, the water company's reservoirs on the Santa Fe River came so close to running dry that severe penalty charges were imposed to reduce water consumption by 25 percent. The crisis lent credibility to forecasts by city planners that given the present growth rate, the water supply would be inadequate to support the population in a *normal* year by 1999. Santa Fe has no water rights to the Río Grande, which is reserved for agricultural use in southern New Mexico and Texas. Wells on Buckman Road near the Río Grande have been used increasingly to supplement the water supply from the Santa Fe River, but it now appears that the aquifer is being tapped to its limits and will not support more large wells.

The currently favored solution to the water crisis is for the city, which recently acquired the formerly private water company, to issue municipal bonds and buy unused water rights to the Chama River from the Jicarilla Apache Reservation or other places in northern New Mexico, where the population is declining. The theory, which raises some tricky legal questions, is that since the Chama River flows *into* the Río Grande, Santa Fe could draw water from the Río Grande—even though it would be the same water that is now reserved for other users to the south. Analysts estimate that this approach could accommodate a population of up to 90,000 on the city water system. Growth in the county would depend on the availability of individual well permits.

Buying up out-of-town water rights is opposed by a sizable antigrowth faction, which sees the water limitation as a desirable restraint on land development. The antidevelopment plan for dealing with the water crisis is to tighten land use restrictions to the point where population growth would become virtually impossible; but this option poses problems of its own. It would accelerate the rise in housing costs, exacerbating the shortage of affordable housing and the exodus of long-time residents to Española and Chimayo. A side effect would be to speed the increase in Anglo population and decline in Spanish population that has taken place in Santa Fe in recent years.

Assuming that population growth will continue at some level, the main thrust of future development will depend on the route of the planned Northwest Bypass, which would create easy access to large expanses of open land near the Río Grande and the Buckman Road wells, where water delivery

Fine Arts Museum of New Mexico, c. 1919. An excellent rendition of ancient Spanish and pueblo buildings. *Photograph courtesy Museum of New Mexico, neg. 28861.*

would be easiest. Completion of the $80 million bypass project seems to hinge on U.S. Department of Energy funding, based on the city's contention that the bypass is needed before the DOE can safely transport nuclear waste from Los Alamos National Laboratory to the proposed Waste Isolation Pilot Project (WIPP) in southeastern New Mexico, the opening of which has been blocked by community activists since 1987. To complicate the situation further, no right-of-way has been arranged for the northern portion of the bypass. The obvious routes cut through either an Indian reservation or an exclusive suburb in the piñon-covered hills northwest of town. Both have expressed grave reservations about being on a nuclear waste route.

Especially in the northwest sector, new housing construction has taken the form of exclusive custom homes, which add more to the property tax base relative to the demand for public utilities than tract homes or apartments do. Many locals are outspoken in their opposition to this approach to growth because the lack of affordable housing has increasingly skewed the city's demographic toward independently wealthy, often part-time residents. Although this is not necessarily a bad thing for a community with an uncertain private-sector economy, it is another factor pushing the cost of living upward.

The most ambitious experiment so far in providing an alternative to custom home development is Frijoles Village, a controversial plan that recently won approval from the city/county extraterritorial zoning commission. The subdivision, to be located northwest of town near the planned bypass, would place 433 homes on 139 acres while leaving 205 acres as community areas, including parks, a plaza, a school site, and a wilderness belt. Five percent of the residential lots would be set aside for low- to moderate-income housing, and all homes would be within 7 minutes' walk of a central plaza. The project would be built jointly by 14 developers, who propose to establish a private county water company and purchase Río Grande water rights from agricultural users in southern New Mexico. The main obstacle is opposition by residents of the northwest area, where all present home sites are 2.5 acres or larger. They view Frijoles Village as a scheme to put higher-density housing in the area, which they fear would lower existing property values.

Economic development is also a factor shaping Santa Fe's future. Today, Santa Fe's five largest employers—the state of New Mexico, the Santa Fe School District, the federal government, St. Vincent's Hospital and the city of Santa Fe—account for about 25 percent of all jobs. The largest private sector employers include Wal-Mart (300 jobs), the Eldorado Hotel (270 jobs), and Furr's Supermarkets (260 jobs). About half of all jobs in Santa Fe—or two-thirds of private-sector jobs—are in companies with fewer than 20 employees. City forecasts of population growth as high as 40,000 additional residents

Delgado Bridge after a thunderstorm. Water rarely flows in the Santa Fe River. *Photograph by Richard Harris.*

by the year 2015 are accompanied by optomistic projections of 40 percent increases in both government and tourist industry employment—a questionable assumption at best. The recent trend has been toward streamlining state government, and the number of overnight visitors to Santa Fe has remained virtually unchanged during the 1990s. It is true that Santa Fe's artistic community back in the 1920s would certainly have dismissed the prospect of 200 art galleries as a fantasy, and early hotel entrepreneurs such as Fred Harvey and Conrad Hilton would have scoffed at the absurd thought of a hospitality industry that could accommodate up to 85,000 tourists a month. Still, one must wonder where 40 percent more tourists could possibly find parking places within walking distance of the Plaza.

The city has put considerable effort into attracting industry to Santa Fe without a great deal of success. Some officials have hoped that the proximity of Los Alamos National Laboratory would stimulate new industries capitalizing on the lab's highly touted technology-sharing programs, but these high-tech companies have not materialized. Santa Fe is a disadvantageous location for most manufacturing companies because remoteness from major urban markets means higher shipping costs. The lack of postgraduate educational opportunities also discourages technology companies from locating in Santa Fe.

Perhaps the most promising direction for future economic growth in Santa Fe lies with information-based industries. Book and magazine publishing is the fastest-growing industry in Santa Fe today. A growing number of Santa Fe residents are engaged in software development and related occupations where telecommuting—working for a distant employer from home via computer modem—is an increasingly widespread practice. An airline recently announced that it was considering Santa Fe as a site for its central reservation service, which would create 400 to 600 local jobs, instantly making it one of the largest private-sector employers in the city.

Whatever shape Santa Fe's future may take, there is little doubt that Santa Fe–style architectural design will remain in vogue and keep on evolving through creative experimentation. Enchanted by the novelty, newcomers quickly develop at least as much enthusiasm as longtime residents for Santa Fe's low-rise earthtone buildings with *vigas* and portals, not to mention other local eccentricities, such as smothering breakfast eggs in green chile, wearing cowboy boots with evening gowns, arriving 10 or 20 minutes late for appointments, answering the phone with a cheerful "Bueno, hey!"—all the trappings of a unique twentieth-century frontier town where provincialism still counts for something.

7

Northern
Santa Fe County

N orth of the city lies a vast expanse of empty land sloping down from the Sangre de Cristo and Jemez mountain ranges to the Río Grande. The area contains little private property; it is divided between state and federal public lands and five Indian Pueblo grants. Most of the present-day pueblos were established in the seventeenth century. At that time the Pueblo people had already been living in the same areas for centuries, but in pre-Columbian times most villages had been built on high plateaus and in hidden canyons where they were easier to defend.

With the arrival of Spanish soldiers, the Pueblo people shared in the benefits of military protection against nomadic marauders. Meanwhile, Franciscan missionaries established their churches in open areas near the Río Grande and its tributaries, where crop irrigation was easier, and smaller, scattered Indian communities were gradually consolidated into these new pueblos.

Today, most northern Indian pueblos consist of an old village center built around a large dance plaza with one or two ceremonial kivas and a Catholic mission church. Modern houses, from handbuilt adobe homes to plain brown stucco government housing units radiate outward from the town center. The ruins of a large ancestral pueblo, typically occupied from around 1300 to 1600, usually stand from 1 mile to 7 or 8 miles from the present pueblo, and smaller unexcavated ruins are found throughout the area. Each present-day pueblo owns a land grant, similar in legal status to a reservation

Opposite: Shrine to the Virgin of Guadalupe, Iglesia de Santa Cruz, Santa Cruz, N.M. *Photograph by Richard Harris.*

except that the pueblo originally acquired it by grant from the king of Spain instead of by treaty with the U.S. government. Land near the river is used to grow corn and other crops in communal fields, and many pueblos, including Nambe, Tesuque, and Santa Clara, maintain fishing lakes or other recreational areas in scenic areas of their grants, charging admission fees to non-Indian users. Large areas of the tribal grants, however, are arid, hilly land that is used only for such purposes as gathering clay for pottery and providing open range for tribally owned, semiwild horses.

The roads of northern Santa Fe County form an hourglass pattern. All routes north from the capital merge with U.S. Highway 84/285 before reaching Camel Rock on the Tesuque Pueblo grant. There is no back road or scenic detour between Tesuque Pueblo and Pojoaque, where the highway fans out into routes that head west toward Los Alamos and Bandelier National Monument, north toward Taos, and east toward the villages in the wooded foothills of the Sangre de Cristos. The county itself is bounded by the Río Grande on the west, the high peaks of the Pecos Wilderness on the east, and—with slight adjustments for political reasons—the Santa Cruz River on the north.

In Santa Fe County, the Indian pueblos west of the highway, near the Río Grande, have shunned intermarriage with non-Indians for centuries. Catholicism has been tolerated but not widely embraced. Customs and ceremonies at these pueblos are thought by anthropologists to represent a continuation of postclassic Pueblo and Anasazi civilization. In communities east of the highway—Pojoaque, Nambe, and the now predominantly Hispanic community of Chimayó—harsh living conditions during colonial times brought more interdependence between Spanish settlers and Indians, and this was the only area in New Mexico where the two groups intermarried.

The effects of this cultural merging are reflected in the area's agriculture, weaving, building methods, language, spiritual faith, and family life. It is here, in the pueblos and villages of the Sangre de Cristo foothills, that many uniquely New Mexican traditions have their origins. Ironically, communities in this area have been slow to accept Anglo newcomers. Since the mid-1980s, however, a few artists, writers, and modern-day pioneers have learned to adapt to the old ways and rhythms of village life, confident that their blue-eyed families, art studios, and small bed and breakfasts will become an integral part of the community in only four or five generations.

DRIVING TOUR OF NORTHERN SANTA FE COUNTY

An exploration of northern Santa Fe County fits in with a day trip to any of several major destinations farther north, such as Bandelier National Monument, Abiquiu, or Taos. These and other options are described later in the chapter.

The village of **Tesuque,** located 7 miles north of town, has become one of the most desirable places to live in the Santa Fe area. Separated from the city and the main highway by high, piñon-covered ridges, Tesuque has a secluded feel. Apple orchards and the natural cottonwood bosque that lines Tesuque Creek make for lush greenery in the summer months. Many homes near the village are valued in the millions of dollars, and most of the motion picture and television celebrities who make their homes-away-from-Hollywood in the Santa Fe area choose to live in Tesuque. Among the mansions, though, are many modest old adobe homes, some of them centuries old. The village was founded in 1740, and the valley was farmed by Franciscan monks from the mission at nearby Tesuque Pueblo a century earlier.

You can reach Tesuque village on State Route 590, a loop road that branches off to the east from U.S. Highway 84/285 and rejoins the main highway 3 miles farther north near Tesuque Pueblo. A more scenic route, though, is to follow Bishop's Lodge Road, an extension of Washington Avenue, north from downtown. Most Tesuque homes are along this road, as is one of the Santa Fe area's most unique sightseeing attractions, **Shidoni Art Foundry,** where artists come from around the world to cast large works in bronze. Extensive, parklike gardens serve as an open-air gallery for a constantly changing assortment of 40 or 50 statues and metal sculptures. The gardens are open to the public daily. Visitors can watch bronze pourings on Saturdays. The indoor contemporary gallery doubles as a community center where village residents hold public meetings and events. A mile or so farther on, where Bishop's Lodge Road meets SR 590, Tesuque's only two commercial buildings mark the village center. **The Tesuque Market,** part small-town general store

El Nido. *Photograph by Richard Harris.*

and part gourmet deli and café, is one of the most fascinating places in the Santa Fe area to linger over a latté and watch (or meet) an intriguing assortment of locals. Nearby, **El Nido Restaurant** (the name means "The Nest") offers fine dining in a nineteenth-century adobe hacienda that is reputed to have been used as a house of prostitution in the 1920s.

Tesuque Pueblo is on the other side of Highway 84/285 from the village of Tesuque, along the same stream, which changes designations from Tesuque Creek to the Río Tesuque or Tesuque River as it passes the pueblo. Originally known as *Te-Tsu-Geh,* meaning "Cottonwood Tree Place" in the Tewa language still spoken at most Indian pueblos north of Santa Fe, the pueblo dates back to the fourteenth century and was visited by conquistador Francisco Vásquez de Coronado in 1540. As the nearest Indian pueblo to Santa Fe, it was one of the first places where Franciscan missionaries established a church in the early seventeenth century. The mission, San Lorenzo de Tesuque, was completely destroyed in the Pueblo Revolt of 1680, and after the Spanish reconquest, a new mission was established under the name San Diego de Tesuque. The mission church and monastery at the pueblo were abandoned in the early nineteenth century and subsequently collapsed, but the original sacristy was restored in the 1920s to become the church that faces the Plaza today. About 400 people live in Tesuque Pueblo, which is one of the most traditional pueblos in New Mexico. The Tesuque land grant encompasses 17,024 acres, including two detached sacred sites in the Sangre de Cristo Mountains northwest of the Santa Fe Ski Basin. U.S. Highway 84/285 runs diagonally across the grant for about 6 miles north of Trader Jack's Flea Market.

Although the people of Tesuque Pueblo have a reputation for being inhospitable to non-Indian visitors to the pueblo itself, they operate an assortment of commercial enterprises along the main highway, including the Camel Rock RV Campground and the **Camel Rock Casino.** The 60,000-square-foot building with its grandiose porte-cochére and vast parking lot, one of 12 operated by Pueblo and Apache tribes in New Mexico, was completed in 1994. Soon afterward, a series of state supreme court decisions invalidated the compacts that had purported to give the tribes the legal right to conduct casino gambling. The Indian casinos continued to operate in defiance of the law until March of 1997, when the state legislature voted down a bill that would have legalized them. Then, in a surprise move in the final hours of the legislative session, the bill was revived and passed—by one vote. Whether gambling is good or bad for New Mexico, the benefits to Tesuque Pueblo have been tangible. The center of the old pueblo, which had fallen into disrepair, has been beautifully restored. The ancient ceremonial kiva and buildings surrounding the dance plaza have new protective coatings of adobe, giving the pueblo a just-like-new look. Gaming proceeds have also financed expansion of **Tesuque Natural Farms,** a pueblo enterprise that grows specialty crops such as amaranth, the staple grain of the pre-Columbian Aztecs, and breeds llamas.

Camel Rock marks the entrance to Tesuque Pueblo. *Cameras are prohibited at the pueblo itself.* *Photograph by Richard Harris.*

Camel Rock Casino. *Photograph by Richard Harris.*

The pueblo also operates a fishing lake and riding stables, and parts of the reservation have been used as locations for motion picture and television productions. A permit is required for photography or sketching at the pueblo, and photographing the interior of the church and most dances is strictly prohibited. Outsiders are not allowed inside the kiva at any time. Major ceremonial dances that are open to the public include the San Antonio Feast Day corn dance on the first weekend in June, the San Diego Feast Day dances on November 12, and matachina dances on Christmas Day.

Eight miles north of Tesuque Pueblo is **Pojoaque,** the smallest Indian pueblo in New Mexico in terms of population. The name is a Spanish corruption of the original Tewa name, *P'o-Suwae-Geh,* meaning "Drinking Water Place." (Ironically, one of Pojoaque's major problems today is groundwater pollution, which makes well water unsafe to drink.) The pueblo's location at the confluence of the Tesuque, Pojoaque, and Nambe rivers made it a natural crossroads in ancient times. Another pueblo, **Cuyamungue** (from the Tewa for "Stone-Throwing Place"), was located about 2 miles to the south. A smallpox epidemic around 1900 all but wiped out the population of Pojoaque and Cuyamungue, and the few survivors abandoned the original pueblos, which deteriorated and collapsed. In 1932, a group of 14 descendents of the Pojoaque people obtained a federal land patent on the original 11,593-acre grants to Pojoaque and Cuyamungue pueblos and began commercial development along the highway, creating a shopping center to serve the population of area ranches and Indian pueblos and in the process eradicating all remnants of the old adobe pueblo.

Today, Pojoaque has restaurants, a supermarket, a hardware store, a branch bank, service stations, a drugstore, a video rental store, a liquor store, a candle factory, and a medical and professional office complex, all owned by non-Indian investors who lease their land from the tribal government. Most of the pueblo's approximately 150 members live in a trailer park on the edge of the commercial district. The **Poeh Cultural Center and Museum,** built in 1990 near the south end of town, serves as the main visitors' center for all of the Tewa-speaking pueblos and also houses the Pojoaque Pueblo Indian Vocational Education Program, open to members of all the Tewa pueblos, with a curriculum that focuses on traditional pottery making, stone sculpture, and business administration. At the north end of town, the former high school has been converted into **Cities of Gold Casino.** One of the largest casinos in the state, Cities of Gold employs 550 people—more than three times as many as the total number of men, women, and children who are members of the pueblo—and occupies a central role in planning for future economic development. Incidentally, Pojoaque was the first pueblo to elect a woman governor.

The surrounding pueblo land grant, much of which is a maze of arid badlands known as **El Barranco,** is not used for agriculture or livestock grazing, although the pueblo grazes a small herd of bison on its land as part of the

Reconstructed Pojoaque Pueblo. *Photograph by Richard Harris.*

Intertribal Bison Cooperative. El Barranco, also called the Santa Fe Marl, is said to be one of the most nearly perfect exposed seabeds in existence; its treacherous cliffs and ravines trapped numerous mammoths and other Pleiocene-era mammals whose fossil remains have been dug up and shipped to museums, especially the Museum of Natural History in New York City.

The crossroads at Pojoaque presents a choice of three diverging routes, all rewarding. U.S. Highway 84/285 continues northward from Pojoaque, leaving Santa Fe County near the city limits of Española. Another major highway, State Route 502, heads west past San Ildefonso Pueblo and across the Río Grande, then leaves Santa Fe County just past a fork in the highway where one road goes to the town of Los Alamos and the other to Bandelier National Monument. A smaller but no less scenic highway, State Route 503 leads east from Pojoaque and eventually veers north, passing Nambe Pueblo and winding its way northward to the large village of Chimayo on the northern boundary of Santa Fe County.

If you choose to go west on State Route 502, consider taking a detour on the old river road that parallels the main highway on the north. To reach it, turn north (right) on either of two unpaved roads marked to **Jacona** and Jaconita; each joins the road along the Pojoaque River in a quarter of a mile. Proceed west (left) on the narrow paved road. Almost completely surrounded by the Pojoaque and San Ildefonso Pueblo grants, the non-Indian settlements along the river date back to before 1700. Pojoaque Pueblo had been temporarily abandoned in 1696 following an unsuccessful uprising against the Spanish settlers, and the portion of the pueblo grant that was most suitable for agriculture was transferred to Captain Jacinto Pelaez as a reward for his leadership in quelling the rebellion. Pelaez transferred the Jacona portion of the grant, which had been the site of another small pueblo abandoned at the same time and never reoccupied, to his brother-in-law, Ignacio de Roybal, in 1705. Roybal's hacienda, much altered enlarged over the centuries, still stands near the junction of the Jacona road and the river road. Soon the Indians returned to Pojoaque Pueblo and asserted their claim to their old land grant, and title to the land along the river remained in dispute in the courts of Spain, Mexico, and the United States for more than two centuries. It was finally given to the non-Indian ranch owners in 1937 in a quiet-title* suit under the law of adverse possession. (Irrigation rights to the water in the Pojoaque River became the subject of yet another court battle that continued until the mid-1980s and employed more than 100 lawyers in Santa Fe.) Before the 1937 decision, title to land in Jaconita, Jacona, and El Rancho could not be legally transferred. Instead, it was passed down from generation to generation. Parcels of the land were given to newlyweds, and family lands were typically subdivided between all male heirs each time an owner died. Since water rights depended on river frontage, the land was subdivided into narrow strips as little as 50 feet wide at the river bank and as much as a mile long, and the villages grew to a population of several hundred. Shortly after the 1937 quiet-title action, the Roybal family sold the original hacienda to author Jon Glidden, who wrote western novels under the pen name of Peter Dawson. Other adobe houses along the river were bought in the 1940s by author Edith Warner, sculptor Allan Clark, and painter Cady Wells, the forerunners of the writers and artists who make up a sizable percentage of the population in the area today.

Continuing south along the river road, Jacona merges seamlessly into **El Rancho,** a larger village with a community center, a bar, and a recently refurbished Catholic church. Unlike Jacona, El Rancho has houses on both sides of the river. Those on the north side are reached by a long one-lane bridge. Although the Pojoaque River is less than 10 feet wide and only a few inches deep most of the time, it meanders along an expanse of bare sand more than 100 yards across. Once or twice a year, a flash flood swells the river until it fills the entire sand bed, running deep enough to carry uprooted pine trees along and drown cattle. Such floods sometimes wash the bridge away, too, stranding residents on the north bank with no way to come and go except to drive across the soft sand and through the river once it subsides.

Past El Rancho, the pavement ends as the river road enters the **San Ildefonso Pueblo** grant. Known to the people who live there as *Po-Woh-Ge-Oweenge* ("Where the Water Cuts Through") because of its location where the

---

*A quiet-title action is a suit for a judicial decree that the plaintiff owns title to real property; it "quiets," or lays to rest claims of others—known or unknown—to the property.

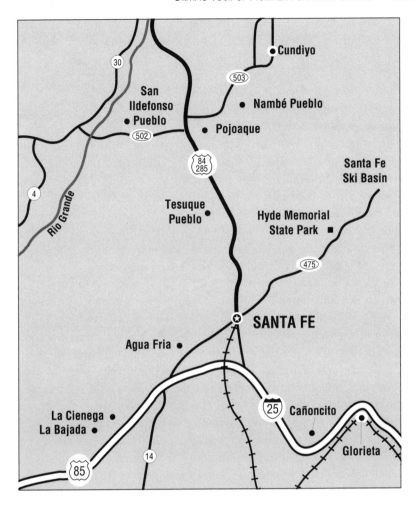

Northern Santa Fe County

Pojoaque River flows into the Río Grande, San Ildefolso is the largest Indian pueblo in Santa Fe County, with a population of about 800. It was established around 1600 by descendents of the people who built the thirteenth-century pueblos now known as Frijoles Ruin and Tsankawi Ruin at Bandelier National Monument. Franciscan friars built a mission church and monastery at San Ildefonso in 1617. The mission operated in harmony with the pueblo for nearly 60 years, but both were ultimately torn apart by violence. In 1675, the father superior of the monastery at San Ildefonso accused tribal healers of bewitching him and his brother and sister-in-law. Forty-seven Indian men were arrested for conspiracy in the witchcraft plot, and as punishment all were sold into slavery except four, who were hanged at other Río Grande pueblos to set an example. The incident sparked hostility between the Indians and the Spanish, which culminated in the Pueblo Revolt of 1680, during which the missionaries at San Ildefonso were murdered. When Governor De Vargas returned to reconquer New Mexico 12 years later, the people of San Ildefonso moved to a new pueblo on top of Black Mesa, the 1000-foot-high volcanic butte that towers above the present village. De Vargas laid seige to the mesatop pueblo in 1694 and forced the Indians to allow missionaries back into the pueblo. Two years later, during an uprising of Pueblo settlements in the Pojoaque area, the San Ildefonso people locked the missionaries in the church and set it on fire, burning them alive, and once more retreated to the pueblo on top of the mesa. As before, Spanish soldiers laid seige to Black Mesa and forced the people to surrender and accept the missionaries. A new church was built in the early eighteenth century and used until 1900, when it was replaced by a very plain adobe chapel. In 1968, pueblo members finished the present church, a replica of the original 1617 mission church.

Today, the pueblo on top of Black Mesa is in ruins, and the mesa itself—known to the Indians as Tunyo—is a sacred site forbidden to non-Indians. According to Tewa legend, the mesa is the home of Tsabiyo, a mythical giant who is used by Tewa mothers to frighten children into obedience. In some Tewa pueblos, a man playing the role of Tsabiyo appears after fall harvest time, armed with a whip, to punish people who have broken pueblo laws during the year.

Although the old adobe buildings surrounding San Ildefonso's two dance plazas are overshadowed by extensive housing developments of modern vintage, the people of the pueblo continue to cling to ancient traditions. Corn farming is a main occupation. The pueblo is best known for its arts and crafts —embroidery, silversmithing, watercolor painting, moccasin making, and especially pottery. Its distinctive raku-like black pottery, developed in 1919 by María and Julian Martinez, whose work highlights many museum collections, is the most highly valued Pueblo pottery of the twentieth century. The pueblo has an arts and crafts museum, and a number of residents operate pottery shops in their homes. The major ceremonial feast day is held on January 22 and 23, when dancers dressed as animals conduct private nighttime ceremonies on top of Black Mesa and then descend in a procession at dawn, continuing the animal dances throughout the day. Other major dances include a corn dance to bring rain on San Antonio Feast Day in early June and a thanksgiving corn dance at harvest time in early September. San Ildefonso is unique among modern pueblos in having two separate kiva clans that alternate dances on ceremonial days. Anthropologists believe that multiple-kiva clans were far more common among the ancient Anasazi and pre-Columbian Pueblo people. Photography is restricted. Except on ceremonial days, all visitors to the pueblo must register with the tribal governor's office before walking around either the pueblo or tribal lands. Across the highway from the pueblo, on the east side of the Río Grande near the site of a postclassic pueblo ruin called Boye that was still occupied when Don Juan de Oñate arrived in 1898, a low rock ridge displays some of the finest examples of ancient shamanic petroglyphs found in the Tewa region.

After crossing the Río Grande and climbing to an intermediate level of the Pajarito Plateau, the highway divides. State Route 502 continues up a sheer canyon wall to Los Alamos, while SR 4 heads south to the bedroom community of White Rock. Both towns are in Los Alamos County, New Mexico's smallest and newest county, which separated from Rio Arriba County in 1949 to free these communities, made up of Anglo newcomers, from political domination by the traditional, mainly Hispano population of the much larger Rio Arriba County. Just short of the county line is the **Tsankawi** unit of Bandelier National Monument. This 7-square-mile area, detached from the main national monument unit to the south, contains the ruins of a fourteenth-century pueblo reached by hiking an ancient foot trail along the side of a cliff. Unlike the ruins in the main part of the national monument, Tsankawi is completely unexcavated, and such artifacts as pottery shards and fragments of stone tools lie scattered among the ruins. Set on a promontory, the ruins overlook the Río Grande, San Ildefonso Pueblo, and Black Mesa.

Maria Martinez firing pottery, 1950. *Photograph by Tyler Dingee, courtesy Museum of New Mexico, neg. 73449,*

Pottery shards at Tsankawi. *Photograph by Richard Harris.*

Driving east from Pojoaque on State Route 503, you will pass through the village of Nambe, consisting of mainly modern homes and a large dairy farm, before reaching the turnoff to **Nambé Pueblo.** The name *Nambé* means "Mound of Earth in the Corner" in the Tewa language and refers to the location of an older pueblo, now a barely visible ruin, about a mile downstream from the present pueblo on a rounded rise overlooking Pojoaque Creek. This pueblo has been inhabited since about A.D. 1300 and has a present-day population of 650. It was the site of one of the first Franciscan missions in New Mexico, established around 1600. The original church was destroyed in the Pueblo Revolt of 1680, and a new one was not built until 49 years later. The 1729 mission church lasted until 1909, when it suffered structural damage during replacement of the roof and collapsed during a rainstorm.

Of approximately 200 structures that formed the pueblo when the early missionaries arrived, fewer than 20 have survived. The modern pueblo consists mainly of individual houses set well apart to form a fairly large village. Unlike most of the other Tewa pueblos, the people of Nambé often intermarried with their Spanish neighbors during the colonial era, and their traditions represent a mixture of Indian and Norteño beliefs. Nambé is one of the few Indian pueblos where photographing ceremonial dances is sometimes permitted. Dances are held on Christmas, Easter, and the Fourth of July, as well as on October 3–4, the Feast of St. Francis, the pueblo's patron saint.

Nambé Pueblo is on a mountainous 19,075-acre land grant that adjoins the Pecos Wilderness. A primary source of tribal income is the use fees that visitors pay to fish in Nambé Lake or picnic by Nambé Falls. A small herd of bison, formerly owned by the state of New Mexico and transferred to the Indians in 1996 as a budget-cutting measure, also roams the backcountry of the pueblo grant. The pueblo operates the only tour company in New Mexico owned and operated by Indians.

As it makes its way north, the road divides. State Route 503 goes west to the small, traditional hilltop village of **Cundiyó.** Alhough Cundiyó has been predominantly Spanish since its founding in 1743, the name comes from the Tewa, meaning "mound of the little bells," which was the name of a large Indian pueblo, the ruins of which are at the foot of a small rounded hill about 100 feet above the town, probably built by ancestors of the Nambé people. State Route 520 goes north to **Chimayó,** one of the largest Norteño villages, situated exactly on the Santa Fe County boundary line. Chimayó takes its name from the ancient pueblo of Tsimajó, which was located where the Santuario de Chimayó stands today. The Tewa Indian name means "obsidian," which was quarried here to make arrowheads, knives and other tools.

In the seventeenth century, Chimayó marked the eastern edge of the colony of Nuevo Mexico. Since there was no prison in the territory, petty criminals were banished to Chimayó, which served as a sort of penal colony without guards and a buffer between Spanish territory and raiding parties of nomadic Athabascans. Its inhabitants were wiped out during the Pueblo Revolt of 1680, and it was reestablished after the Spanish reconquest as a respectable village under the name San Buenaventura de Chimayó. It is the heart of a sheltered agricultural valley where apples, chile, Indian corn, and other crops are grown; much of the harvest is sold from roadside stands along the main highway in nearby Española. Sheep herding is also a key industry here, and Chimayó is famous for its wool weaving. In its early days as a place of exile, when supplies were hard to get, Chimayó's inhabitants learned how to weave wool blankets for warmth in the winter from the local Indians, who had been weaving textiles from cotton and turkey feathers for centuries. The results were utilitarian but hardly beautiful. In 1805, the Spanish governor in Santa Fe sent to the city of Saltillo, Mexico, for master weavers to teach their art to New Mexicans. The teachers, Ignacio and Juan Bazán, did not care for Santa Fe and moved to Chimayó, where they taught Saltillo-style blanket weaving to all the young men and women of the village, establishing a local tradition that has endured to the present day. The Ortega family, owners of the largest weaving shops in the village, has been practicing the craft continuously for eight generations. After the arrival of the railroad in Santa Fe, many Chimayó weavers bought commercially manufactured yarn instead of spinning it from local sheep's wool, but in recent years, as their work has gained the stature of collectible folk art, there has been a return to traditional hand spinning of local wool and use of vegetable dyes from plants gathered locally. The **Plaza del Cerro,** Chimayó's old village square, has a defensive *torreón* and surrounding wall of adobe buildings. Built in the 1740s, it is the best example in New Mexico of the fortified plazas that were designed to protect remote settlements in Spanish colonial times.

As many as 30,000 pilgrims from all over northern New Mexico line the roadsides on Good Friday as they make their way to Chimayó on foot. The **Santuario de Chimayó** is probably the most revered Catholic sacred site in New Mexico. It was built in 1814–1816 by Don Bernardo Abeyta as an act of thanksgiving. According to legend, while deathly ill and in a delerium of fever, a vision drew Abeyta to this spot, where he was instantly cured. He then saw a light emanating from the ground and, digging a small hole, discovered a crucifix with a dark Christ figure, which local people interpreted as a miraculous sign comparable to the Black Christ of Esquipulas, Guatemala, or the dark-skinned Virgin of Guadalupe. It is said that springs near the spot had long been considered sacred by the local Indians for their healing properties, and that penitente brothers used to throw earth from the hole in the ground where the crucifix was found into a fire to calm thunderstorms. Today, the faithful of northern New Mexico come to Chimayó to be healed as European Catholics might go to Lourdes. Crutches, amulets, and handwritten prayers of thanks cover the walls of the small anteroom to the left of the church altar, where flickering candles illuminate the crucifix Don Bernardo found, and *curanderas*—village healers—can often be heard in murmured rituals beside *el pozito,* the "little well" of holy earth in the smaller room to the rear. At no other place can visitors experience so profoundly the intensity of northern New Mexico's provincial Catholicism.

The Santuario de Chimayó is a quaint, perfectly preserved adobe mission church with twin square bell towers and a wide main portal and a gallery-level covered porch reached by a doorway from the choir loft. Locals like to point out that it was built without nails, as if this were itself a miracle. Inside, a handpainted altar screen provides the backdrop for a collection of hand-carved wooden *bultos,* or saints' images, and a 6-foot Black Christ figure. It is an enlarged version of Don Bernardo's original crucifix and also—miraculously, some say—an almost exact replica of the Black Christ of Esquipulas. (The revered Guatemalan Christ figure was carved in 1595, so it is quite possible that the crucifix Don Bernardo found was a miniature of that one.)

The Santuario de Chimayó was privately owned by the Abeyta family until 1929, when author Mary Austin, a chronicler of the penitente faith in northern New Mexico, persuaded an anonymous donor to give $6000 to the Society for the Preservation and Restoration of New Mexico Churches, which purchased the property from the Abeytas and gave it to the Catholic church. Nearby, just beyond the Santuario parking lot and the little *ristra* shop with the sign that reads "Chimayó Holy Chile—Yes, It's Heavenly," is the privately

Santuario de Chimayo. *Photograph by Richard Harris.*

owned **Chapel of the Santo Niño de Atocha.** Pregnant mothers go there to have their unborn children blessed. Local legend says that the Santo Niño Perdido, or Holy Lost Child, whose image adorns the chapel's altar, comes to life at night and wanders the roads helping the poor, so it is traditional for those who seek the child saint's blessing to bring offerings of baby shoes or doll shoes. Toy-size miniature churches decorate the wall around the small atrium in front of the chapel.

State Route 76, the main road through Chimayó, runs northeast into the foothills of the Sangre de Cristos and is commonly known as the High Road to Taos. If you turn west instead, SR 76 will return you to U.S. Highway 84/285 at Española, a large, busy, and not particularly charming crossroads town just over the county line in Rio Arriba County. The slow 10-mile route between Chimayó and Española takes you through the village of **Santa Cruz,** where one of the largest adobe mission churches in New Mexico faces the plaza. The well-preserved church dates back to 1733, but the village is much older.

The second-oldest Spanish settlement in New Mexico, established by the Oñate expedition in 1598, Santa Cruz held a strategic position along the main

road between Santa Fe and Taos for three centuries before the modern highway rechanneled traffic through Española. In 1807, U.S. Army captain Zebulon
Pike was escorted through northern New Mexico after Spanish soldiers arrested his expedition as a spies during their exploration of Colorado. Pike's journal records that Santa Cruz then had a population of 2000—the largest city in
the north, only slightly smaller than the capital.

In August 1837, Santa Cruz mayor Juan Esquival joined other Norteño
leaders in a revolt known as the Chimayó Rebellion against the Mexican government. The Mexican territorial governor in Santa Fe mounted a force of 200
men for a disciplinary expedition, but when they reached Santa Cruz and met
the rebel army, many of the Mexican soldiers deserted and the governor's army
was reduced to 23 survivors, who fled back to Santa Fe. The next day, the governor fled for Mexico City but made only 20 miles before meeting a group of
disgruntled Indians from Santo Domingo, who killed him and looted his
belongings. The governor's head was hacked off and carried back to Santa
Cruz, where it was displayed on a stake as a victory trophy. The rebels took over
Santa Fe and elected Taos native José Gonzales as governor. Before any
attempt to form an independent government could be brought to fruition,
however, the Mexican army arrived in January 1838 and retook control of the
capital as Esquival and the other rebels retreated into the northern hills. No
friendlier toward U.S. authorities than Mexican ones, the people of Santa Cruz
took up arms again 10 years later, in 1847, to block American occupation
troops on their way to Taos to punish the assassins of Governor Bent. This time
they lost.

DAY TRIPS NORTH OF SANTA FE

Here are the major day-trip destinations of historical interest beyond Santa Fe
County in northern New Mexico. All driving distances and times are one-way
from Santa Fe:

BANDELIER NATIONAL MONUMENT

40 miles / 60 minutes from Santa Fe

*Take U.S. Highway 84/285 to Pojoaque, then Route 502 turning south on Route
4; OR follow the route outlined to Tesuque, Pojoaque, Jacona, El Rancho, San
Ildefonso Pueblo, and Tsankawi, continuing on Route 4 through White Rock to the
national monument entrance.*

This area of rugged canyons carved into the volcanic Pajarito Plateau was the
birthplace of Adolph Bandelier, a self-taught archaeologist who originated
the idea of excavating and stabilizing Indian ruins instead of merely looting
them for artifacts. The fourteenth-century Frijoles Ruin and associated cliff

Tuyuoni ruins, Rito de los Frijoles, Bandelier National Monument. *Photograph by Jesse L. Nusbaum, courtesy Museum of New Mexico, neg. 28693.*

dwellings and ceremonial caves up the canyon from the visitors center are the crowning achievement of Bandelier's 34 years of work. Only low walls remain of the fortress-like walled town, which once stood three stories high. The road reaches only a corner of the nearly 33,000-acre monument; the rest is wilderness. You can hike down the canyon through pine forest and along the side of colorful volcanic tuff cliffs to a pair of waterfalls above a remote part of the Río Grande or take a more ambitious all-day hike through the backcountry, crossing two other deep canyons, to the Stone Lions Shrine, a pair of reclining cougars carved from stone in ancient times and still used as a site for secret ceremonies by the descendents of the people who built the large unexcavated ruin nearby. The most popular national park unit in northern New Mexico, Bandelier National Monument can be very crowded in the summer tourist season.

217

Puye Cliff Dwellings. *Photograph by Richard Harris.*

Los Alamos

30 miles / 45 minutes from Santa Fe

Take U.S. Highway 84/285 to Pojoaque, then Route 502; OR follow the route outlined to Tesuque, Pojoaque, Jacona, El Rancho, and San Ildefonso Pueblo, continuing on Route 502 to Los Alamos.

The U.S. Department of Energy's Los Alamos National Laboratory was the birthplace of the atomic bomb during World War II. Today, despite budget cuts and an ambiguous mission, LANL continues to develop improved nuclear weapons technology, with gene mapping and geothermal energy tests as backup projects. Virtually everybody in this California suburbs–style town of 7000 sprawled across the tops of several mesas works with LANL or its employees in some capacity. Before Los Alamos was taken over by the army during the war, it was the Los Alamos Ranch School, where wealthy families from the east sent sickly sons to get healthy through outdoor living. Sharing the original log ranch school buildings with the local art center, the Los Alamos County Historical Museum tells about the old ranch days as well as the war years. There are genuine antique atomic bombs at LANL's Bradbury Science Museum.

PUYE CLIFF DWELLINGS

33 miles / 45 minutes from Santa Fe

Take U.S. Highway 84/285 to Pojoaque, then Route 502 and Route 30 to the marked turnoff; OR follow the route outlined to Tesuque, Pojoaque, Jacona, El Rancho. and San Ildefonso Pueblo, crossing the Río Grande and turning north on Route 30.

The ancestral home of the Santa Clara Pueblo people, this 740-room mesa-top pueblo and extensive cliff dwellings complex dates to the twelfth century A.D., when it was inhabited by 1500 people. The pueblo, with its reconstructed kiva, is still used by the Santa Clara people for ceremonial dances. A museum is housed in the old Harvey House, part of the 1920s Fred Harvey Tour Company, which housed guests here during overnight horseback trips from La Fonda in Santa Fe. The ruins and their setting are equal to those of Bandelier National Monument, and the crowds are smaller, although the admission price is higher. Fees for visiting the ruins and nearby Santa Clara Canyon are a major source of income for Santa Clara Pueblo, which does not operate a casino.

ESPAÑOLA

23 miles / 30 minutes from Santa Fe

Take U.S. Highway 84/285; OR follow the route outlined through Tesuque and Pojoaque.

This small city along the main highway between Santa Fe and Taos was the site of San Gabriel de los Caballeros, the first settlement in Spanish colonial New Mexico, established in 1598 by Don Juan de Oñate but subsequently abandoned. There is a commemorative monument with a statue of Oñate on the northern outskirts of town. Española itself was founded in the 1880s as a railroad town on the Denver & Rio Grande's "Chili Line." In recent years, its population has swelled with longtime Hispano residents of Santa Fe who have moved north in search of more affordable housing. Two Indian pueblos adjoin the town. Santa Clara Pueblo, known to its residents as Kha P'o (Tewa for "Valley of the Roses") is the second largest of the Tewa pueblos; its people are known for their craftsmanship in beadwork, painting, sculpture, pottery, and embroidery. Much of urban Española is on Santa Clara grant land leased from the pueblo. On the north side of town, San Juan Pueblo, known to its people as Ohkay Owingeh ("Strong People"), is the largest of the Tewa pueblos. The modern pueblo operates Ohkay Oweenge Towa Gardens Cooperative, a large farm that grows ancestral crops using traditional pueblo methods, as well as the Ohkay Casino. Española is also the U.S. headquarters of the Sikh religion, which maintains a large permanent residential and spiritual center in the southeast part of town and operates several businesses, including an auto dealership and northern New Mexico's leading security guard agency.

ABIQUIU

45 miles / 1 hour from Santa Fe
Take U.S. Highway 84/285 to Española, then follow Highway 84 northwest.

Georgia O'Keeffe, New Mexico's best-known painter, made her home next to the main plaza of this small Indian–Spanish town for more than 40 years. Located along the Río Chama, the town dates back to 1734, when it was established as a community of genízaros (Indians without tribal affiliations) to protect the Spanish colonists from marauding Apaches. Today, the town center retains its original charm (photography is prohibited on the town plaza), while ranch estates near town are the homes-away-from-home of such celebrities as actresses Shirley MacLaine and Marsha Mason, psychiatrist and bestselling author Harville Hendricks, and the King of Saudi Arabia. A few miles out of town, the former dude ranch that is now Ghost Ranch Conference Center has a paleontology museum exhibiting dinosaur skeletons found at quarries on the ranch, including the Coelophysis, New Mexico's state fossil. A road near Ghost Ranch leads to Christ in the Desert Monastery, a free-form adobe monastery established by the Benedictine order in 1964. Monks there are known for their sacred choral compositions and are among the few monks anywhere who continue the practice of copying illuminated manuscripts by hand. A short distance east of town are the ruins of Poshu'ouingue, a fifteenth-century Indian pueblo.

THE HIGH ROAD TO TAOS

75 miles / 2 hours 30 minutes from Santa Fe
Take Route 503 northeast from Pojoaque or Route 76 east from Española to where the two routes meet at Chimayó. Continue northeast on Route 76 to Picuris Pueblo, jog 6 miles east on Route 75, and continue north on Route 518 to Ranchos de Taos.

The original route linking Santa Fe with Taos, this scenic route hugs the foothills of the Sangre de Cristos as it makes its way among traditional villages and through Carson National Forest. Along the way are Las Truchas ("The Trout"), a Spanish village in a spectacular setting at the base of 13,102-foot Truchas Peak, known for its wool weaving; Las Trampas ("The Traps"), with a well-preserved and still used mission church dating back to 1751; and Picuris Pueblo, one of the oldest Indian pueblos in the region, dating back to A.D. 750. Picuris was one of the largest northern pueblos,

Truchas in winter, 1939. *Photograph courtesy Museum of New Mexico, neg. 11580.*

with a population of 5000 at the time of the Pueblo Revolt of 1680, but most residents were relocated after the Spanish reconquest. Today, Pueblo inhabitants number fewer than 350. There is a small museum, and guided walking tours of the old pueblo are available. Near Picuris Pueblo are the Spanish village of Peñasco and Santa Barbara Campground, the northern gateway to the Pecos Wilderness and the trailhead for climbing Truchas Peak.

TAOS

70 miles / 1 hour 20 minutes from Santa Fe

Take U.S. Highway 84/285 to Española and follow Route 68 north to Taos; OR follow the High Road to Taos.

The Anasazi people colonized Taos as early as A.D. 900, and the multi-story dwellings seen at present-day Taos Pueblo (known to its Tiwa-speaking inhabitants as Tua-Tah — "Our Village" —) were already in use when conquistador Hernando de Alvarado arrived in 1540. The first Franciscan mission in New Mexico was established at the pueblo in 1600, and the Spanish colonial village of Taos was founded in 1617. Following U.S. occupation, Taos was the scene of a rebellion in 1847 that started with the assassination of New

Old church tower, Taos Pueblo. *Photograph by Richard Harris.*

Mexico Territory's first Anglo governor and ended with the execution of more than 150 Indians; historians still disagree about whether the Spanish or the Indians were responsible for the revolt. Sixty-five years later, Taos once more gained prominence as the locale of the southwest's premiere writers' and artists' colony, more than a decade before the first painter showed up on the streets of Santa Fe, and today Taos is said to have more artists, galleries, and studios per capita than any other U.S. town. Besides the Indian pueblo, which is still inhabited and attracts more tourists than any other Indian community in the United States, Taos has the eighteenth-century Martinez Hacienda, the nineteenth-century Kit Carson Home and Museum, and Governor Bent Museum, the studios-turned-museums of early Taos artists Ernest Blumenschein and Nicolai Fechin, and the Millicent Rogers Museum, one of the southwest's finest private collections of Indian and Spanish colonial art works. In the winter, Taos Ski Area attracts more out-of-state visitors than any other place in New Mexico.

CHACO CULTURE NATIONAL HISTORICAL PARK

156 miles / 4 hours from Santa Fe

Take U.S. Highway 84/285 to Española, then Highway 84 through Abiquiu; turning west (left) at Abiquiu Lake, follow Route 96 through Coyote and Regina to Cuba; go north on Route 44 to Nageezi Trading Post and take the well-marked, unpaved road 26 miles west to the park.

As a day trip, this ambitious expedition means getting up at the crack of dawn and dragging back to Santa Fe, cheerfully exhausted, long after dark. Still, it deserves mention not only as the origin of today's Río Grande Pueblo Indian culture but also as the largest and most magnificent pre-Columbian city north of central Mexico. Read the next section for more about the ancient Chacoans. There is almost nothing in the way of sleeping accommodations nearby, and the campground has become overburdened, spawning several de facto recreational-vehicle campgrounds on Navajo land outside the park boundary.

NORTHERN NEW MEXICO'S INDIAN HERITAGE

American Indians have lived in New Mexico for at least 10,000 years. During the last Ice Age, mammoths and giant bison grazed the rich, green countryside just beyond the reach of the glaciers, as nomadic hunters schemed to kill them with pointed sticks or chase them over cliffs. Artifacts such as those found at Sandia Man Cave, 50 miles southwest of Santa Fe, are believed to be some of the earliest evidence of human habitation in the United States. Little

Ruins of Pueblo Bonito, Chaco Culture National Historic Park. This Pueblo was the largest multifamily residence built anywhere in the world before the 20th century. *Photograph courtesy Museum of New Mexico, neg. 48563.*

is known about these archaic people; time has eradicated all traces of them except for a few stone points and bone tool fragments.

Sometime between A.D. 250 and 800, the people of the southwest learned to grow corn, a food crop developed by the Maya Indians over a span of 2000 years from a species of Central American grass and apparently brought to the southwest by Toltec traders from central Mexico. As the hunters and gatherers settled into a more comfortable agricultural lifestyle, they traded for other Mexican crops, including squash, beans, melons, and of course, chile peppers. At first, Indian farmers lived in solitary pit houses, one- or two-room dwellings excavated about 4 feet below ground level and covered by roofs elevated several feet above the ground. It did not take the people long to learn that, in farming, cooperation equals efficiency, and little by little, formerly nomadic people were drawn together into permanent communities.

By the year 900, many Indians in the southwest were banding together to build what are known today as pueblos (the Spanish word for "village")— multifamily dwellings built around common areas used for ceremonies and communal work. The design principles of Indian pueblos were similar to Santa Fe's Spanish Pueblo Revival style, although the usual building materials were flat stones and puddled adobe. The pueblo builders of the so-called Classic Period—A.D. 900 to 1250—are now referred to as Anasazi, from the Navajo word for "enemy ancestors" (that is, ancestors of the Pueblo people, who were often seen as enemies of the Navajo).

Of the hundreds of large pueblos and cliff dwellings built by various Anasazi groups throughout the Four Corners region of New Mexico, Arizona, Utah, and Colorado, the most magnificent was at Chaco Canyon, 120 miles northwest of Santa Fe in the San Juan Basin. From archaeological evidence, Chaco appears to have been the largest pre-Columbian settlement in the southwest and probably in all of what is now the United States. Population estimates range from 3000 to 10,000 residents in this cluster of nine "great houses," the largest of which was five stories, the largest of which stood five stories high, contained 650 dwelling units and 37 kivas, and was built of more than 50 million individual sandstone "bricks." The 215,000 ponderosa pine tree trunks, many of them up to 10 inches in diameter and 50 feet long, that were used as *vigas* in the Chaco great houses had to be carried for at least 60 miles on foot. Equally impressive was the network of roads that radiated from Chaco to outlying pueblos up to 100 miles away. At least 20 such roads, each nearly 30 feet wide, ran in straight lines regardless of the terrain, surmounting sheer cliffs with hand-carved stairways and crossing deep arroyos with wood-beam ramps and scaffolds. The purpose of the roads is a mystery, since the Anasazi had neither wheeled vehicles nor horses but traveled on foot.

Agriculture, permanent towns, and trade with the Mexican Toltecs empowered the Anasazi to develop spiritual practices, knowledge of astronomy, and material wealth unknown among other pre-Columbian people north of the tropics. But around A.D. 1200, the pueblos of Chaco Canyon were suddenly abandoned, and within the next 50 years almost all other Anasazi pueblos in the southwest were also left to ruin. Scientists have proposed many theories to explain the sudden collapse of the Anasazi civilization—war, disease, famine, environmental disaster, or perhaps some change in the nature of the people's shared spiritual vision—but nobody knows the reason for sure. Virtually all the people left the Four Corners area. The Chacoans migrated to the canyons and valleys of the upper Río Grande watershed, where they built hundreds of smaller, widely dispersed pueblos and cliff dwelling complexes at sites that seem to have been chosen with defense in mind.

Around the same time that the Anasazi cities were abandoned, another major Indian migration was taking place. Small groups of nomadic Athabascan people from western Canada began a slow migration down the Front Range of the Rocky Mountains, moving southward at an average rate of about 20 miles a year. When they reached the southern tip of the Rockies in New Mexico, they encountered the wealthy, sedentary Pueblo people and began to raid them. The threat of marauding Indians from the outlands continued as a major problem facing Pueblo Indians as well as later Spanish settlers over a period of nearly 500 years.

By the fourteenth century, the Tanoan Pueblo people—ancestors of the Tewa-, Tiwa-, and Towa-speaking tribes today—had colonized the area around Santa Fe so thoroughly that several areas, including the Galisteo Basin, the Pajarito Plateau around present-day Bandelier National Monument and Los Alamos, and the foothills of the Sangre de Cristos around Nambé and Chimayó, were home to many more people than live there today. This loose network of villages seems to have had no central capital like those that had characterized the Anasazi civilization. Instead, the largest Postclassic Pueblo towns were at Taos, on the northern border of the Tano people's domain, and Pecos, on the eastern border. It was here that trade and diplomacy took place with the Plains Indian tribes, who were not allowed to travel farther into the Pueblo lands. At Pecos, a massive wall defined the area set aside for visitors' encampments.

When the Spanish colonists arrived, the Pueblo people were spared the resettlement or extermination that faced so many other North American Indians partly because the existence of permanent, architecturally sophisticated villages led European newcomers to view them in human terms rather than as a sort of dangerous wildlife like nomadic tribes. In addition, the Vatican had conditioned Spain's permission to colonize the Americas on success in converting the *indigenes,* or native people, to Catholicism. Franciscan missionaries were cast in the role of protecting the Indians from abuse by the Spanish authorities, even as the colonial army protected the Pueblo people as well as the Spanish settlers from Athabascan raiding parties. The Indians shared their crops, building methods, and survival techniques with the Norteño settlers, and many joined the Franciscan missions, although the ancient Indian religion was still practiced in secret.

In Mexico and other Spanish colonies, forced Indian labor was commonly used in the construction of buildings and clearing of farmlands. In seventeenth-century New Mexico, both missionaries and civil authorities required Indians to do unpaid part-time labor as a form of tribute in lieu of taxes. Slavery was relatively rare, although Indians charged with crimes were sometimes sold into slavery as a form of punishment. This practice was one of the causes of the Pueblo Revolt of 1680, in which hundreds of Spanish settlers died and the survivors suffered a 12-year exile. After the Spanish returned to New Mexico and quelled the last of several smaller Indian insurrections in the 1690s, the independence of the Pueblo people was respected, and forced labor was no longer required. Instead, the Spanish imported Aztec slaves from Mexico and later bought them at a slave market in Taos, where Navajo warriors brought captives seized from Zuni and other remote pueblos far to the west.

One of the most profound effects of the Pueblo Revolt of 1680 was to separate the Athabascan nomads into the Navajos, who had made an agreement with the Puebloans to support the uprising in exchange for sheep and horses from the Spanish ranches, and the Apaches, who did not participate in the revolt and continued their traditional way of life. The first Indians to master the arts of horsemanship and sheepherding, the Navajo drifted westward into the Four Corners to rule the same land that the Pueblo people's Anasazi ancestors

Home interior, San Ildefonso Pueblo, Museum of New Mexico. *T. Harmon Parkhurst.*

had abandoned. There they reigned unchallenged until 1864, when U.S. Army Colonel Kit Carson led an expedition into the Navajo lands, burning the Indian cornfields to flush them out of hiding. Carson's troops marched the Navajo people, who numbered about 8000, along with 2000 horses and 10,000 sheep and goats, for a distance of 300 miles to a camp at Fort Sumner in eastern New Mexico. Many died along the trail, and the rest suffered famine in the ill-supplied concentration camp. American surveyors could find nothing desirable about the former Navajo lands. Four years later, the army marched the surviving Navajo people and their flocks back to their homeland, which the tribe—now numbering nearly 200,000—has inhabited peacefully ever since.

As for the Apaches, they roamed in small groups throughout western Texas, New Mexico, and Arizona, discouraging Spanish and Anglo settlers by horrible acts of torture and terrorism. Finally, in the 1880s, the U.S. Army waged its final Indian war against the Apaches. Unlike most other Indians the army had fought, the nearly invisible Apaches employed small-scale guerrilla tactics, relying on the rugged landscape for concealment and protection. The war against the Apaches was played out without large or decisive battles. Instead, taking control of the Apache lands a little bit at a time, the army gradually forced the Indians to retreat into remote mountain wilderness, and then declared these mountain areas as Apache reservations and prohibited the people from leaving. In New Mexico, the Apaches inhabit the Jicarilla Reservation 80 miles northwest of Santa Fe and the Mescalero Reservation 160 miles south.

The Pueblo people around Santa Fe managed to avoid strife with the new-comers from the United States during the nineteenth century, observing as bystanders the cultural tensions between Anglos and Hispanos. Trouble did not arise until 1921, when the Pueblos filed a series of lawsuits in federal court to recover ancestral land grants and water rights from non-Indians — including some of the wealthiest and most politically powerful people in the state. In 1922, Holm O. Bursum, U.S. Senator from New Mexico, introduced the Bursum Indian Bill, designed to protect non-Indian land titles from the Indians' ancestral claims. The bill passed the Senate quietly, since Indians were not eligible to vote, but was brought to public attention during hearings in the House of Representatives. A Santa Fe–based coalition of archaeologists, writers, and artists, Catholic clergy, and the National Federation of Women's Clubs organized a protest that captured national media attention and brought about the defeat of the Bursum Bill and the restoration of Pueblo grant lands.

But the anti-Indian forces were not about to give up so easily. Less than a week after the Bursum Bill was voted down, the senator's political allies, Interior Secretary Albert B. Fall and Bureau of Indian Affairs Commissioner Charles H. Burke, implemented a new regulation prohibiting all ceremonial dances. Additional regulations were proposed to discourage teaching Indian children their native languages and to promote assimilation of Indians into the mainstream population with an eye toward eventual elimination of Indian reservations. The Santa Fe coalition for Indian rights escalated its protests, finally resulting in a scandal that forced a reorganization of the Bureau of Indian Affairs.

Many New Mexican Indians served with distinction in World War II, notably the Navajo "code-talkers," who served as radio operators throughout the Pacific theater of operations. Their job was to transmit secret messages in the Navajo language, the only American "code" that Japanese cryptographers never succeeded in breaking. In the glow of heroism after the war, public sentiment in favor of the Indians spread throughout New Mexico, and Indians were finally granted the right to vote in 1948.

In the decades since, Indian arts and crafts have become a central aspect of the unique character of Santa Fe and northern New Mexico. Nearly 90 retail stores in Santa Fe alone specialize in traditional and contemporary Indian arts, and both the Santa Fe Indian Market and the Eight Northern Pueblos Arts and Crafts Show top the list of the largest and most prestigious Indian art shows in the country. Prized by many American and European collectors, such items as Pueblo pottery and jewelry bring from 50 to 100 times the prices comparable items sold for in the 1940s.

However, Indians continue to suffer the most widespread and severe poverty of any subculture in New Mexico, with a standard of living even lower than that of recent Mexican immigrants. The biggest factor is not racial discrimination but a peculiarity in the federal law that provides limited sovereignty for Indian pueblos and reservations. Under the law, outsiders cannot serve legal papers, attach property, or collect debts on Indian land without express permission from the tribal governor. Designed to protect Indians against fraud, the law has had unintended consequences. For instance, the only mortgage loans available for housing on Indian reservations come from federal programs that contain technical requirements concerning construction specifications; a requirement having to do with insulation R-factors has been interpreted to disqualify adobe structures from federal financing, forcing pueblos to change from traditional building materials to wood frame and stucco.

Worse yet, protection from bill collectors means that banks and other financial institutions will not lend money to Indians. Tribal business ventures can only be financed from the dwindling funds of a special government program created for the purpose. While a few pueblos have devised creative schemes for financing businesses off the reservation—such as the Hotel

Eagle dancers from San Ildefonso Pueblo perform at Seton Village, 1931. *Photograph by Harold Kellogg, courtesy Museum of New Mexico, neg. 77474.*

Santa Fe, controlled by Picuris Pueblo but located in Santa Fe—more have resorted to casino gambling as a method of generating income to finance other pueblo enterprises. From 1994 to 1997, the doubtful legal status of Indian gaming has grown into one of the most controversial political issues in the recent history of New Mexico. Antigambling citizens' organizations and church groups formed a strange alliance with non-Indian gambling interests such as the influential horse-racing lobby to shut down Indian casinos, while tribal leaders threatened consequences from imposing steep tolls on the use of highways crossing Indian land to leasing reservation land for nuclear waste disposal if they were deprived of the casino revenues. The New Mexico legislature approved a compact to legalize Indian casinos in the final hours of the 1997 legislative session.

Meanwhile, despite attempts by several governments over the centuries to suppress their heritage, many New Mexico pueblos hold to their ancient language and social structure, in which farm and grazing land is communally owned, women own the houses and most personal property and pass them down from mother to daughter, men have primary responsibility for religious rituals through their kiva clans, and both men and women share in the secular decisions of the tribe. The people of all pueblos continue to practice their ancient religion and hold ceremonial dances.

Public dances, at which non-Indian spectators and members of other pueblos are welcome, are held on major religious holidays, including the feast days of one or more patron saints bestowed upon the pueblo centuries ago by Spanish priests and Three Kings Day (January 6), when all pueblos change tribal leadership annually and ceremonially pass the Canes of Authority given to them by President Lincoln to the new governor and council. Yet the pueblo ceremonial dances are no more Catholic than touristic. Held on religious days as an age-old compromise to reconcile the division in most pueblos between Catholic believers and non-Christians, they are part of a spiritual tradition that goes back many centuries.

The dances are meant to harmonize the community with the well-being of the earth. They are seasonal. In the warm months, corn dances—the proper term for what non-Indians often call "rain dances"—put the people in touch with the forces that make crops grow, and in the winter animal dances symbolize the spiritual link between tribal hunters and their traditional prey, the deer, pronghorn, and bison. Kiva clans also hold secret ceremonies about which anthropologists know little, often at ancient ruins, caves, or other sacred sites in the mountains. Some pueblos also hold other ceremonial dances such as matachinas, a custom of reenacting the arrival of the Spanish that was imported from Mexico and is used to unify the pueblo in its dealings with non-Indians. Some pueblos also sponsor powwows, in which Indians gather for trade, socializing, and politics centered around nonreligious dance contests. Powwows are intertribal by nature. Indian children practice competition dances as a physical fitness exercise, and many young adult dancers travel from one powwow to the next around North America hoping to win prize money. Photography is usually allowed at powwows, though rarely at ceremonial dances.

As the twentieth century draws to a close, there is little doubt that northern New Mexico's Indian pueblos will endure. Tradition and cultural pride have never been higher among the Tewa people since New Mexico became U.S. territory. Yet whether the Indians will continue as an economic underclass or emerge into a new era of prosperity on their own terms remains an open question.

8

Southern Santa Fe County

U
nlike the northern part of the county, where cars with out-of-state plates crowd the highway all summer, few visitors take time to explore southern Santa Fe County. The area is an often surprising grab bag of Spanish colonial haciendas, old mission churches, Indian ruins, the state penitentiary, factory outlet malls, horse ranches, New Age retreats, film stars' mansions, Old West movie sets, and a former ghost town turned artist colony can all be found within a 20-mile radius.

The history of the southern part of the county revolves around the late nineteenth century. Long before, the Galisteo Basin had been home to a dozen Pueblo Indian communities, but the five pueblos that were still active when the Spanish arrived were wiped out by warfare and smallpox before 1800, leaving the area almost totally uninhabited. It was not until 1880 that the arrival of the railroad gave life to villages such as Galisteo, Lamy and Cerrillos as well as the coal mining boom town of Madrid, bigger in its heyday than Albuquerque. Around the same time, gold and silver were discovered in the Cerrillos Hills and the Ortiz Mountains, creating a flurry of mining activity and a string of new towns that vanished from the map a few years later when the ore ran out.

The mountains, valleys, and weird rock formations of southern Santa Fe County are almost all on privately owned ranchland that is posted against tresspassers, so hikers head for the mountains and canyons of the north

Opposite: Penitente morada, las Golondrinas. *Photograph by Richard Harris.*

instead. The only national forest area in the southern county is Glorieta Mesa, a rarely visited, 30-mile-long island in the sky of rolling piñon forest edged by cliffs that tower 1500 feet above the Galisteo Basin. The occasional cyclists who find their way up the switchback road to the top of the mesa (it starts from the village of Rowe in San Miguel County) find themselves in mountain bike paradise. The rest of the southern Santa Fe County landscape is best seen through a windshield.

DRIVING TOUR OF SOUTHERN SANTA FE COUNTY

Any of the three highways that runs south from Santa Fe—Interstate 25, State Route 14, and U.S. 285—makes for a scenic and historically interesting drive in the country. The three routes can be combined into an all-day adventure by following the unpaved, well-maintained back roads that connect them.

Begin your tour with Rancho de las Golondrinas, an essential stop for anyone interested in the history and traditional architecture of the Santa Fe area. To get there, take **Interstate 25** southbound from Santa Fe, in the direction of Albuquerque. Go 6 miles south of the Cerrillos Road/Route 14 exit (the last Santa Fe exit), passing the **Downs at Santa Fe** horse racetrack. Horse racing has traditionally been a favorite sport in New Mexico, although its importance seems to be on the decline because of competition from rival parimutuel tracks in neighboring states as well as from Indian casinos and New Mexico's recently passed state lottery. Races are held four days a week from mid-June through August, and in the spring the Downs offers betting on closed-circuit simulcast horse races in Albuquerque. Take Exit 271: La Cienega and follow the paved access road for several miles, encouraged by occasional signs that say "Las Golondrinas." The road curves back behind the racetrack to the bedroom community of La Cienega (Spanish for "the swamp").

El Rancho de las Golondrinas (the Ranch of the Swallows) is the last intact paraje on the old Camino Real trade route that linked Santa Fe with Chihuahua and Mexico City. The parajes were waystations situated at intervals of a day's travel along the route. The word literally means place or spot and was originally applied to suitable campsites. Eventually, country inns were established at most of these traditional rest areas to accommodate travelers in relative luxury, and the inns themselves came to be called parajes. El Rancho de las Golondrinas was the last such overnight stop before reaching Santa Fe—or the first on the seven-week journey to Mexico City. The ranch dates back to at least 1710, when it was purchased by Miguel Vega y Coca. The main house was built in 1721. The ranch later passed by marriage into the prominent Baca family of Santa Fe, which owned and operated it for two

Rancho de las Golondrinas. *Photograph by Richard Harris.*

centuries. It was acquired in 1932 by the Curtin–Paloheimo family, who undertook a painstaking restoration of the original buildings. Over a period of 40 years, the family relocated other historic structures from around New Mexico to various locations on the 200-acre property, creating the most impressive collection of its kind in the state. In 1972 it became an open-air museum owned and managed by the Rancho de las Golondrinas Charitable Trust and an affiliate of the Association for Living Historical Farms and Agricultural Museums. The old ranch comes to life on weekends, especially Spring Festival at the beginning of June, Summer Festival in early August, and Harvest Festival in October. During the festivals, scores of volunteers in eighteenth-century period costume demonstrate such traditional skills as shearing sheep, spinning wool, threshing wheat, stringing chile ristras, and extracting molasses from sorghum stalks. On Wednesdays through Sundays from June through September, visitors are welcome to stroll around the ranch and observe the farmwork.

El Rancho de las Golondrinas is set in a bowl-shaped valley that hides the twentieth century from view. The thick-walled adobe hacienda contains 12 rooms, including a chapel, weaving workshop, and prisoners' room, all opening onto a central placita courtyard with a well and a pair of large horno ovens. The ranch house was designed to serve as a fortress if necessary and has a tall defensive torreón overlooking the valley below. Adjoining the east side of the hacienda is a barnyard with burro corrals, sheep pens, a chicken coop, and a goat barn. Beyond the livestock area are miscellaneous outbuildings, among them a country store, a root cellar, a tin shop, a molasses mill, and a butchering area.

Horno ovens, Rancho de las Golondrinas. *Photograph by Richard Harris.*

From the hacienda, a trail leads down to a 200-year-old irrigation ace-quia and past fields of blue and red corn, chile plants, squash, and pump-kins. Near the creek bank is a *descanso* or resting place, where those who died at the ranch would lie in state outdoors to receive the respects of friends and relatives before the funeral and burial. It was traditional for the family of the deceased person to place a simple wooden cross at the des-canso as a permanent marker, although poor families would place a rock there instead. The monument of crosses and stones at this spot eloquently reveals the numbers of people who have made Los Golondrinas their home over the centuries.

On the other side of the creek are apple orchards and vineyards. Farther along, a mile-long loop trail leads to various buildings collected from other sites around New Mexico. There are a nineteenth-century schoolhouse from Ratón, a penitente *morada* or religious meetinghouse from Abiquiu, and beside a lovely willow-shaded mill pond, a working grist mill from Mora powered by a large waterwheel. The nearby Casa de Madrid is the only structure on the property that is not historic in origin; the frontier Victorian-style house was built in the 1970s, when the ranch was used as a filming location of the made-for-TV movie Butch and Sundance: The Early Years. The main trail leads on to a group of a dozen or so smaller houses, stores, and farm buildings, with a small chapel, that offer a glimpse of living conditions in Norteño mountain villages of the nineteenth century.

For a loop trip through the southern part of the county, it is best to follow State Route 586 south from the La Cienega exit. If you have plenty of time to explore, however, there is another detour of historical interest a few miles farther down the interstate. Continue past the Waldo exit (you can't miss it, thanks to the huge new factory outlet mall there, but the ghost town of Waldo itself is easier to reach from Cerrillos); continue for 3 more miles to exit 264: **La Bajada.** The name means "The Descent" and refers to the steep escarpment that drops 700 feet from the plateau around Santa Fe to the Río Grande Valley. The steep grade was the biggest obstacle on the entire Camino Real; after coming nearly 1000 miles from Mexico City, wagons had to stop at the foot of La Bajada, unload their wagons, carry their cargo uphill on burros, haul the wagons up empty, and reload them at the top. La Bajada was such a significant landmark that the Spanish Colonial land below it became known as Río Abajo (Lower River) and above it, Río Arriba (Upper River); today, the descent roughly marks the western boundary of Santa Fe County and the east edge of the Santo Domingo Pueblo Grant. In colonial times, El Camino Real did not follow exactly the same route as the modern interstate. Instead, it made its way by switchbacks up the steep climb at the **Village of La Bajada,** at the foot of a cut where the Santa Fe River pours down from the plateau to the Río Grande. Although the village is less than 3 miles north of the interstate, to get there you must follow State Route 16 east for about 4 miles along the Indian reservation boundary and then turn back northwest on an unpaved road for 3 more miles. The village dates back to the earliest years of Spanish colonization, when it was briefly considered as a site for the capital because of its strategic defensive position. It is still inhabited by a handful of artists and farmers. There are scattered adobe ruins and a chapel that dates back to the 1830s and has recently been restored.

Back at the La Cienega exit from Interstate 25, a frontage road parallels the superhighway for 4 miles to the Waldo exit. Midway along, the frontage road intersects State Route 586, which goes south to the village of Los Cerrillos. Route 286 skirts a twin butte called Cerro Bonanza. Small deposits of silver and lead were discovered at almost a dozen sites in the hills along the south side of the butte, giving brief life to several mining camps. **Bonanza,** founded in 1879 at a site 1½ miles south of the interstate, reached a peak population of 2000 before the mines played out three years later. An

Old La Bajada Highway, 1928 Santa Fe Railroad. *Photograph courtesy Museum of New Mexico, neg. 92219.*

abandoned two-story hotel and casino stood on the site until World War II and was notorious as a rendezvous for rumrunners and other criminals during Prohibition. **Carbonateville,** 2 miles farther down the road, was smaller but lasted longer—until 1899. Nearby are the ruins of the Mina de la Tierra, Chalchihuitl, and Cash Entry silver mines, as well as the Gem Turquoise Mine, one of several sites in the area that were used first by the Anasazi Indians and later by the Spanish. **The Gem Turquoise Mine** was a minor tourist attraction until the 1930s, charging visitors 25 cents to see the turquoise diggings. Today, there is no visible trace of Bonanza or Carbonateville, and it is easier to visit old turquoise mines from Los Cerrillos, on the south side of the mining district.

State Route 586 meets State Route 14 (the extension of Santa Fe's Cerrillos Road, commonly referred to as the **Turquoise Trail**) about 10 miles south of the city. The only sight motorists miss by taking the shortcut from La Cienega is the state penitentiary, located on SR 14 midway between Santa Fe and Los Cerrillos. The modern semirural subdivision that has sprung up around the intersection of routes 14 and 586 marks the approximate site of a major Indian pueblo that existed when Santa Fe was founded. The Spanish dubbed the pueblo **San Marcos** and forced the occupants to work in the Mina del Tiro, the first colonial silver mine in what is now the United States. The people of San Marcos Pueblo were among the instigators of the Pueblo Revolt of 1680. A few Indians still lived at San Marcos in the early years of the twentieth century, when a number of Indian and mestizo communities were called upon to choose whether they wanted their towns regarded as sovereign Indian pueblos under federal jurisdiction or as villages under state jurisdiction; the people of San Marcos elected not to be an Indian reservation, and most of the San Marcos Pueblo grant was later sold to non-Indian developers and subdivided.

The village of **Los Cerrillos,** commonly just called Cerrillos, is located a short distance west of Route 14, 24 miles south of Santa Fe. Although both Indians and Spanish settlers had lived in the vicinity for centuries, Los Cerrillos was officially founded in 1879, when prospectors from Colorado found minor deposits of gold there and established the townsite pursuant to the federal Mining Act of 1872, which let mining companies claim real estate to build towns near working mines. The following year, the Atchison, Topeka & Santa Fe Railroad came through Los Cerrillos, and the town boomed to a population of 800, boasting four hotels and 21 saloons. Lack of water prevented large-scale mining development and blocked further growth, however, and population declined to about 100 residents by 1970. Today, artists and others have recolonized Los Cerrillos to some extent. Most of the old adobe houses in the 10-square-block village are now occupied, and some have been renovated and enlarged. The village church has been beautifully restored. A few stores and art galleries, as well as a bar, operate there, along with the rambling adobe Casa Grande, a 20-room adobe compound whose owners of 25 years have gradually converted it into a quaintly eccentric tourist shop, turquoise mining museum, bed and breakfast, and petting zoo. Guided four-wheel-drive tours of the old Indian and Spanish turquoise diggings in the nearby hills can be arranged there. The authentic nineteenth-century storefronts that line one side of the village's main street still bear

Los Cerrillos main street. *Photograph by Richard Harris.*

Casa Grande. *Photograph by Richard Harris.*

signs such as the Wortley Hotel and the Murphy & Dolan Store, which were actually the names of establishments in the southern New Mexico town of Lincoln. Cerrillos was used as a film location for *Young Guns,* a movie about Billy the Kid and the Lincoln County War, in 1988, and the locals keep the signs as a matter of local pride.

Waldo, a nearly vanished ghost town, is located 2 miles northwest of Los Cerrillos. To reach it, follow the main street across the railroad tracks, bear left, and follow the unpaved road out of town. (If you veer right instead at the first fork in the road, you will find yourself in the maze of small, unstable hills where turquoise has been mined since ancient times. The Pueblo Indians and their Anasazi ancestors held turquoise sacred and valued it above all other minerals. The mines in the Cerrillos hills were the turquoise source for the pueblos of Chaco Canyon, the largest of the ancient Anasazi cities. From there, the stone was traded throughout the southwest and far south into Mexico.) Waldo was founded in 1892 at the railroad junction where a spur line ran to the coal mines of Madrid. It was the site of several coke ovens operated by Colorado Fuel & Iron, the Rockefeller family's steel company based in Pueblo, Colorado. Wells in Waldo pumped 150,000 gallons of water a day, which were carried to the Madrid coal mines in railroad tankcars. Waldo reached a peak population of 100 in 1925. It declined gradually and was abandoned in 1954. Today, all that remains are stone building foundations and the forgotten ruins of the old coke ovens.

The richest mineral deposit in Santa Fe County was not gold, silver, or turquoise, but coal. Vast seams of both bituminous (soft) and anthracite (hard) coal honeycomb 30 square miles of the mountainsides surrounding the town of **Madrid,** 3 miles south of Los Cerrillos on SR 14. Both Spanish settlers and the U.S. Army brought coal from there to Santa Fe, but the town was not founded until 1869. It boomed with the arrival of the railroad, especially after a spur track was run to Madrid from the main Atchison, Topeka & Santa Fe line. In the 1890s, when up to 250,000 tons of coal a year were being mined, Madrid briefly had a population larger than Albuquerque. Several thousand people made their homes there through the 1930s. The town had its own automobile dealership, golf course, and baseball stadium. Thanks to the abundant supply of fuel, it was the first city in the state to have unlimited electric service, and in the 1920s and 1930s Madrid became nationally famous for its spectacular Christmas light displays. Early-day airlines used to reroute their nighttime flights during the holiday season to take in a bird's-eye view of Madrid's lights. Coal from Madrid was used to power the national nuclear laboratory at Los Alamos in the 1940s. But as natural gas replaced coal for heating and diesel-powered train engines replaced steam locomotives, Madrid's coal production declined until 1954, when the mines were closed for good.

Madrid had always been a company town, owned by the Albuquerque and Cerrillos Coal Company, which provided the frontier Victorian-style wood-frame row houses to workers at minimal rates. When it closed the mines, the coal company listed the entire town and surrounding land for sale but found no takers. When the tanker trains from Waldo stopped run-

Madrid Boarding House. *Photograph by Richard Harris.*

Madrid fixer-upper. *Photograph by Richard Harris.*

ning, Madrid residents found themselves without a water supply, and the town was all but abandoned. By 1970, the census population was a mere 45 residents—all but a few of them hippie squatters occupying dilapidated old homes without electricity or heat. In 1975, to reduce its property taxes, the former coal company began selling off the buildings of Madrid individually for nominal prices—and the resurrection of the town began. The Mine Shaft Tavern started as a bikers' roadhouse but soon developed a reputation for live rock music that drew crowds from Santa Fe. The Mining Museum grew into a modest but profitable tourist attraction along the scenic route between Santa Fe and Albuquerque. The Madrid Melodrama, presenting Victorian-era plays in the old railroad barn during the summer, gained recognition as one of the West's most authentic old-time theaters. Over the years since, Madrid has grown steadily as most, though not all, of its old homes and storefronts have been restored.

Today, the community seems to consist entirely of artists. The dozens of studio–galleries that line the main street outnumber all other retail business-es combined. By all appearances, Madrid ranks among the most successful of the creative communities formed by New Mexico artists seeking to leave Santa Fe in search of more peaceful surroundings and lower rents. Such buildings as the huge boarding house, the town amusement hall, and the Catholic church still lend an authentically historic air. Madrid once again stages spectacular lighting displays at Christmas, and the old baseball stadi-um is now used for several annual music events, including the acclaimed Madrid Bluegrass Festival. Water shortages continue to be a serious problem.

South of Madrid, SR 14 crests the **Ortiz Mountains.** They are not a large mountain range compared to the nearby Sandia Crest and Sangre de Cristo and Jemez mountains, but they played a significant role in New Mexico history as the site of the first placer gold strike in what is now the United States and one of the few places in New Mexico where gold has ever been found in mineable concentrations. Unfortunately, the lack of water prevented efficient extraction of gold from the rock, so mining companies could only sort through massive quantities of ore for the small percentage that was of high enough grade to justify shipping it elsewhere for refining. Inventor Thomas Edison established a laboratory in the heart of the mountains for the purpose of developing an electrostatic method of extracting gold with minimal water use, but his efforts were unsuccessful. Today, the gold mining area is off-limits to sightseers because a mining company is experimenting with a modern cyanide leeching method that involves recycling limited quantities of water, hoping to reprocess the vast heaps of low-grade gold ore that could not be concentrated by the process used 100 years ago. Because of the toxic chemicals used, however, the gold project has become a hotly contested environmental issue.

On the other side of the Ortiz Mountains, 11 miles south of Madrid at the foot of a smaller range called the San Pedros, lies the old mining town of **Golden**. An old Spanish settlement known as La Villa Real de San Francisco began at the site around 1835, when placer gold was found in a nearby arroyo, but was soon abandoned. The town of Golden was founded in 1879, and a major mine operated there through the mid-1880s, reaching a peak population of 400. After mining ceased, the town struggled along as a ranching center, although it declined to a low of 15 residents. Today, some old buildings have been renovated and some custom homes have been built in the area, although redevelopment is slow because the location makes commuting to either Santa Fe or Albuquerque impractical. Old foundations still outnumber habitable structures. San Francisco Church, which dates back to the original 1830s Spanish settlement, was restored in 1960 through the efforts of New Mexico's celebrated historian, Fray Angelico Chavez.

Just beyond Golden, SR 14 leaves Santa Fe County. It continues for another 17 miles to intersect Interstate 40 about 15 miles east of Albuquerque. As a scenic route between Santa Fe and Albuquerque, the Turquoise Trail takes about half an hour longer than the faster, though not much shorter, Interstate 25.

Motorists touring southern Santa Fe County may wish to turn around at either Madrid or Golden and retrace their route back past Los Cerrillos. About 5 miles northeast of Cerrillos, an unpaved road turns off to the east (right). It is one of several similar-looking ranch roads along this stretch of highway; watch for the small sign to Galisteo.

The back road makes its way across open ranchlands scattered with modern houses for about 10 miles before reaching the village of **Galisteo.**

Galisteo church. *Photograph by Richard Harris.*

Originally a Tano Indian pueblo that was reported by Coronado's 1541 expedition, the village was variously called Ximena, San Lucas, Santa Ana, Santa María, and finally, Nuestra Señora de los Remedios de Galisteo. It was one of 10 pueblos along the Galisteo River that were still occupied when the colonial era began, and one of the earliest Franciscan missions was established there in 1614. Comanche raids and disease decimated the Indian population throughout the basin until, by 1780, the people of Galisteo Pueblo numbered fewer than 100. They and all other surviving residents of the Galisteo Basin were relocated to Santo Domingo Pueblo in 1782. A few descendents of the Galisteo people still live at Santo Domingo and speak a different language from the rest of the Pueblo. The present village traces its origins to the Mexican Period—1821 to 1846—when it was resettled by Spanish and mestizo farmers. The church that stands at the center of the village dates back to 1882, and gravestone enthusiasts cite the old cemetery up the hill nearby as one of the best in the state. Galisteo was down to fewer than two dozen inhabitants in 1959, when the U.S. Post Office shut down, although the Ortiz y Pino family continued to run a small country store in part of their ancestral hacienda across the street from the church. The most recent recolonization of Galisteo began in the 1960s, when TV personality Arthur Godfrey bought a horse ranch nearby. Other celebrities moved into the area, along with a New Age institute, an ultraexclusive spa resort, and a luxury bed and breakfast. In the past few years, most of the abandoned buildings have been renovated as the village has been recolonized by artists. The Galisteo Art Association sponsors a studio tour weekend in mid-October.

Visible from Galisteo looking south is the skyline of the **Silverado movie set** on the Cook Ranch. Built in 1985 for the movie Silverado, the 45-building town has also been used as the location for other westerns, including Wyatt Earp, Buffalo Girls, and Lonesome Dove. It is the largest of four movie towns in the area. The others are Bonanza Creek Ranch off State Route 586 and Eaves Western Town and Rancho Alegre Mexican Village, both off State Route 14 between Santa Fe and Los Cerrillos. None of the movie sets is open to the public.

If you were to go south on State Route 41, in 18 straight, traffic-free miles you would reach the tiny ranching "town" of **Stanley**, a cluster of mostly abandoned buildings near the southern boundary of Santa Fe County. There is nothing of interest, although the surrounding landscape is a favorite haunt of pronghorn antelope. Ten miles farther on, just over the county line, the highway joins Interstate 40 at Moriarty, a community of 1860 people that is the largest town for many miles around.

Proceeding north on paved State Route 41, you cross the San Cristobal Ranch, one of the largest and oldest in the county. Six miles' drive from Galisteo is the intersection with U.S. Highway 285, a main highway that con-

Lamy Railroad Station. *Photograph by Richard Harris.*

tinues south for 200 miles through empty rangeland before reaching Roswell and Carlsbad in the southeastern part of the state. Instead, turn north (left) on Highway 285 to return to Santa Fe. Along the way, take a short detour from the highway to see the village of **Lamy.** Originally established in 1880 as an Atchison, Topeka & Santa Fe Railroad station, the spot was named after Archbishop Lamy, who persuaded the railroad to run a spur line into Santa Fe from that point. Today, the train station is still the main reason for Lamy's existence. It serves passengers taking Amtrak to and from Santa Fe, with one eastbound and one westbound train daily. Regularly scheduled rail service into the city was discontinued in 1926, but since the early 1990s the independent Santa Fe Southern Railroad has operated excursion trains between Santa Fe and Lamy for tourists. The parking area is picturesquely littered with rusting old railroad cars, and a large park on the east side of the station makes for a shady picnic spot. Aside from a handful of residences, the other major buildings in town are a boarded-up Catholic church and the Legal Tender, a restaurant and saloon in a turn-of-the-century false-front Victorian building with a modern addition.

Across Highway 285 from Lamy lies **El Dorado,** a large, modern development with its own elementary school, fire department, and community center. Like older communities of southern Santa Fe County, Eldorado suffers from an uncertain water supply that has sometimes forced severe emergency rationing. This drawback has held home prices and rents significantly lower than in the city. Seven miles north, Highway 285 crosses Interstate 25 and joins Old Las Vegas Highway at **Cañoncito,** a metal-roofed old church and cluster of adobe houses. Santa Fe is another 7 miles west.

Interstate 25 northbound actually runs southeast from Santa Fe as it makes its way through the narrow pass between the southern tip of the Sangre de Cristo Range and the vast, uninhabited island in the sky known as Glorieta Mesa. At the top of the pass is the small village of **Glorieta,** established in the early nineteenth century as a rest area along the Santa Fe Trail and later a loading station for the Atchison, Topeka & Santa Fe Railroad. Visitors today drive through Glorieta on their way to Pecos just over the county line in San Miguel County.

Glorieta is best known as the site of the Battle of Glorieta, the decisive Civil War battle in New Mexico, fought on March 26–28, 1862. A month earlier, following a defeat at the hands of Confederate soldiers from Texas in the Battle of Valverde south of Albuquerque, Union troops had abandoned Santa Fe, allowing the Rebels to occupy the capital without opposition. Reinforced by a detachment of Colorado Volunteers, the Union army surprised a train of Confederate supply wagons bound for Santa Fe as it made its way over Glorieta Pass. Three days of running battles through the nearby woods and ranchlands left 5 Union soldiers and 32 Confederate soldiers dead, 14 Union

Abandoned church, Lamy. *Photograph by Richard Harris.*

soldiers and 43 Confederate soldiers wounded, and 71 Confederate soldiers taken as prisoners of war. The battle ended indecisively, as the Confederate troops withdrew to Santa Fe and the federal troops to Fort Union in eastern New Mexico, but complete destruction of the supply train made it impossible for the Confederate troops to remain in Santa Fe. They withdrew on April 8, 1862, ending Civil War hostilities in New Mexico.

Today, the Battle of Glorieta is the subject of a small museum midway between Glorieta and Pecos that is part of **Pecos National Historical Park.** Costumed participants reenact the battle each spring, and quite a few of Glorieta's 300 residents keep collections of Civil War cannonballs and musket balls that they have found in the surrounding woods. Across the interstate from the village is the **Glorieta Baptist Assembly Conference Center,** a large complex of retreat cabins built by Southern Baptist churches in Texas around a central meeting and worship facility. The trailhead for a popular hiking trail to the summit of 10,199-foot Glorieta Baldy is located behind the center.

DAY TRIPS SOUTH OF SANTA FE

Here are the major day-trip destinations of historical interest south of Santa Fe County. All driving distances and times are one-way from Santa Fe:

PECOS

21 miles / 30 minutes from Santa Fe

Take interstate 25 nothbound to Glorieta and follow Route 50 to the village of Pecos.

This small Hispano settlement developed unofficially in the early eighteenth century on the outskirts of Pecos Pueblo and Mission, which was originally known by its Towa name, Cicuyé. Then, as now, its inhabitants were primarily woodcutters who supplied the firewood needs of Santa Fe. It was abandoned along with the pueblo in 1838 but reestablished soon afterward as a rest stop on the Santa Fe Trail and called Levy. The name was changed to Pecos in 1883. Today, the general store, restaurants, bars, and public utilities located in this town of 1200 serve dozens of tiny, scattered Spanish-speaking villages scattered through the surrounding national forest.

Three miles south of town, the main unit of Pecos National Historical Park preserves Pecos Pueblo, a large Indian town built in the thirteenth century at the eastern gateway to the Tanoan Pueblo lands. The 600-room, four- to five-story pueblo was inhabited by craftspeople who traded extensively with the Plains Indians, specializing in pottery and turquoise jewelry. Fray

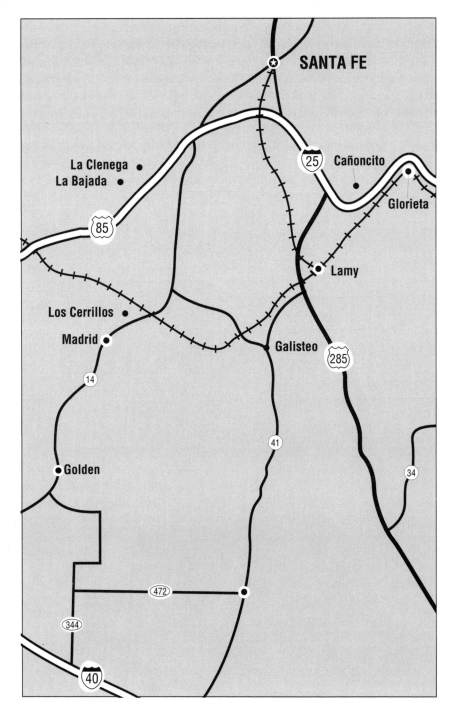

Southern Santa Fe County

Luis de Escalona, a priest with Coronado's expedition, stayed in Pecos to found a mission in 1541 and presumably became New Mexico's first Christian martyr. Franciscan brothers built a large adobe mission church adjoining the ancient pueblo in 1617 and maintained one of their most successful missions there until they were forced to flee during the Pueblo Revolt of 1680. Tree ring data show that the imposing mission church was rebuilt or restored shortly after the Spanish reconquest in 1692 but suffered many hardships throughout the eighteenth century. Apache and Comanche attacks plagued the pueblo and mission from 1720 through 1750, when Cicuyé sent its entire male Indian population into the eastern plains to battle the marauders, who ambushed the Pueblo men and slaughtered all but one. In 1768 a smallpox epidemic reduced the population at Pecos to 180, and in 1805 a choleralike disease known as mountain fever left only 102 survivors, too few to effectively farm the communal fields. Famine followed, and the pueblo at Pecos had only 17 Indian residents in 1838, when the priests abandoned the mission and relocated the survivors to Jemez Pueblo, north of Albuquerque. Today, more than 200 descendents of the Pecos people live at Jemez, speaking a separate dialect and conducting separate religious rituals from the other Jemez residents. The 365-acre pueblo and mission site was donated to the Museum of New Mexico in 1915 and subsequently transfered to the National Park Service as a national monument. In 1992, actress Greer Garson donated her entire 5500-acre ranch, which surrounded the pueblo, to the park service to protect it from subdivision and development by future owners. The park service designated the former monument and the ranch as

Mission church ruin, Pecos National Historical Park. *Photograph by Richard Harris.*

Pecos National Historical Park, although none of the newly added land has been opened to the public because of fears about how a sudden expansion of national park facilities might affect the traditional way of life of nearby village residents.

North of the village of Pecos, the Pecos River Canyon is a popular catch-and-release trout fishing area with enclaves of vacation cabins. A turnoff from the main road leads up Dalton Canyon, the hideout of the notorious train-robbing Dalton Gang in the late nineteenth century. The pavement ends at Terrero General Store, all that remains of a large turn-of-the-century gold mine and mill town. A rocky unpaved road continues to a series of national forest campgrounds and trailheads providing access to the Pecos Wilderness.

COCHITÍ PUEBLO

29 miles / 30 minutes from Santa Fe

Take interstate 25 southbound to the La Bajada interchange and follow Route 16 northwest.

Continuously inhabited since the twelfth century, this Keres-speaking pueblo on the Río Grande consists of single-story houses surrounding two ceremonial kivas and a mission church, San Buenaventura de Cochití, a mission church originally built in 1628 and rebuilt following the Pueblo Revolt. Today, Cochití pueblo is known for its distinctive crafts, which include double-headed drums, traditional turquoise heishi jewelry, and the "storyteller" pottery figures originally created here by Helen Cordero in the 1960s and a familiar sight in Santa Fe's Indian arts galleries. Besides Christmas, Three Kings Day, and Easter ceremonies, the pueblo holds corn dances on May 3, the Feast of Santa Cruz, and July 14, the Feast of San Buenaventura.

Near the pueblo is Cochiti Lake, a large reservoir on the Río Grande just above the Santa Fe River confluence. The reservoir neither provides drinking water nor generates electricity, but was built by the U.S. Army Corps of Engineers for flood control, capturing spring runoff to ensure adequate irrigation water for the chile and pecan farms of southern New Mexico and Texas. The lake is a popular recreation area, with a beach and facilities for boat launching and wind surfing, as well as a huge campground and a golf course. Adjacent to the lake, the suburban-style village of Cochiti Lake originally provided housing during dam construction and has since become a vacation and retirement community. Development is limited, despite its beautiful setting and recreational advantages, because the land on which the residential neighborhood is located is on a long-term lease from Cochiti Pueblo, making the future terms of home ownership uncertain. Past the village of Cochiti Lake, the pavement ends and the road winds through apple orchards and up Cochiti Canyon to Tent Rocks, a locally popular hiking area that few visitors know about, where ancient geothermal steam vents hardened volcanic ash to form weird 30-foot-tall tepee-shaped rock formations.

SANTO DOMINGO PUEBLO

29 miles / 30 minutes from Santa Fe
Take interstate 25 south to the Santo Domingo interchange and follow Route 22 north.

The largest of the Río Grande pueblos, with a population of nearly 6000, Santo Domingo was built in 1700 after a flood destroyed the ancestral pueblo a short distance to the west, where usually dry Galisteo Creek meets the Río Grande. The present pueblo consists of adjoining single-story houses organized in blocks around a large plaza with a kiva and adobe church. The inhabitants are among the most traditional Río Grande Pueblo groups, speaking their ancestral Keres language and adhering to a rigid social structure that predates Spanish colonialism. The economy is based on farming and supplemented by arts and crafts, which are sold at a market area near the interstate highway exit as well as at a tribally owned store in Albuquerque's Old Town shopping district. Attitudes toward non-Indian visitors are hospitable, although photography is strictly prohibited. While the pueblo observes several feast days, including those of San Juan (June 24), San Pedro and San Pablo (June 29), and Santiago (July 25), its most spectacular celebration is on the Feast of Santo Domingo, August 4, when more than 500 dancers participate in an all-day corn dance through the streets of the pueblo. As you approach the pueblo from the interstate, turning right instead of left will bring you to all that remains of the forgotten little railroad town of Thornton—a wonderfully picturesque trading post that has been in operation since the 1930s, when trains stopped here to let tourists visit the pueblo.

SAN FELIPE PUEBLO

38 miles / 40 minutes from Santa Fe
Take interstate 25 south to the San Felipe Pueblo interchange.

The ancestors of the San Felipe Pueblo residents occupied two earlier pueblos a few miles to the north and west before building the present one around 1700. Like neighboring Santo Domingo, San Felipe is a deeply traditional farming pueblo where people cling to their old language, religion, and cultural heritage, resisting outside influences even though the pueblo's location —on the old Camino Real and the AT&SF railroad route and within earshot of the present interstate highway between Santa Fe and Albuquerque—has meant a steady flow of non-Indians passing through for some 400 years. The austere, twin-towered San Felipe Church dates back to the early nineteenth century. The antiquity of the pueblo is vividly evident in the central dance plaza, which has been worn into a bowl shape by 300 years of ceremonies. The largest dance of the year is the all-day corn dance that takes place on the Feast of San Felipe, May 1, with hundreds of dancers and an all-male chorus of chanters. There is also a buffalo dance on the Feast of Candelario, February 2. An unusual craft specialty here is heishi, necklaces of flat circular beads graduating in size, painstakingly made by rolling pieces of turquoise or shell on a flat, rough surface; the art of heishi originated in Anasazi times, and many examples have been found among the ruins at Chaco Canyon.

CORONADO STATE MONUMENT

43 miles / 45 minutes from Santa Fe

Take interstate 25 southbound to the Bernalillo interchange.

Now a ruin, the sprawling fourteenth-century pueblo of Kuaua on the bank of the Río Grande was still occupied in 1540, when conquistador Francisco Vásquez de Coronado and his expedition of 336 Spanish soldiers, together with priests, slaves, and livestock, arrived. It was one of more than a dozen pueblos in what Coronado dubbed the Provincia de Tiguex ("Tiwa Province"), where he established his headquarters while sending explo-

Replicas of Kuaua kiva murals painted by Zena Kavin in 1940 for display at Coronado State Monument. *Photograph courtesy Museum of New Mexico, neg. 44483.*

rations through the southwest from the Grand Canyon to Kansas. Coronado's men were welcomed at first, and the Indians shared their food and supplies in exchange for small gifts, but as the months wore on, trouble broke out over excessive demands and incidents of sexual harrassment, and the Pueblo people rose up against the Spaniards. Coronado responded by destroying two villages and executing participants in the rebellion, then continued to live at the pueblo until the spring of 1542. The expedition's journalist, Pedro de Castañeda, records that Coronado made his headquarters in one of the pueblos of Tigeux, but does not say for sure which one, so whether the ruin preserved at Coronado State Monument was the real base of operations is a matter for speculation. Kuaua was selected for preservation as a monument because archaeologists from the School of American Research and the University of New Mexico discovered the best preserved and finest known examples of kiva murals here. The murals are on public view, protected by plexiglass. Descendents of the people who inhabited Kuaua live today at little Sandia Pueblo on the northern outskirts of Albuquerque and the much larger Isleta Pueblo south of the city.

SANTA FE'S NATURAL ENVIRONMENT

The natural environment is mirrored in virtually every aspect of Santa Fe life. Earth and wood are the fundamental elements of the City Different's buildings. In fact, adobe structures were traditionally built from the earth found on the spot where construction was taking place. Even when imported or synthetic building materials are used, they are disguised with earthtone paint to blend into the natural surroundings. Landscaping, too, emphasizes the natural. With water at a premium, few Santa Feans attempt to grow lawns in front of their homes, although it is common to have a flower garden–size patch of lawn in a walled back yard or courtyard. Yards are typically landscaped with chamisa, juniper, and other flowers, shrubs, and trees that grow naturally in the local environment and require little or no extra water.

Much of the art created and displayed in Santa Fe uses motifs from the natural surroundings, and natural materials such as clay, wood, and plant dyes are often used. Herbs from the surrounding mountains are widely used for medicinal and ritual purposes. For instance, osha root—an herb that is almost unknown outside New Mexico and northern Mexico—is available in most pharmacies and supermarkets and has been used for centuries to cure the common cold. Anyone moving into a new home in Santa Fe is sure to receive gifts of "smudge sticks," tightly rolled bouquets of sage and juniper that are burned like incense to bless the house. Environmental protection is a key issue over which most local and many statewide elections are won or lost.

Pecos Ruins National Monument, 18th century church and stabilized 17th century church foundation. *National Register of Historic Places.*

Proximity is one reason for Santa Feans' heightened awareness of the natural environment. Wherever you are in the City Different, chances are you can see at least one of the four surrounding mountain ranges—the Ortiz Range and Sandia Crest to the south, the Jemez to the west, and the Sangre de Cristos abruptly rising more than a mile in elevation from the eastern city limit. Much of the surrounding land is owned by the public as part of Santa Fe National Forest or as Bureau of Land Management or state-owned grazing land. Unlike in other parts of the west, where dominion over private land is a right to be defended from all tresspassers, if necessary with firearms, northern New Mexico has had a tradition of communal land use for centuries. Pueblo Indians, who have no ancestral concept of land ownership, continue to regard their tribal grant lands as community property free from individual claims, and Norteño Spanish villagers have traditionally viewed the surrounding forests and meadows as ejidos—common land—which all residents of the village are free to use but not abuse. The inclusion of historically ejido lands in the national forest in the 1920s continues to be a source of conflict between local Hispanics and the federal government, but the issue is one of jurisdiction. Unlike in many western states, nobody in northern New Mexico advocates privatization of public lands.

Santa Fe County boasts an amazing variety of "life zones" with different vegetation and wildlife. They are a function of altitude, as the landscape rises from about 6000 feet along the Río Grande and in the extreme southern part of the county to more than 12,000 feet in the Pecos Wilderness. Elevation

Pueblo of Santo Domingo (Kiua), 19 miles aouth of Santa Fe, built 1700. *National Register of Historic Places.*

makes a great difference in precipitation, and temperatures drop by as much as nine degrees for every 1000 feet of elevation gain. At low elevations, where rain or snow is fairly rare, the main vegetation is buffalo grass with scattered sage, cholla, and small prickly pear cactus and occasional small piñon trees. Creeks and rivers are shaded by cottonwood trees; most other trees and shrubs commonly found in these riparian habitats are invaders brought to the area in early times as ornamentals. Russian olive trees and tamarisks, especially, flourish near water in New Mexico and have spread throughout the state.

At elevations of 7000 to 8000 feet, where snow falls in the winter but melts off quickly, piñon and juniper trees grow close together in a dwarf forest. Above 8000 feet, ponderosa pines grow in cool, spacious forests carpeted in pine needles. Above 9000 feet the forest turns to aspen, a slender round-leafed tree that turns bright gold in the first week of October; according to the National Forest Service, the area of the Sangre de Cristo Mountains south of the Santa Fe Ski Basin has the largest contiguous aspen forest on earth. Above 10,000 feet, where the forest remains covered by snow many feet deep until late spring, thick stands of spirelike Douglas fir trees cover the steep hillsides.

Wildlife that ranges within a 30-mile radius of Santa Fe includes foxes, skunks, porcupines, deer, elk, pronghorn antelope, bighorn sheep, and bears. Mountain lions are sighted occasionally. Coyotes are very common and on moonlit nights often roam the arroyos that run through many Santa Fe neighborhoods. The most common large birds within the city are ravens. The hills, canyons, and wetlands around the city are havens for magpies, roadrunners, great horned owls, great blue herons, turkey vultures, and bald and golden eagles. Many migratory birds, from Canada geese to whooping cranes, spend the winter in New Mexico, and newcomers are often surprised to find that all winter Santa Fe has an abundance of robins, most of which fly away at the first sign of spring.

The most controversial bird in northern New Mexico is the elusive Mexican spotted owl, a small nocturnal bird that lives only in ancient forests and for that reason has been classified as "threatened" under the federal Endangered Species Act. Protection of the owl, as well as a little-known salamander found only in the Jemez, has provided environmental activists with grounds for court injunctions halting timber sales in Santa Fe National Forest and other national forests throughout the southwest. Logging of ancient forest areas has been a source of conflict between environmentalists and large wood products corporations for many years, but recent court injunctions have been interpretted as halting small firewood-cutting operations, too, creating hostility between environmental factions and the residents of mountain villages such as Pecos and Truchas, where many people heat only with wood and make their livings cutting firewood in the national forest for sale.

Another land use issue that has attracted attention lately is cattle grazing. In the ranchlands of Santa Fe County, as in other parts of the state, more than a century of overgrazing has turned many areas from grassy prairies to desert. Environmentalists have had little success in persuading the federal and state governments to hike grazing fees or reduce the number of cattle permitted to graze on public lands. Recently, Santa Fe–based environmental organizations have undertaken a different approach, bidding against ranchers for prime grazing leases and using private donations to pay low annual fees for the right not to graze cattle on public lands. Other land use issues that have spurred public protest in the 1990s have included a proposed expansion of the Santa Fe Ski Basin, a proposed pumice quarry in a scenic area of the Jemez, a proposed open-pit copper mine near Picuris Pueblo, and various plans to build homes on top of hills or ridgelines in Santa Fe.

Pollution risks concern many Santa Feans, who value the privilege of living in one of the country's more pristine environments. In arid country where the most valuable of all natural resources is water, the contamination of groundwater presents a serious problem. Such contamination has occurred in isolated areas around Santa Fe because of underground gasoline storage tank leakage, but most water problems have come as a result of illicit waste disposal. For instance, a recent law expanding the scope of hazardous waste regulation inadvertently left restauranteurs with no legal method for disposing of large quantities of kitchen grease. Before the mistake could be corrected, a clandestine industry had developed hauling the contents of restaurants' grease traps out of town and dumping the saturated sludge in arroyos, causing long-term degradation of groundwater quality. Air quality is also a matter for concern, as Santa Fe's visibility often drops to poor levels in the winter because of widespread firewood burning.

The number one environmental issue in Santa Fe for many years has been the perceived nuclear threat posed by the Waste Isolation Pilot Plant, a facility near Carlsbad in southern New Mexico that was designed to bury nuclear waste in huge chambers in drilled out of subterranean salt beds. One main concern of Santa Feans is that the only possible route for shipping nuclear waste from Los Alamos National Laboratory to WIPP is down U.S. Highway 84/285, which runs through Santa Fe as St. Francis Drive, the city's busiest and most accident-prone street. Many believe that this plan makes a nuclear accident all but inevitable. Concerned citizens have mobbed public hearings in unprecedented numbers to protest WIPP, and although the facility was originally scheduled to begin receiving shipments in 1987, its opening was still delayed indefinitely as of November 1996. The positive value of an antinuke stance in Santa Fe is apparent from the signs, familiar to locals but often puzzling to outsiders, displayed by what appears to be a clear majority of stores, gas stations, and offices around town. They read, "Another Business Against WIPP."

Village of Pecos, aerial view. *National Register of Historic Places.*

Cristo Rey Church, detail. *Photograph by Richard Harris.*

¿Y Que Más?

GLOSSARY

acequia—open irrigation ditch shared by farmers who take turns opening gates along the ditch to flood their fields. Acequia user associations were the basic unit of government in Santa Fe until recent times and are still a powerful force in some Norteño villages.
adobe—sun-dried brick of native clay and straw
arroyo—dry wash; intermittent stream

banco—bench built in as part of a wall (interior or exterior)
barrio—neighborhood, especially one occupied by poor people
battered wall—a wall that slants slightly inward toward the top, typical of adobe building construction and artificially created in nonadobe Spanish Pueblo Revival–style buildings to create an adobe look

calle—street
camino—road
canal—roof drain, often erroneously called a *canale* because the plural is *canales*
casa—house
corbel—short timber, usually square and often decoratively carved, placed on top of a roof support post to increase its weight-bearing capacity

coyote fence—a tall fence of vertical juniper poles wired together

farolito—"little lantern," an altar candle inside a brown paper bag weighted with sand, used as a Christmas decoration (called a *luminaria* in Albuquerque and southern New Mexico)
fogón—rounded corner fireplace, often called an *horno* fireplace

genízaro—nomadic Indian of no particular tribe

hacienda—colonial estate or manor house, often fortified
horno—large beehive-shaped outdoor oven, traditionally used by Pueblo Indians

jacal—a type of log cabin construction in which squared cedar logs were planted upright and the gaps between them chinked with adobe

kiva—round Pueblo Indian ceremonial chamber, part above and part below ground level

latilla—peeled wood pole placed between *vigas* to support a roof
luminaria—in Santa Fe, a small street

bonfire where carols are sung on Christmas eve. (In Albuquerque and southern New Mexico, *farolitos* are called *luminarias*.)

mansard roof—a curb roof with an almost vertical lower slope and an almost horizontal upper slope, having the same profile on all four sides of the building. Seventeenth-century French in origin, this Victorian revival style was popular in New York in the 1880s and came to Santa Fe with the railroad.
molina—flour mill
morada—penitente chapel and meetinghouse

Norteño—a native of New Mexico, Chihuahua, or Sonora; a northern New Mexico villager

paraje—literally, place or spot; an overnight stopping place on the Camino Real; an inn or waystation built at such a place
pen tile—a type of gray brick resembling small concrete blocks, manufactured by convicts at the New Mexico State Penitentiary and often used as an inexpensive substitute for adobe bricks from the mid-1920s through the 1940s
placita—patio or courtyard; small plaza
plaza—town square; large courtyard open to the public
portal—roof supported by posts over a sidewalk or porch
puddled adobe—clay poured in layers to form a floor or wall

raja—split wood piece laid between *vigas* to support an earthen roof, a common construction method in eighteenth-century Santa Fe; differs from a latilla in that it is only half round
rancho—ranch
reredos—decorated altar screen of stone, wood, or canvas
retablo—painted altar piece, often depicting a saint
río—river
rito—creek
ristra—string of chile peppers, garlic, or other vegetables hung out to dry in the sun. Red chile ristras are a traditional (and edible) decoration.

torreón—a squat, round tower, originally designed for defense from Indian attacks
Tewa—The language spoken by the people of Pojoaque, Tesuque, Nambe, San Juan, San Ildefonso, and Santa Clara Pueblos. Other Pueblo Indian dialects spoken in northern New Mexico include Tiwa, Towa, and Keres.
trastero—handmade wooden cabinet

viga—rough-hewn roof support beam, exposed in the building interior and often protruding from the exterior facade or wall

¿Y que más?—"And what more?" (asked by waitpersons at the end of a meal in New Mexican restaurants)

zaguán—hallway or vestibule; enclosed portal

NEW MEXICO CUISINE

Santa Feans agree that chile is one of the five basic food groups. As local doctors debate whether it is addictive or just extremely habit-forming, people who leave the City Different to visit other parts of the United States almost always pack canned green chile in a corner of their suitcases for emergency use.

New Mexican chile (the Spanish spelling, never the anglicized "chili") is unique. Cultivated by the Pueblo Indians for centuries before the Spanish arrived, it became a favorite crop on colonial farms and continues to be New Mexico's most important agricultural product today. The state grows more chiles than are grown in all the rest of the United States because New Mexico chiles grown elsewhere, in different soil and climate conditions, prove flavorless. The main chile-growing areas are Hatch in southern New Mexico and Chimayo on the north edge of Santa Fe County. In Hatch, much of the chile is allowed to ripen to a bright red color, then dried and ground into the chili powder sold in supermarkets around the world. Most Chimayo chile is sold within northern New Mexico as either red-chile ristras or roasted green chile.

In the hundred or so Santa Fe restaurants that specialize in New Mexican food, waitpersons will ask you, "Red or green?" Chile, that is. Avoid the common mistake of assuming that green chile must be milder than red. It is not. In fact, since restaurants depend on local customers to survive the long off-season, many places try to offer the hottest green chile in town.

Green chile has a tough, indigestible skin. Roasting the chili pods hardens the skin to the consistency of plastic and makes it slide off easily. It is hard to roast chile pods properly in a conventional oven, so most New Mexicans buy their chile in bulk at harvest time (Labor Day through mid-September), when there is such a surplus that it costs just a few dollars a bushel, and have the seller roast it on the spot in a large, rotating contraption made of steel grating especially for the purpose and heated with a roaring gas burner. Then they freeze the roasted chile pods in plastic storage bags for later use.

After defrosting and peeling, the roasted green chiles are usually diced and simmered in a small amount of broth to create a sauce or stuffed with cheese and fried to make chile rellenos ("filled chiles"). New Mexican restaurants, which use much more green chile than they can freeze at harvest time, buy either whole or diced frozen green chile from one of the several local companies that sell it in wholesale quantities year-round. Frozen green chile is also sold in all supermarkets and is considered far superior to canned green chile.

The reason that canned green chile exists at all is that it is the only reasonable way to transport it to other parts of the country. Santa Feans with kids away at college can tell you that fresh green chile spoils before reaching the east coast, dried green chile tastes nothing like the genuine item, and New Mexican chile seeds refuse to grow outside the state. Shipping frozen chile on dry ice by overnight courier works but costs a fortune. Though the flavor of canned green chile may leave something to be desired, any displaced Santa Fean is thrilled to find it in a care package from home. Sweetly spicy green chile jelly is also easy to transport.

Blue corn, another unusual New Mexican ingredient, is a variety of Indian corn. Non-Indian farmers in Chimayó and the Española Valley grow Indian corn in all colors—blue, purple, red, orange, yellow, and white, mixed in every possible combination. The Pueblo people have been breeding their corn crops selectively for centuries to produce the pure blue strain, which is believed to be sacred. Unlike the sweet corn usually grown in the United States, Indian corn kernels are tough and chewy, so the corn is usually dried and ground into meal. Its distinctive taste is different from that of white or yellow cornmeal.

Blue corn is traditionally made into tortillas or boiled to make a soupy hot cereal called atole, often flavored with honey, anise, or red chile. Pueblo people splash thin atole onto a hot griddle to make a paper-thin bread called piki that is rolled in layers and served at ceremonial feasts. Blue cornmeal (masa harina) is available in all northern New Mexico supermarkets. It can be used in other recipes calling for cornmeal, such as cornbread; substituting buttermilk for regular milk in the recipe will make the bread come out bright blue instead of concrete gray. Much of the blue corn grown today by Indians and non-Indians alike is sold to natural food companies to be made into products such as corn chips and cornflakes. In restaurants, blue corn tortillas are often used to make enchiladas (chicken or cheese rolled in or layered with corn tortillas and smothered in red or green chile sauce) and huevos rancheros (fried eggs served on tortillas—and smothered in red or green chile). Some restaurants use whole kernels of blue corn to make posole, similar to hominy, and serve it as a side dish.

Piñon nuts, a staple in the diet of southwestern Indians since preagricultural times, are thin-shelled nuts that grow inside the cones produced by piñon trees. The slow-growing pines produce nuts only once every seven years; all the trees in a particular area will make nuts at the same time, and it happens in different areas each year. When the nuts ripen, the pine cones open enough to let them fall to the ground. Many local people in the villages of northern New Mexico harvest piñon nuts in the fall and sell them either to wholesalers or direct to buyers at roadside stands. Harvesting is done by spreading a blanket around the base of a tree, throwing a rope around the top, and shaking the tree until the nuts fall out by the thousands. Piñon nuts are roasted, sometimes salted, and sold in the shell as a snack. Many people use them in any kind of recipe that calls for nuts, from muffins to salad to fish filets. But since shelling piñon nuts is an extremely labor-intensive process, shelled pine nuts imported from China, available in many supermarkets, cost a fraction of the price of local ones and taste the same. Piñon nuts are a staple ingredient at Santa Fe restaurants that specialize in "New Southwest" cuisine (similar to the eclectic gourmet cuisine known as California nouveau, but featuring local ingredients).

Many Santa Feans lean toward gourmet cooking at home, too. **Kaune's Foodtown,** 511 Old Santa Fe Trail, is where grocery shoppers go for a more intriguing array of foods than conventional supermarkets offer. The store, started by Henry Spencer Kaune in 1880, is one of Santa Fe's oldest family-run businesses. It was originally located on the south side of the Plaza and moved to its present location in 1950. It has prospered by adapting to new tastes as the city's cultural makeup has changed. A more recent change in food-buying habits is evident at **Alfalfa's Market,** 333 West Cordova Road, and **Wild Oats Community Market,** 1090 South St. Francis Drive, both supermarket-sized natural food stores that belong to chains based in Boulder, Colorado. The stores also offer natural food supplements, herbal remedies, and organic beauty care products, as well as 15-minute "shopper's massages." Each place has a soup and salad bar, bakery, and deli with tables for indoor and outdoor eating. The parking lot views may leave something to be desired, but these two supermarket cafés are perhaps the best places in Santa Fe to meet interesting locals.

RESTAURANTS

Santa Fe has a reputation for fine dining that is unsurpassed in the Rocky Mountain west. The city has more than 200 restaurants. Here is a selection of two dozen of the best, including those that specialize in traditional New Mexican food, those that are in historic buildings, and a few local secrets that I only share with my friends.

New Mexican Food

Tomasita's at 500 South Guadalupe Street (983-5721), in the Guadalupe historic district, is considered by many to be Santa Fe's quintessential New Mexican restaurant. Located in a big brick building expanded from an old trackside warehouse, this restaurant has gotten famous and still doesn't take reservations, so expect long waits, lots of noise and authentic Norteño-style chile rellenos and sopaipillas. The same local family also operates **Tia Sophia's** at 210 West San Francisco Street (982-9880) downtown and **Diego's Café** in De Vargas Mall (983-5101).

The **Guadalupe Café** at 422 Old Santa Fe Trail (982-9762) was Tomasita's face-to-face competition on Guadalupe Street for many years. Now, in its new location across the street from San Miguel Mission and the Lamy Building, you can enjoy the exceptional New Mexican food on an outdoor terrace looking out on a street scene that is entertaining by day and romantic after dark.

The Shed at 113-1/2 East Palace Avenue (982-9030), open only for lunch, serves traditional New Mexican–style tacos and enchiladas in an atmospheric old adobe building that was once the home of New Mexico Territorial Governor Bradford Prince. Come early or late; one of the most popular restaurants among people who work downtown, the Shed can be very crowded during the noon hour.

La Choza at 905 Alarid Street (982-0909), located southwest of downtown off Cerrillos Road near St. Francis Drive, is a favorite among locals who wouldn't think of waiting for a table at Tomasita's. It's a little off the beaten path, over the railroad tracks and across the street from the homeless shelter, but the chicken enchiladas are worth the search.

Tiny's at 1015 Pen Road Shopping Center (982-9817), in an aging minimall on the east side of St. Francis Drive near Cerrillos Road, used to be a neighborhood lounge that served food on the side. At night you could dance to Norteño bands there. Then its reputation spread as the place where Spanish politicians hang out during the legislative session, and they expanded into a major restaurant, though few out-of-towners know about it. The fare is steaks and superb traditional New Mexican food, and the prices are not for tourists.

Maria's New Mexican Kitchen at 555 West Cordova Road (983-7929), off St. Francis Drive across the street from the Coronado Shopping Center, is the *real* quintessential New Mexican restaurant. We don't tell people about it because then we would have to wait a long time for a table. The fajitas are fantastic, and folks tell stories about what happened after Maria's margaritas.

Gabriel's on Highway 84/285 northbound (455-7000), 5 minutes north of the Santa Fe Opera and the flea market on the highway to Pojoaque, sparks up the usual New Mexican food with an Old Mexican flair. Many of the waiters (not to mention the cooks) hablan poco Inglés, and specialties range from New Mexican chile rellenos and south-of-the-border *pollo en mole* (chicken in chile–chocolate–peanut sauce) to a thoroughly contemporary version of vegetarian fajitas.

HISTORIC RESTAURANTS

The **Ore House** at 50 Lincoln Avenue (983-8687) has a menu dominated by steaks, a daily seafood special, and 80 kinds of margaritas. Go there at off-peak hours to get a table on the balcony and enjoy the best view of the Plaza.

La Casa Sena and **La Cantina** at 125 East Palace Avenue (988-9232) in Sena Plaza, under the same management but with different menus—La Cantina is the more affordable—share an old Spanish courtyard with a fountain in the center, certainly the most romantic restaurant location in Santa Fe. The menu features Continental and New Southwest selections. Indoor diners at La Casa Sena are serenaded with opera and Broadway show tunes by some of Santa Fe's most talented waiters and waitresses.

Santacafé at 231 Washington Avenue (984-1788) is in the historic Padre Gallegos house, a Territorial adobe that was occupied by a defrocked priest turned politician and later by Sheldon Parsons, one of the first painters in the Santa Fe artists' colony. One of the finest restaurants in Santa Fe, Santacafé serves imaginative New Southwestern fare that is pricey and worth it.

Upper Crust Pizza, at 329 Old Santa Fe Trail (982-0000), next door to San Miguel Mission, occupies part of the eighteenth-century Barrio de Analco, including the oldest house in Santa Fe. The pizzeria offers traditional or whole wheat crusts and a wide choice of toppings including green chile, chorizo (Mexican sausage), feta cheese, and artichoke hearts.

Geronimo at 724 Canyon Road (982-1500) is the current occupant of the Borrego House, an adobe farmhouse that dates back to the 1850s. The rooms are many and small, with just two or three tables in each, and the food is New Southwestern with a Mediterranean flair, with tempting pasta and seafood choices.

El Farol at 808 Canyon Road (983-9912), Santa Fe's oldest restaurant and bar, offers a tantalizing selection of Spanish-style tapas. From midevening on, live music—anything from flamenco to bluegrass—enlivens this neighborhood bar in one of America's most unique neighborhoods.

La Tertulia at 416 Agua Fria (988-2769) is in the former convent of the Santuario de Guadalupe, later converted into the residence of one of the city's leading Spanish families. Seating is in small, candlelit rooms decorated with traditional Norteño art. Specialties are steaks and paella accompanied by Sangria.

The **Zia Diner** at 326 South Guadalupe Street (988-7008), a popular casual restaurant, serves green chile cheeseburgers, piñon meatloaf and slices of homemade pie in a railroad-era building that used to be an autobody repair garage called the Supreme Body Shop, although you'd never know it from today's sleek Eurostyled interior.

LOCAL SECRETS

The **Downtown Subscription** at 376 Garcia (983-3085) has been the favorite writers' hangout and newsstand ever since it moved from its previous location to escape the tourists that have taken over the sidewalk seating at the café's closest competition, Galisteo News. Besides magazines and newspapers from around the world, the "Sub" serves gourmet coffee, pastries, and a limited choice of lunch items.

The **Aztec Street Coffee House** at 317 Aztec (983-9464), a modest café in a small house just off Guadalupe Street, serves ultra-affordable green chile cheeseburgers and fries to an international assortment of young writers, artists, philosophers, and slackers in a no-frills ambience.

Atalaya Restaurant and Bakery at 320 South Guadalupe Street (982-2709) in the heart of the Guadalupe historic district offers a moderately priced New Southwestern menu of creative salads and sandwiches such as sliced portobello mushroom on herbed focaccio bread, as well as full meals.

The **Cowgirl Hall of Fame** at 319 South Guadalupe Street (982-2565), across the street from Atalaya, features Texas-style barbecue alongside New Mexican and vegetarian dishes. After dark, it transforms into one of Santa Fe's favorite party bars, with live music and comedy in the back room.

Café Oasis at 526 Galisteo (983-9599) south of downtown may make you feel as if you'd stumbled through a time warp into Haight-Ashbury circa 1967. This family-run restaurant in a crazily painted old house features ecclectic furnishings and amateur folk singers. The menu leans toward pasta, fish, and vegetarian food.

The **Cloud Cliff Bakery and Café** at 1805 Second Street (983-6254) beside Second Street Studios does a lively lunch business with a full range of menu options from Southwestern to European fare. At off-peak hours it's a popular espresso-and-pastries artists' hangout and exhibit space.

Harry's Roadhouse on Old Las Vegas Highway (989-4629), a homey little place about 5 miles southeast of town with outdoor dining in a spacious back-yard landscaped with streams and little waterfalls, is my personal favorite among Santa Fe restaurants. Prices are moderate, and the food ranges from seafood and pasta to creative variations on traditional New Mexican fare such as a black bean and eggplant burrito big enough to feed a family.

HOTELS AND LODGINGS

Most major Santa Fe hotels are located in the downtown historic district, within a short walk of the Plaza. Almost all are expensive by southwestern standards, and some are very expensive. All recommendations here are in historic areas. Many midrange motels and motor inns can be found along busy Cerrillos Road southwest of downtown.

Calling in advance for reservations is advisable—and absolutely essential in July and August. If you are planning to visit during Indian Market, the third weekend in August, be advised that hotels and motels are booked solid for this weekend by the end of April. All phone numbers are in area code 505

La Fonda at 100 East San Francisco Street (982-5511), on the southeast corner of the Plaza, was the last major project of architect I. H. Rapp, the originator of Santa Fe style. It is the oldest hotel still operating in Santa Fe and stands on the site of the first hotel in town. Southwestern hotelier Fred Harvey's masterpiece, it epitomizes Spanish Pueblo Revival design. The lobby is dark, atmospheric, and busy, and the 170 rooms, furnished in Spanish colonial style, blend luxury with tradition. There is an indoor swimming pool. $$$$

The **Inn at Loretto** at 211 Old Santa Fe Trail (988-5531), a Best Western motor inn a block north of the Plaza, is a beautiful contemporary adaptation of Spanish Pueblo Revival architecture to a large structure. There are 140 rooms and an outdoor swimming pool. The inn occupies the former location of the Loretto Academy, a Catholic-run girls' school in territorial times, and its most special feature is the Chapel of Our Lady of Light (Loretto Chapel), which stands on the grounds. $$$

Garrett's Desert Inn at 311 Old Santa Fe Trail (982-1851) is the most ordinary motel in the downtown historic district and the most affordable (although rates are higher than for comparable places on Cerrillos Road). The 88 rooms are clean and modern, with the usual motor inn amenities. The location—on the south bank of the Santa Fe River, two blocks from the Plaza—makes it special. $$

The **Inn of the Anasazi** at 113 Washington Avenue (988-3030) is one of the most centrally located hotels in downtown Santa Fe, half a block from the Plaza. Although the 59-room inn is one of the newest buildings in the historic district, built in 1991, its masterfully contemporary Spanish Pueblo Revival design speaks eloquently of the continuum between past and present in the City Different. Inside, fireplaces and indirect lighting cast a glow through the curving, cavelike little lobby, restaurant, and bar, focusing attention on the artwork that hangs on every wall. Guest rooms have *viga* ceilings, four-poster beds, gas fireplaces, and Navajo rugs. $$$$

The **Hotel Plaza Real** at 125 Washington Avenue (988-4900) was built around the same time as the Inn of the Anasazi next door, but that's where the resemblance ends. The classic Territorial Revival building surrounds a small courtyard and garden. The 100 guest rooms are light, airy, and simply furnished. Many have woodburning fireplaces, and some have balconies. $$$

La Posada de Santa Fe at 330 East Palace Avenue (986-0000) has casitas on 6 acres of shady grounds and rose gardens around a central inn that was originally the Victorian mansion of prominent local merchant Abraham Staab, whose wife's ghost is said to haunt the hallways. La Posada has expanded little by little over the years, so the 119 rooms, suites, and casitas vary widely in style, amenities, and rates. There is an outdoor swimming pool. $$$

The **Hotel St. Francis** at 210 Don Gaspar Avenue (983-5700) has been a hotel since 1923, when it was built on the site of an older hotel that had burned to the ground. Formerly the De Vargas Hotel, this National Historic Landmark had declined into disreputability before an investment group took it over and completely renovated it in 1986. Like the lobby, the rather small guest rooms radiate turn-of-the-century elegance. $$$

The **Eldorado Hotel** at 309 West San Francisco Street (988-4455), the biggest building in the downtown area and the biggest hotel in the city, is cited by some as proof that Spanish Pueblo Revival style was never meant for five-story, 218-room hotels. The Clarion hotel chain tried hard to add touches of Santa Fe charm when it built the Eldorado in 1986, but somehow the place seems like it ought to be in Los Angeles instead. It is slightly historic, though. Threatened by public opposition over the nineteenth-century adobe house that stood on the sight where they planned to erect the hotel, the developers left the house standing, built around it, and made it the Old House Restaurant. $$$$

The **Hilton of Santa Fe** at 100 Sandoval (988-2811), a sprawling, two-story, 159-room Territorial-style hotel, was built around an old adobe house dating back to the late eighteenth century that, legend has it, became a brothel in Santa Fe Trail days. Today, it is the preferred home-away-from-home of politicians in town for the annual January–February legislative session. $$$

The **Territorial Inn** at 215 Washington Avenue (989-7737), a 10-room bed and breakfast two blocks from the Plaza, was originally the home of a merchant from Philadelphia. Sheltered from the city street by shade trees, the inn has a hot tub in the backyard gazebo and fireplaces in some rooms. $$$

The **Grant Corner Inn** at 122 Grant Avenue (983-6678) was one of the first bed and breakfast inns in town. Two blocks from the Plaza, this old, though unexceptional, two-story brick house has 11 rooms of varying sizes with all the usual bed and breakfast trappings—brass and tester beds, comfy old-fashioned quilts, and TVs hidden in armoires. The breakfast, served fireside in winter and on the big wraparound porch in summer, is so good that people who aren't staying there go there to eat. $$$

The **Preston House Bed and Breakfast** at 106 Faithway (982-3465), several blocks east of downtown off Palace Avenue, was the home of an infamous lawyer and member of the Santa Fe Ring in the 1880s. Today, the city's best example of Queen Anne Victorian architecture is an elegant eight-room bed and breakfast. $$

The **Inn of the Turquoise Bear** at 342 Buena Vista (983-0798), the home of poet Witter Bynner for decades and the birthplace of Santa Fe's literary community, has recently been converted into a bed and breakfast establishment. By coincidence, one of the resident co-owners is Robert Frost. (Not *that* Robert Frost. . . .) $$

The **Hotel Santa Fe** at 1501 Paseo de Peralta (982-1200) offers a level of luxury comparable to the best downtown hotels at a somewhat lower rate and offers a free shuttle to the Plaza, six blocks away. This 131-room Spanish Pueblo Revival style hotel is coowned and operated by Picuris Pueblo, the smallest Indian pueblo in New Mexico and one of the most isolated, on the High Road to Taos. $$$

The **Santa Fe Motel** at 510 Cerrillos Road (982-1039), not to be confused with the nearby Hotel Santa Fe, is one of the few moderate-priced motels within walking distance of the Plaza. $$

The **Travelodge Santa Fe Plaza** at 646 Cerrillos Road (982-3551) looks pretty much like most small Travelodges but is the most affordable motel near downtown. $$

The **Bishop's Lodge** on Bishop's Lodge Road (983-6377) between downtown Santa Fe and the village of Tesuque, grew from the retreat and private chapel of Archbishop Lamy, the French cleric sent to dehispanicize New Mexico's Catholic church in the mid-nineteenth century. Today, The Bishop's Lodge is a self-contained 88-unit, 1000-acre resort with tennis courts, a swimming pool, riding and hiking trails, and a skeet shooting range, all in a secluded setting within 10 minutes' drive of the Plaza. $$$$

Hacienda Rancho de Chimayó on Highway 76 (351-4444) in Chimayó, 25 miles north of Santa Fe, has seven casita-style rooms with locally handwoven draperies and rugs and *horno* fireplaces surrounding a pretty courtyard across the highway from the rancho's restaurant, which is famous for its traditional New Mexican food. This place is a dream-vacation home base for exploring the mountain villages and Indian pueblos of northern New Mexico. $$$

The **Galisteo Inn** (466-4000), 22 miles south of Santa Fe in the village of Galisteo, offers a rare opportunity to experience rural New Mexico village life in near-luxurious comfort. The 11-room Territorial-style inn on the bank of the Galisteo River has an outdoor swimming pool and a wonderful, practically undiscovered restaurant. $$

FIESTAS AND EVENTS

As in most Latin American cultures, local fiestas, markets, and other celebrations are all essential elements of community life in Santa Fe and the surrounding area. Visitors may wish to plan their stays to coincide with (or avoid) these events:

January—Most Indian pueblos hold ceremonial dances on **New Year's Day** (January 1) and also on **Three Kings' Day** (January 6), when leadership of each pueblo is transferred annually. San Ildefonso Pueblo observes the **Feast of San Ildefonso** with animal dances on January 22–23.

February—The Santa Fe Ski Basin hosts the **Jimmy Huega Express** race on the first weekend, the **University of New Mexico NCAA Race** on the second weekend, and **Winterfiesta,** including the Governor's Cup and Tesuque Peak Flyer's Invitational races, on the last weekend in February.

March—The Santa Fe Ski Basin hosts the **Hispano Chamber Ski Fiesta** on the first weekend and the **Gladfelter Memorial Bump Run** and **Southwest Snowboard Championships** on the last weekend in March.

April—The Santa Fe Ski Basin celebrates its scheduled closing day with **Surf 'n' Ski** on the first weekend in April. As many as 30,000 New Mexicans take part in the annual **Good Friday Pilgrimage** to the Santuario de Chimayó. Most Indian pueblos hold ceremonial dances on **Easter Sunday.**

May—A **Battle of Glorieta Pass Reenactment** is held at El Rancho de las Golondrinas on the second weekend in May. The Southwest Indian Arts Association sponsors its **Spring Powwow and Indian Market** the last weekend in May at Pojoaque Pueblo.

June—The annual **Santa Fe Run Around** 5K and 10K foot races are held on the first weekend in June, as is **El Rancho de las Golondrinas Spring Festival.** The Santa Fe Opera has its **Gala Opening Celebration** at the end of June. The corn dance at Santo Domingo Pueblo on **San Pedro Feast Day** (June 29) is one of the largest Indian ceremonial dances in the state.

July—The **Santa Fe Opera, Chamber Music Festival,** and **Desert Chorale** perform throughout July and August. The **Fourth of July** is observed with a pancake breakfast on the Plaza and a fireworks display at the Downs of Santa Fe. Nambe Pueblo holds its annual **Nambe Falls Celebration** on July 4, too. Starting with a rodeo parade on the Plaza, the **Rodeo de Santa Fe** takes place the second week of July. El Rancho de las Golondrinas hosts a **Wine Festival** the third weekend of July, and the annual **Eight Northern Pueblos Arts and Crafts Show,** one of the largest Indian markets in the United States, is held the same weekend at a different pueblo each year. The **Galisteo Rodeo** takes place in the village of Galisteo on the last weekend of the month, and **Spanish Market** is held on the Santa Fe Plaza the same weekend.

August—St. John's College hosts **Shakespeare in Santa Fe,** with free weekend performances throughout the month. The Rodeo Grounds is the scene of the **All Women's Rodeo** in early August. El Rancho de las Golondrinas holds its **Summer Festival and Frontier Market** the first weekend of the month. During the second week, the Palace of the Governors sponsors a five-day **Mountain Man Rendezvous and Trade Fair.** The **Santa Fe Indian Market,** the largest event of the year, takes place on the third weekend in August. San Ildefonso Pueblo holds a **Corn Dance** late in August.

September—On the weekend after Labor Day, the **Fiestas de Santa Fe** mark the end of tourist season with the burning of Zozobra, grand ball, Children's Pet Parade, Historical/Hysterical parade, and candlelight religious processions. San Ildefonso Pueblo holds a corn dance on the **Feast of the Nativity of Mary** (September 8).

October—Nambe Pueblo celebrates the **Feast of San Francisco** on October 3 and 4. El Rancho de las Golondrinas holds its **Harvest Festival** the first weekend in October.

November—Tesuque Pueblo celebrates the **Feast of San Diego** on November 12. The Santa Fe Ski Basin officially opens the day after **Thanksgiving.**

December—The town of Madrid stages a lighting ceremony as part of its **Christmas Open House** the first weekend in December. Pojoaque Pueblo observes the **Feast of Guadalupe** (December 12). The Palace of the Governors sponsors **Christmas at the Palace** from the second weekend in the month through New Year's Day. On the third Sunday of the month, Santa Fe holds its traditional **Las Posadas** procession. **Christmas Eve** is observed with a luminaria walk on Canyon Road and a buffalo dance and torchlight procession at Nambe Pueblo. Most Indian pueblos hold matachinas and other dances on **Christmas Day.**

BOOKSTORES AND BOOKS

Those in the market for books on the history and culture of the Santa Fe area will do well to start with the gift shops of the major museums. The **Palace of the Governors Shop** specializes in books on American Indian, Hispanic, and New Mexican history and literature, anthropology, and arts and crafts. The **Museum of Fine Arts Shop** features books on many New Mexico artists among other books on art and photography. **The Museum of Indian Arts and Culture Shop,** the **Institute of American Indian Arts Museum Shop,** and the **Case Trading Post** in the **Wheelwright Museum** all carry extensive selections of books on Indian topics.

Any of the more than 40 booksellers in Santa Fe will tell you that local reading tastes are atypical. The large sections on literature by local writers and nonfiction ranging from history to hiking guides and cookbooks show that Santa Feans buy more books about New Mexico than they do national best-sellers. Among the best selections of local interest books are found at the **Collected Works Bookshop,** 208-B West San Francisco Street; **Old Santa Fe Trail Books & Coffeehouse,** 613 Old Santa Fe Trail; **Garcia Street Books,**

376 Garcia Street; **Palace Avenue Books,** 209 East Palace Avenue; **Railyard Books,** 340 Read Street; and the **La Fonda Newsstand** in La Fonda hotel. One of the city's most unusual bookstores, **The Ark** at 133 Romero Street, a block west of the railroad yards, specializes in healing, psychology, and New Age titles and stocks an outstanding selection of local interest and local author books, metaphysical and otherwise. The city's only chain bookstores, **Waldenbooks** in the Villa Linda Mall and **Hastings Books, Music & Video** in the De Vargas Mall, also stock local titles.

Classic and current books that cover aspects of Santa Fe history and culture that are available in Santa Fe bookstores as of the 1996 Christmas season include:

Adobe Angels: The Ghosts of Santa Fe and Taos by Antonio R. Garcez (Santa Fe, NM: Red Rabbit Press, 1995)

Artists of the Canyons and Caminos: Santa Fe, the Early Years by Edna Robertson and Sarah Nestor (Santa Fe, NM: Ancient City Press, 1996)

The Centuries of Santa Fe by Paul Horgan (Albuquerque, NM: University of New Mexico Press, 1956)

The City Different and the Palace by Rosemary Nusbaum (Santa Fe, NM: Sunstone Press, 1974)

Contemporary New Mexico, 1940–1990 edited by Richard W. Etulain (Albuquerque, NM: University of New Mexico Press, 1994)

Creator of the Santa Fe Style: Isaac Hamilton Rapp, Architect by Carl D. Sheppard (Albuquerque, NM: University of New Mexico Press, 1988)

Enchanted Lifeways: The History, Museums, Arts and Festivals of New Mexico compiled by the New Mexico Office of Cultural Affairs, Ellen Kleiner, editor (Santa Fe, NM: New Mexico Magazine, 1995)

From Santa Fe to O'Keeffe Country: A One-Day Journey Through the Soul of New Mexico by Rhoda Barker and Peter Sinclaire (Santa Fe, NM: Ocean Tree Books, 1996)

Great Excavations: Tales of Early Southwestern Archaeology, 1888–1939 by Melinda Elliott (Santa Fe, NM: SAR Press, 1995)

Hidden New Mexico by Richard Harris et al. (Berkeley, CA: Ulysses Press, 1997)

The Illustrated History of New Mexico by Thomas E. Chávez (Niwot, CO: University of Colorado Press, 1992)

The Insider's Guide to Santa Fe by Bill Jamison (Boston: Harvard Common Press, 1987)

John Gaw Meem: Pioneer in Historic Preservation by Beatrice Chauvenet (Santa Fe, NM: Museum of New Mexico Press, 1985)

John Gaw Meem: Southwest Architect by Bainbridge Bunting (Santa Fe, NM: School of American Research/Albuquerque, NM: University of New Mexico Press, 1983)

Journey to the High Southwest by Robert L. Casey (Seattle, WA: Pacific Search Press, 1986)

New Mexico in Maps edited by Jerry L. Williams and Paul E. McAllister (Albuquerque, NM: University of New Mexico Press, 1979)

New Mexico in the Nineteenth Century: A Pictorial History by Andrew K. Gregg (Albuquerque, NM: University of New Mexico Press, 1968)

New Mexico Style: A Sourcebook of Traditional Architectural Details by Nancy Hunter Warren (Santa Fe, NM: Museum of New Mexico Press, 1995)

New Mexico's Best Ghost Towns by Philip Varney (Albuquerque, NM: University of New Mexico Press, 1987)

Old Santa Fe Today by the Historic Santa Fe Foundation (4th edition Albuquerque, NM: University of New Mexico Press, 1991)

The Palace of the Governors by J. K. Shishkin (Santa Fe, NM: Museum of New Mexico, 1972)

The Roads of New Mexico (Fredericksburg, TX: Shearer Publishing, 1990)

Roadside History of New Mexico by Francis L. and Roberta B. Fugate (Missoula, MT: Mountain Press, 1989)

Santa Fe by Lawrence W. Cheek (New York: Compass American Guides/Fodor's Travel Publications, 1996)

Santa Fe: The Autobiography of a Southwestern Town by Oliver La Farge (Norman, OK: University of Oklahoma Press, 1959)

Santa Fe: A Pictorial History by John Sherman (Norfolk, VA: Donning Company Publishers, 1983)

Santa Fe and Taos: The Writer's Era, 1916–1941 by Marta Weigle and Kyle Fiore (Santa Fe, NM: Ancient City Press, 1994)

Santa Fe on Foot by Elaine Pinkerton (Santa Fe, NM: Ocean Tree Books, 1986)

The Smithsonian Guide to Historic America: The Desert States by Michael S. Durham (New York: Stewart, Tabori & Chang, 1990)

The WPA Guide to 1930s New Mexico by the Writers' Program of the Work Projects Administration in the State of New Mexico (American Guide Series, 1940, original title: *New Mexico: A Guide to the Colorful State;* reprinted by the University of Arizona Press, 1989)

FOR MORE INFORMATION

TOURIST INFORMATION AGENCIES

Santa Fe County Chamber of Commerce, 510 North Guadalupe Street, Suite N (988-3279), located in De Vargas Mall North, has information for visitors, real estate buyers, and small businesses and sells a "Santa Fe Stats" booklet with current demographic and economic figures.

Santa Fe Convention and Visitors Bureau, Sweeney Center, 201 West Marcy Street (984-6760), publishes the annual Santa Fe Visitors Guide.

New Mexico Tourism Department, 459 Old Santa Fe Trail (827-7336), has a visitors center that distributes free brochures and publications on all areas of New Mexico.

Eight Northern Indian Pueblos Council, San Juan Pueblo (852-4265) produces an annual 8 Northern Indian Pueblos Visitors Guide and can provide current information on dances, ceremonials, arts and crafts shows, and pow-wows.

HISTORIC PRESERVATION AGENCIES

City of Santa Fe Planning Division, 200 Lincoln Avenue (984-6605), sells copies of the city's historic design ordinances, historical maps, and various surveys that have been commissioned over the years, including the *Guadalupe Neighborhood Historic Survey* (1981), the *Don Gaspar Architectural Historic Survey* (1983), the *Historical District Handbook* (1986), the *Santa Fe Historic Plaza Study I with Translations from Spanish Colonial Documents* (1990), and the *Santa Fe Historic Plaza Study II: Plaza Excavation Final Report* (1992).

State of New Mexico Historic Preservation, 228 East Palace Avenue (827-6320), maintains public files on every historic building in the state that has applied for listing on the State Register of Cultural Properties and the National Register of Historic Places. There are more than 10,000 in Santa Fe alone.

PERIODICALS

New Mexico Magazine, Lew Wallace Building, 495 Old Santa Fe Trail (827-7447), the first state travel magazine in the United States, has been published monthly since soon after New Mexico became a state in 1912. It contains many articles of historical and cultural interest and is available at most newsstands. Complete sets of back issues can be found at the Santa Fe Public Library and the New Mexico State Library.

El Palacio, Museum of New Mexico Press, 228 East Palace Avenue (827-6454), publishes scholarly articles on New Mexico history. Complete sets of back issues can be found at the Santa Fe Public Library and the New Mexico State Library.

Index